VEHICLES OF HOPE:

Serving Others on the Road to Satisfaction

Written by

Carol Tebo
with
Larry Tebo

This book is a work of non-fiction. The people and places are real, and the events and situations are true.

ISBN: 1-4033-8952-7 (e-book)
ISBN: 1-4033-8953-5 (Softcover)

Library of Congress Control Number: 2002095441

This book is printed on acid free paper.

Printed in the United States of America
Bloomington, IN

1stBooks – rev. 02/18/03

*For our
children and grandchildren*

TABLE OF CONTENTS

FROM THE AUTHOR

On September 11, 2001, preparations were being made in Indianapolis, Indiana, for the 25th anniversary celebration of Habitat for Humanity's successful mission to improve the lives of people around the world through partnering with them to build simple, decent homes in which to live and provide a brighter future for their children. Thousands from the U.S. and other countries were expected to attend.

Those already there, stunned and saddened by the unfolding events, were faced with a momentous decision: out of deference for what had taken place, should they cancel the festivities or should they go ahead with them? Their prayerful conclusion was that in the wake of such blatant evil, it was important to honor the power of love. Though many were unable to make it there, the celebration (altered in some ways, and perhaps one of the first major counters to the terrorists' statement) became a reverent, moving and uplifting affirmation that goodness abounds.

With the exception of updates, this manuscript was complete when the catastrophic events of September 11 occurred. People seemed surprised and awed by the sacrifices that so many made for strangers and the great outpouring of love and aid. But, as my husband Larry and I watched the collision of the forces of good and evil unfold, we realized that the scenario was a familiar one. Since selling our home and possessions and becoming full-time RVers in 1996, we had dedicated a large portion of our time to working with Habitat for Humanity and helping at natural disaster sites, and we had observed those very same benevolent responses taking place in grand and small ways every day, all over our land. The reason so many were surprised on September 11 is because, unfortunately, goodness does not normally sell newspapers.

Herein is an account of the personal pilgrimage of two ordinary people who, one day, chose to follow their dream and to let Spirit[*] lead them on an incredible adventure of discovery and fulfillment. I chose to share our journey for several reasons.

---

[*] In many cases I have chosen to substitute *Spirit* or *Creator* when referring to God. For me, this helps avoid the image of a "man in the sky" and eliminates the necessity of gender pronouns, while at the same time capturing both the omnipresent nature of Spirit as well as its personal presence within each of us.

First, so many people asked how we found the courage to give up the security of home and income. Often they have confided both their longings and their fears of following their hearts' desires. I hope that learning about how our needs have been supplied, as well as the rich personal rewards we have reaped, will help alleviate their concerns and inspire them to make whatever major shift in their lives they feel called to make.

Second, through our work with Habitat for Humanity and at disaster sites, we feel we have been privy to the noblest potentiality, as well as the incredible strength and resilience, of the human spirit. I believe that we are all connected in Spirit and that life is designed to be a shared experience. I want to convey the deep satisfaction that is derived by both giver and receiver when we fulfill our highest calling—to serve one another.

A third motive surfaced as we began relating our unfolding saga to others. Besides enjoying hearing about our travel adventures, people wanted to know more about how Habitat for Humanity worked and were fascinated by the dynamics of a crew of volunteers building multiple houses in one week. Likewise, many were mesmerized by our accounts of working at disaster sites and were especially moved by the courage of survivors and the outpouring of compassion and aid. Too often, television viewers are left only with images of destruction and grief. They never see the miraculous process of rebirth. Therefore, it is also my intention to enable readers to observe, through our eyes, the uplifting and far-reaching effects of Habitat for Humanity and disaster relief and recovery work.

My final purpose in writing this book is to convey a message of hope. For, without hope that there is an indomitable force of goodness at the core of life, it becomes much easier to disconnect ourselves. On the other hand, seeing hope in an apparently hopeless situation renews our energy and gives us the impetus to contribute our own efforts so that, one by one by one, we become a mighty force for overcoming. It is my prayer that *Vehicles of Hope* will bolster your hope and stir you to become a vehicle of hope to others.

Carol Tebo

ACKNOWLEDGMENTS

So many people have contributed to this book, both directly and indirectly, and deserve a huge THANK YOU—

Our full-time RVing mentors, Topsy and Alex Jarvie, for showing us that anything is possible when you have the right attitude.

Our children and friends, for their support and encouragement, even though they may have wondered if we really knew what we were doing.

The Habitat homeowners, disaster survivors, volunteers, ministers and leaders of disaster response organizations who gave generously of their time and themselves to share their stories.

Millard and Linda Fuller, co-founders, and Habitat for Humanity for providing an avenue for us, and thousands of others, to express our faith in concrete action.

Our daughters Jeannette Campbell and Tanya Rybarczyk, as well as friends Jenna Delorey and Margaret High, for reading this manuscript and giving insightful suggestions and editing advice.

Jill Claflin, Director of Creative Services at Habitat for Humanity, for reviewing, editing and advising on text related to Habitat.

Julie Hall and Rena Adams for proofreading.

Ernie Angelicola for invaluable computer formatting assistance.

Carolina Landing and Natchez Trace, Thousand Trails & NACO preserves, for providing office space to work on the manuscript.

Koinonia Partners for providing space to work on the manuscript, and the community members for their support, encouragement and love.

Our adaptable feline travel companions, the late Ross and the charismatic Patches.

Each other, for the willingness to risk comfort and security to follow our dream.

The Divine Spirit, for steering us in the right direction and providing for our needs at every turn in the road.

With heartfelt appreciation,
Carol and Larry Tebo

MAP OF BIRMINGHAM STORM PATH

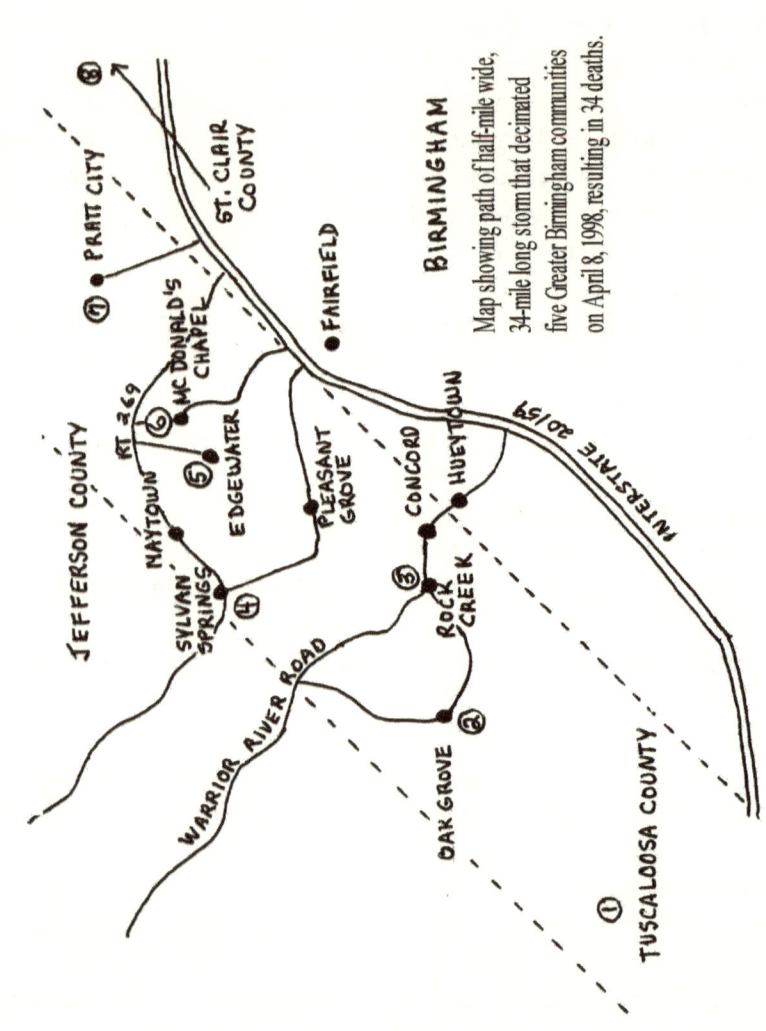

BIRMINGHAM

Map showing path of half-mile wide, 34-mile long storm that decimated five Greater Birmingham communities on April 8, 1998, resulting in 34 deaths.

PROLOGUE

Deadly Rampage

On April 8, 1998, the Wednesday before Easter, a storm developed in Tuscaloosa County, Alabama, spawning a tornado that chewed up several miles of timberland. Mustering strength, it made its way into western Jefferson County on the outskirts of Birmingham, reaching the densely wooded community of Oak Grove around 8 p.m. There, packing winds of 200 mph, it claimed the lives of 4 people and completely leveled the 80-year-old Oak Grove School attended by children from kindergarten through high school.

As the storm advanced to nearby Rock Creek, the winds accelerated to 300 mph, qualifying it as an F-5—the most powerful designation for a tornado. It summarily ravaged that community, felling hundreds of trees and demolishing the Rock Creek Church of God Family Life Center and the Concord Fire Station. Obliterating dozens of homes, it left 10 fatalities in its wake.

Relentlessly slashing a half-mile-wide swath on its 30-mile deadly rampage, it hit Sylvan Springs next, taking 4 more lives. After that, it slammed into the communities of Edgewater and McDonald Chapel, killing another 14 people. Then, dropping down to F-3 strength, it battered Pratt City before disappearing into the night sky and later touching down in St. Clair County, where the last two deaths occurred.

In the heart of the Bible Belt, many of the residents had been at Wednesday night church services. That fact accounted, in great measure, for the phenomenally low loss of life—34 altogether. Not a single person inside a church was killed.

If Only . . .

Many times my husband Larry and I had sat in our living room watching news of such an event on TV and remarked, "If only we could just pick up and go help those people." In that statement lay the seeds of a dream

1

that finally came to fruition a week after the Birmingham tornado struck. Dressed in work clothes, with a streamer of blue cloth tied to our belt loops (evidence that we were officially checked in at the registration tent), we sat in a van with a half dozen strangers, headed to McDonald Chapel for our first day of clean-up.

The driver was sharing one of those incredible stories that always emerge from disasters. A large dog was found lying in the driveway of a man who lived in Rock Creek. It appeared to be dead, but when the man approached, it opened its eyes, shook its head, and sat up. Leading the dog to his house, the man called the number on its identification tag and discovered that the owner lived in Tuscaloosa. Two days later, the fortunate dog was reunited with its family, seemingly unscathed after its miraculous 40-mile journey by air.

Our First Real Look

The van turned to enter the community of McDonald Chapel, which had consisted primarily of small, tightly packed homes—a mining camp during the years when Birmingham grew so quickly as a major producer of iron ore that it became known as the "Magic City." The driver of our Birmingham Baptist Association van stopped at the entrance until the National Guard officer waved us through.

As we slowly approached our work site, my eyes darted about, taking in the macabre scene; my mind, however, could only process in slow motion what it was taking in. McDonald Chapel looked in many ways how I imagined a war zone must appear after a bombing attack.

The steel frame of a doublewide trailer was wrapped around a sheered-off tree—as though someone had tied it in a knot. Clothing, insulation, curtains, pieces of metal, and even cars were wedged between tree branches. Only the lower portion of many trees remained, the splintered tops of which bore evidence that they had been literally pulled apart by the sucking force of the tornado.

A small church had imploded, the plush red pew cushions of the newly built chapel standing out starkly amid the crumble of white bricks. All that remained of another small chapel was its marquee which read, "Spring—A Time of Rebirth." Up and down every street and hillside were piles of rubble, which a little over a week ago had been the homes of several hundred people—some leveled to their foundations, others with a wall or two left standing, a few looking relatively untouched on the outside except for a missing roof, and two that had been pulled together by the powerful tornadic vacuum.

So, this is what it *really* looks like, I marveled—much more intense and ghastly than it appears on TV. Everyone in the van was silent with their own thoughts. It was hard to believe that it wasn't a nightmare and that Larry and I were actually there.

Nevertheless, being in that place at that time was the next natural step in a progression of events that had led us to divest ourselves of the majority of our possessions, sell our home, and climb into our travel trailer with our cat Ross to begin a journey that would have unimagined impact on our lives.

I. THE ROAD TO SATISFACTION

. . . our greatest joy is in helping others meet their basic needs rather than piling up more and more for ourselves. We think it is a better way to live.

Millard Fuller, **The Theology of the Hammer**

I-1. A DREAM COME TRUE

Now faith is the turning of dreams into deeds;
it is betting your life on the unseen realities.

Hebrews 11:1 (Cotton Patch Version)

Making Music Together

Larry and I have common roots in the soil of Michigan. Both children of first-generation Americans, we were raised with an emphasis on becoming part of the whole, rather than highlighting our diversity—likely one reason we now find it easy to blend in wherever we are. Because we moved frequently in our childhoods, we learned early to adapt to new environments.

Neither of our families was affluent, but both were comfortably middle class. Larry's father was in construction; mine was a newspaper photographer. Our mothers were full-time homemakers. As young children in the forties, our lives were relatively carefree and unprogrammed. Nature was our playground and the things of nature our playmates. We both recall hours spent lying on our backs watching the clouds, observing the workings of anthills, and having the freedom to explore "our territory."

We were teenagers during the 50's, both of us good students and involved in sports. Life was fairly predictable, standards of conduct clear, and we adhered to them without much resistance. Personal responsibility was one of the most emphasized virtues in our upbringing; therefore, although the Cold War loomed over us, it was never an excuse for not moving forward with our lives. Though Larry was Catholic and I Protestant, we had each pursued a relationship with God independent of our families. Faith was central to our lives.

So, when we met on a rainy summer evening in 1976 at a Parents Without Partners sing-along, our commonality drew us to each other. Sitting on the floor in the middle of a crowded room singing Judy Collins' "Send in

7

the Clowns," everyone and everything disappeared. We were completely alone as our voices blended. At that moment, our lives touched and became forever connected. We felt that we had "come home to each other."

Two years later, with Larry's four children and my two beside us, we were married amidst towering pines in my minister's back yard. Our honeymoon was spent camping in the magnificent environs of Lake Placid in upstate New York—an apt beginning to a story that would eventually, by way of a long and winding road, come full-circle.

Different Views

Remarried with children in the late seventies, we were embarking down a road not yet on the map. There were few guideposts. The word *blended* had not yet become attached to *family* in everyday usage. Suffice it to say, there were monumental highs and lows. We did the best we could, but it wasn't always pretty.

Our wedding scripture, Matthew 6:19-21; 25-34, (chosen both for spiritual and practical reasons) reminded us not to worry about material things, but to put our faith and trust in God—as do the "birds of the air" and "the lilies of the field"—and the rest would be taken care of. With six children to support, four of whom would live with us, we anticipated there would be some lean times ahead. We were right.

As we began to get on our feet financially, Larry made a gutsy decision to quit his job that had become emotionally draining and unviable. Shortly after, we were presented with an opportunity to work for a year in Nigeria. With little hesitation, and to the surprise of many, we decided to go. I absolutely believe that some of the best and most far-reaching decisions are often made "impulsively"—motivated by a strong, clear voice inside which says, "Yes, this is what you need to do!"—before all the *other voices,* shouting "it's crazy, impractical, or impossible," crowd in.

Along with two of our children (the older two had already left the house), we lived a very primal existence in Nigeria. Though housing and basic needs were provided beyond our expectations, we went to market almost daily, boiled and filtered our water, ate three sit-down meals every day together, and washed all our clothes and bedding by hand. Evenings in the compound, which we shared with Nigerians and other Americans, were for enjoying each other.

Our brief travel through southern Europe on our way home showed us yet another life scenario. There, we observed a culture that seemed to have struck a critical balance between having a comfortable level of advancement and conveniences and knowing when enough was enough. The relentless drive for more did not appear to have overtaken their lives.

Upon our return to the U.S., we became acutely aware of the contrasts to our own society—one which cannot afford to have its stores closed on Sundays because its members are working six days a week in pursuit of the next gadget or technology to make their lives "better." It sparked a conscious desire in us to find and maintain a balance in our own lives.

However, a year after moving to Salt Lake City and purchasing a home there, Larry lost his job due to a plant buy-out. As a result of several very tough years financially, we redirected our focus to the need to make money. That's when we began to run into trouble.

A House Divided

The first hint we had that we were headed in the wrong direction was when we made another impulsive decision. A year after we secured excellent, well-paying positions in southern New Hampshire, we purchased a piece of camping property on the Connecticut River in the "North Country," as well as a truck and small travel trailer.

In the North Country, we found that progress is tempered by tradition and common sense. We looked forward to our time at camp, relishing our weekend immersions in small-town life and becoming increasingly aware of the contrast to our life down state. We soon found ourselves dreading heading back to our work-a-day world on Sunday evenings. Additionally, we began to question which of our two worlds was the real one—or at least, the one we wanted to invest the rest of our lives in.

We also met Topsy and Alex, full-time RVers who spent their summers on a piece of property just up the road from us. We became intrigued by their lifestyle and spent many hours prodding them for details. It was obvious that they were extremely content and amazingly undaunted by seeming inconveniences or challenges. The more we learned of their story, the more we admired their spirit and approach to life.

Larry and I began to talk seriously about full-time RVing. Simplifying our lives and having more time for service work became a frequent topic of our conversations. But we didn't get it yet. We thought the way to make it happen was to accumulate a certain amount of money to assure our security, get all our "ducks in a row," and then we could live the way our heart was telling us to live. However, life often has a way of not cooperating when we don't pay attention to what we're being called to do.

After two more periods of unemployment, we hitched up the trailer and returned to Salt Lake City. We planned to move back into our house that had been rented, look for jobs, and settle there indefinitely. We ceased talking about our dream.

Our decision seemed to be validated by Larry's acquiring a good position in his field and my securing a job as secretary for a small private school across town. For a year we worked hard at our jobs and feverishly remodeled our house and re-groomed our yard. Nothing we did was extravagant, but the end result was fresh, pleasant and functional. We replaced all our early-attic furnishings with modestly priced new ones, and as we nestled in our cozy recliners in our softly lit living room, we assured ourselves that we loved our home and that we were happy.

We were paying a price for that happiness, however, and it was a high one. As Lily Tomlin reminded people, "If you win the rat race, you're still a rat!" Although my job was satisfying, the demanding hours and long commute, added to all we were doing at home and my normal household responsibilities, were beginning to take their toll.

Larry soon found (though it should have come as no great surprise) that he was once again feeling frustrated and unfulfilled. Management was indecisive and he was jerked back and forth between day and night shifts. Furthermore, his eleven-mile commute often took an hour and a half due to the growing congestion in the Salt Lake Valley.

And, since we had invested our earnings into remodeling and furnishing the house, we still were not in any better shape financially. But worst of all, we had buried *our dream* and settled for the conventional one —a job, a home, and security.

One Road At A Time

I am convinced that most of us know in our hearts (often from an early age) what we should be doing with our lives. However, unless or until we do it, we continue to find ourselves trapped in the same mindless cycle, wondering how we arrived here again, but deep down inside, knowing why. Like Bill Murray in the movie "Ground Hog Day," we live the same day over and over until we find the courage to make the leap of faith to do it differently. Increasingly aware of what we were doing, Larry and I began to analyze what was holding us back.

Our reluctance seemed to have nothing to do with feeling we couldn't live without all our "stuff" (one of the first things we are often asked about), for we had lived happily in Nigeria with the contents of three trunks and two duffel bags.

Nor did we have concerns about living in the spatial confines of a modest-sized trailer. The many weekends spent in our 24-foot trailer at camp had shown us clearly that we lacked none of the necessities for living comfortably.

Likewise, it wasn't because we questioned whether we were suited for the nomadic life, for we had become experts at adapting and adjusting to new environments as a result of our repeated work-related moves. In fact, we had found the frequent changes both exhilarating and refreshing. They kept our senses from becoming dulled by the familiar and routine, and expanded our horizons beyond the confines of our individual worlds. Since most of our families and friends were scattered all over the country, "leaving home" wasn't a pivotal factor, either. On the contrary, we would be able to visit them more easily and more often.

In addition, life had obviously been readying us to become full-time RVers. We already had the truck and trailer plus the mentoring of Topsy and Alex.

However, despite their testimony that full-time RVing was the least expensive way to live (they had done it for nine years on Social Security income alone), we were held firmly in the grips of a scary monster: *security*! Unlike many RVers, because of our frequent job changes we would not have the cushioning benefit of a retirement pension or health insurance. Nor did we have any investments, and we were always hearing that one should have at least a half-million dollars stashed away to secure old age!

As the Bible reminds us, a house divided against itself must eventually crumble. It became clear that we could no longer hold back the tide of discontent, which surfaced as depression in me and bone-weariness in Larry. One day, as he dragged in from work after his hot commute, we looked at each other and said, "What are we doing? It's time!"

I-2. GETTING INTO THE RHYTHM

We are whole creatures in potential,
and the true purpose of desire
is to unfold that wholeness,
to become what we can be.

Eric Butterworth, *Spiritual Economics*

Freedom To Choose

"We escaped," we squealed, as we turned the corner and could no longer see what had been our home in Sandy, Utah. "We're free!" It wouldn't begin to dawn on us what awesome implications freedom had until we had made our way across country to deposit a few belongings at our camp in New Hampshire, visited several of our children, and were finally settled in at Carolina Landing in Fair Play, South Carolina (our home park in the Thousand Trails & NACO [TTN] private campground network). We had purchased Topsy and Alex's membership when they retired from RVing because of health reasons.

We quickly discovered that we would have to learn a whole new way of living. An important part of the process involved reminding ourselves that we had traded our stuff and obligations for *time*. It was ours to use and to shape. We could choose to squander it, filling it with busyness—thus diminishing our freedom by locking ourselves into schedules and things to do—or we could use it to contemplate, reflect, and wait for authentic desires to well up from within us, then use our new-found freedom to respond to them.

When we first started out, I got up every morning and swept the vinyl mat in our screen room. Seasoned full-timers must have enjoyed a hearty laugh from that. It also took Larry awhile to figure out that he didn't have to wash and wax the truck and trailer in one day. The compulsion to keep busy required diligence to resist, even though we were becoming aware of how bone-tired we actually were from the furious pace most of us call living.

Busyness is seductive because it is familiar, and those who dread boredom feel driven to continually fill their time. It can also be an act of avoidance, masking our fear of looking at ourselves and challenging ourselves, for if we stay busy and in our comfort zones, we don't have to risk. But we hadn't come all that way to be comfortable!

Letting The Lines Come

I have always been a very organized person who prided herself on accomplishment. In years past, my daily "to do" lists often boxed me in, putting pressure on me when the day wasn't going the way I had envisioned. On occasion, however, I would wake up with no particular agenda and, at the end of a day of doing only what I felt like doing, I was almost always amazed at what I had accomplished quite effortlessly. My goal, now, is to live each day in that manner.

I've also discovered that time expands when it isn't planned. I believe as we humans mature, we realize that, in this life anyway, time isn't limitless; we begin to see it as a gift to cherish rather than race through. When my life was more programmed, I was always thinking about what I had to do in the future, and my present slipped by me unnoticed. I would often find myself asking where the week, month, or year had gone. Now I am more likely to say to Larry, "Didn't that month seem long?" It is an acknowledgment and appreciation that we have really "lived" that month; that we have truly experienced each day.

I compare my new outlook on living to when I acted in plays. Just before I went on stage, I would experience a momentary fear that I wouldn't remember my lines. I would try to think ahead, but my mind would be blank. I quickly learned that the only line I really had to remember was the first one. Then, as I let myself become immersed in the flow of the action, the lines came as I needed them.

Living freely, I'm finding, is much like that. If we wait for the lines to come, for the inclinations or opportunities to present themselves, we don't have to struggle to know what to do. If we try too hard to "remember ahead," our minds are blocked and we are filled with anxiety and fear; whereas, if we respond to life as it comes to us, we see that we have all we need to meet each moment.

13

In time, we recognized that life on the road is in some ways like life anywhere. It has its rhythms and cycles, its highs and lows, its mundaneness and its challenges. It is most easily lived when we keep ourselves in the flow—day by day, minute by minute —rather than forcing it or resisting it. In time, we learned to relax and become part of the rhythm.

Focusing On The Unbroken Line

Prior to becoming RVers, we made several cross-country treks by car. Sometimes, I found myself driving at night on an unfamiliar, unlit, two-lane winding road. Often only able to use my low beams due to oncoming traffic, it was difficult to distinguish the curves until I was upon them, and I would feel the apprehension mounting as I searched the road ahead, trying to discern which way it was going to bend.

On one such occasion, after driving in an anxious state for an extended time, I decided that instead of straining to see down the road, I would focus my vision on the solid white line along the shoulder right in front of the car. To my immediate relief, I found I could drive in that manner seeing exactly what I needed in time to negotiate any twists and turns in the road.

In a sudden revelation it occurred to me: *This is exactly how I am supposed to live life!* So often I have become tense and anxious trying to see beyond today, trying to anticipate outcomes, worrying about situations I have not yet encountered, and robbing myself of today's happiness by taking on tomorrow's problems, when all I needed to do was focus on the moment at hand.

That is how Larry and I now try to approach living: to stay focused on that solid, unbroken line, attending only to the present moment, to what is right in front of us. As we have attempted to live in this manner, we have found that life is much easier to navigate, even when it takes unanticipated twists and turns. Since we can't negotiate a turn until we're upon it, we may as well conserve our energy for when it's really needed.

In terms of living our vision, it meant moving forward with no reservations, no preconceived notions or guarantees of what lay around the bend. We just sat back and let Spirit do the driving!

I-3. BORN TO SERVE

Service is not just something we do
out of the goodness of our hearts or from principle;
it is a deep, archetypal experience of the soul,
for which we have both a need and an instinct.

Thomas Moore, *Voices From The Heart*

The Joy Of Serving

Though meant humorously, I always feel a twinge of sadness when I see a bumper sticker that proclaims "Born to Shop." I often fantasize about how life might be if we were moved to declare instead, "Born to Serve!"

During my teens and early twenties, I was a member of the Church of the Brethren, a denomination stemming from the Anabaptist movement in Europe in the 1500s. The basic tenants of the Brethren are pacifism, individual spiritual responsibility, simple living, and service.

Between my junior and senior years of college, I interrupted my schooling to enter Brethren Volunteer Service—a network of service projects around the world originally established for conscientious objectors to fulfill their military obligation. After two months of intense introspection and training in a unit of 30 other young people, I was assigned to an inner-city church in Harrisburg, Pennsylvania. My duties were to survey and visit the neighborhood families, be a liaison between them and the church, and conduct after-school clubs for the neighborhood children. The experience changed my life.

The church had split over the issue of remaining in the city to minister to the surrounding community instead of relocating to the suburbs. Those who stayed maintained that "God doesn't relocate," and their actions bore vivid testimony to their convictions. Members, including Lois and Jerry Byrem, with whom I lived, gave up new homes, cars, vacations, and many special pleasures to donate as much as 30% of their incomes to the building of a new education wing which would be a center for community activities and services. Housewives worked almost full-time carrying out committee assignments. Lois's dining room was the center for the bond campaign. Numerous men, like Jerry, forfeited their lunch hours and days off to sell bonds, inspect the building, and do some of the construction work themselves.

The most powerful witness to me, however, was the obvious joy and fulfillment those people received from their servanthood. I knew then that I could never be content to live my life simply for "me and mine."

For Larry, the call to serious service came when he returned home from Vietnam. Though always a kind, helpful and generous person with a zest for living, his appreciation for life was deepened by his war experience, and he gained a new purpose and meaning for his existence. He served on a local school board, took leadership positions in his church, and helped found The Bridge Center in Schenectady, New York, a highly successful residential drug rehabilitation center for young people.

From our own experiences and subsequent events and observations, we have become convinced that the deepest satisfaction in life is derived from serving others. In fact, I will go even further and say that to live a life centered only on ourselves is failing to recognize that we are all part of the larger body of humanity and leads ultimately to isolation, despair and emptiness. *I believe we were created and born to serve one another.*

Servanthood Is Infectious

The word *servant* calls to mind numerous connotations, many conveying a lowly image with which most of us do not care to identify ourselves. Jesus maintained, however, that the highest position in the kingdom of God was that of a servant. He said to his disciples, ". . . whoever wants to be great among you must be your servant" (Matt. 20:26, NIV).

When we were members of Windham Presbyterian Church in New Hampshire, Larry and I participated in their first mission trip to work with the Rural Community Action Ministry (RCAM) in central Maine. This ongoing program uses volunteer mission teams to repair homes, build handicap ramps, and minister in other concrete ways to the poor, elderly and disabled. For us, it was an especially rewarding experience because we made a heart connection with the family whose home we worked on and have maintained a mutually caring connection over the years.

However, in addition to our personal experience, it was instructive to watch the transformation of the youth from our church who participated. Most of them had been "dragged" there by their parents. When the week was over, there wasn't one paint-stained teen who wanted to leave, and their enthusiasm and compassion were contagious. It was they who suggested the idea of sharing a meal with all the families we had served, a joyous culmination to the week that has become an annual tradition. The next year, when the mission trip sign-up sheet was posted, the youth were the first to add their names.

Our second summer on the road, we had the opportunity to join our former church for the 10th annual work trip. We were amazed to see three there from that first group, now beautiful young women and men embarking on their own lives, and to learn that two of them had participated in every single mission trip over the years! They all attested to the impact those experiences had in developing their sensitivity to the needs of others and the deep personal satisfaction it had given them. This story is not an anomaly; we have seen varying versions of it many times. It is typical of what happens when people of any age become introduced to the infectious joy of serving others.

Giving And Receiving

In our sometimes frantic and self-conscious search for happiness, we often place misguided emphasis on getting and accumulating, only to find that no matter how much we store up, our lives continue to feel empty. That is because in the laws of life, giving and receiving are always linked. "We are a profoundly egocentric culture," says Thomas Moore in the preface to *Voices From The Heart*. "Popular psychology recommends a strong sense of self, well-maintained ego boundaries, and wholesome self-esteem—all ego concerns that turn our attention inward and increase anxiety. The religious and spiritual traditions offer a completely different point of view. They say that we find our soul only when we lose our highly prized sense of self."

Giving and receiving should be as natural as breathing in and breathing out—both functions being essential to a healthy life. An extreme in one direction or the other tilts one's life out of skew. On the one hand, there are well-meaning do-gooders whose inability to receive results in a relationship of inequality—dispiriting rather than uplifting those they aim to help. On the other, are people either content to live off the welfare of others or who lavish all of their resources on themselves—both of whom do not understand the adverse effects their failure to contribute has on their own lives.

It is important to "give back" in order to keep the resources of the universe circulating. When we give back to life, we quickly discover that life bestows its bounty upon us in numerous, unanticipated ways. Chief among the benefits is a sense of fulfillment that no amount of money can generate.

So many people expend fruitless time, energy and resources trying to find meaning and purpose in their lives, not realizing it can most readily be found by simply reaching out to others. Consider the dissatisfied millionaires who finally discover this secret and are compelled to give away most of their fortunes to alleviate their feelings of inner bankruptcy, and to experience the joy that had for so long eluded them.

Millard Fuller, founder of Habitat for Humanity, is a relevant example. A successful businessman, lawyer and self-made millionaire by age 29, he was consumed by a drive to make and accumulate wealth. But his world was suddenly turned on end when his wife Linda confronted him with the emptiness of their lives, and left him. Deep soul-searching brought them back together with a renewed commitment to each other and a vow to dedicate themselves to serving God. Giving away all they had, they retreated to the Christian community at Koinonia Farm near Americus, Georgia, to receive guidance and direction from its co-founder and spiritual leader Clarence Jordan. It was there that the idea for partnership housing eventually was birthed and implemented. A few years later, after the death of Clarence, Millard and Linda founded Habitat for Humanity and have guided it into one of the most effective and life-changing worldwide ministries

Mobile Service

As we began traveling, we were quite surprised and pleased to learn that so many RVers are using their freedom and mobility not only for seeing the country, but also for bringing hope and a helping hand to others. They are building homes and churches, helping at disaster sites, working at youth camps and orphanages and involving themselves in numerous ways in communities where they spend a period of time. RVers are in a unique position to render service. Their flexible schedules allow them to respond quickly if need be and give them the option to stay somewhere for an extended time. Housing is not an issue, because their homes are with them.

We also discovered that there are a number of service groups specifically tailored for RVers. In general, they are structured to give participants a choice of short-term work projects throughout the country year round. Most schedule a four-day workweek, 6-7 hours a day, which allows ample time and energy for fellowship and sightseeing.

However, as new RVers, we wanted to maintain our freedom to respond to a variety of opportunities. When we met Eugene and Nancy Martin, who had been full-timing about as long as we had, we were intrigued by the way they combined working with organizations and finding avenues of service on their own.

The Martins often choose an area they want to visit, then approach a local church to exchange service for a place to park. My ears especially perked up when they mentioned making their own connections to help after a tornado hit Winter Garden, Florida. As it turned out, we adopted a mode of operation very similar to theirs. It complemented our desire to remain open and available to Spirit's leading, rather than predetermining where we would go and what we would do.

We Are Family

Some of our friends expressed concern that as full-time RVers we would miss being part of a supportive and caring community. However, we have not found that to be the case at all. If anything, RVing has broadened our sense of community. Just as there are everyday opportunities in neighborhoods or at work to help others, so there are many occasions on a daily basis to be sensitive and minister to "our neighbors" in campgrounds. They can be as diverse as helping make repairs on a rig, taking someone to the hospital, caring for the campground cats, or sharing a meal with a person traveling alone.

Perhaps *because* of the transitory nature of the lifestyle, RVers learn to make instant connections. They often go out of their way for strangers to a degree one might ordinarily only expect from family or close friends. There are very few RVers who will look the other way when someone needs help. In fact, the motto of our Thousand Trails & NACO campground system is "We Are Family," and the standard greeting between the 55,000 members of the *Escapees* RV organization is a warm hug.

What a different world this might be if we *all* treated each other as family and greeted each other with hugs!

II. THE HABITAT CONNECTION

*. . . it isn't easy to find a project that is at the same time
exciting, somewhat controversial, inspirational,
challenging, unpredictable, worthwhile, successful,
and international in scope. But such is
Habitat for Humanity.*

Jimmy and Rosalynn Carter, ***Everything to Gain***

II-4. THUMBS UP FOR HABITAT

What will count when we die is:
Did we change the life of one person for the better?

Betty Fine Collins,
Jefferson County (Alabama) Commissioner

A Hand Up

We were drawn to Habitat for Humanity as a vehicle of service for a variety of reasons. First, Larry and I have always preferred to contribute to people in a way that promotes a lasting or ongoing effect in their lives. Though we have donated our share of Thanksgiving meals and Christmas presents, and often worked at our local soup kitchen and various other service projects, we saw those efforts as filling an immediate and vital need that, unfortunately, seldom enabled people to significantly alter their circumstances. Habitat provides the opportunity to help make a far-reaching difference in a family's life. By helping families move out of undesirable living conditions into new, modest, fully-equipped homes of their own, we would be enabling them to change their entire environment, as well as giving them hope for a more promising future and, perhaps, a more favorable outlook on people and life.

Second, we support the idea of giving people "a hand up" rather than a handout. This is the concept we find is most often misunderstood when we encounter people unfamiliar with Habitat's structure. Habitat for Humanity is not a welfare organization; the homeowners are not "given" the homes. By *partnering* with Habitat, they are simply being given an *opportunity* to own a home, an opportunity they otherwise might not have. The two greatest obstacles to home ownership for the poor are the down payment and mortgage payments that take too big a bite out of their income.

Habitat homeowners make a small down payment ($500 is typical in the U.S.) that can be accumulated while they are investing their "sweat equity"—300-500 hours of labor on their home or helping to build other Habitat homes. The cost of the home is kept low by using volunteer labor, and the payments are made affordable by employing the "economics of Jesus," as founder Millard Fuller calls it—charging no interest and realizing no profit on the sale of the house or on the loan.

In most cases, Habitat mortgage payments in the U.S. are around $120 a month on a 30-year mortgage (more if the homeowner chooses a 15- or 20-year repayment), and are usually much less than what the family was paying in rent for often deplorable places. In addition, a nurturing committee works with recipients to educate them about finances and home ownership, thus helping to ensure that they will make their payments faithfully and become responsible homeowners.

Larry and I had also enjoyed the personal connection we made with the homeowner family during a brief prior building experience with Habitat. Unlike when we sent off a check (also an indispensable form of service), we were later able to picture a particular family and remember the enthusiasm of the children as they watched the walls of "their house" being erected.

Another component of our high regard for Habitat for Humanity is that it provides an opportunity for people to physically and practically express God's love to others through "the theology of the hammer," which Millard Fuller outlines in his book of the same title. Habitat is a Christian organization based on Christian principles, but it neither serves only Christians, nor has any expectations or makes any demands upon the recipients in regard to religion. It is an organization that transcends denominations and dogma, races and creeds, bringing together for a common focus and purpose all who are drawn to its ministry.

Demonstration Plot

As mentioned earlier, that ministry has its roots about six miles outside the city limits of Americus, Georgia, in the complex originally named Koinonia (the Greek word for "fellowship" or "community") Farm. The sign as one approaches the Koinonia Villages and farm operations reads: WELCOME TO KOINONIA—A Christian community seeking to be a Demonstration Plot for the Kingdom of God.

Clarence Jordan, co-founder of Koinonia, held that one's beliefs were not something to be merely discussed, but rather to be lived. ". . . it's so much more pleasant to be sky people than it is to be earth people," he maintained. This physically imposing, charismatic, highly intelligent and educated Southern white man, who had a degree in agriculture and a Ph.D. in New Testament Greek, saw all around him in his native state of Georgia good Christian folk who had found a way to dichotomize their religion, allowing them on the one hand to profess faith in a loving savior, while at the same time committing unspeakable acts of hatred and degradation toward their brothers and sisters who had a different skin color.

According to Lena Hofer-McCaughtrie, who had left her Hutterite community in Canada as a young woman and lived at Koinonia while pursuing her dream to become a nurse, "Clarence always said, 'If you don't live it, don't preach it!'" "Living it" was what Clarence referred to as *incarnational theology.*

In 1942 (long before the Civil Rights Movement), his family joined with another in purchasing a 440-acre farm in Sumter County, Georgia, for the purpose of creating an interracial farming community and providing jobs and support for the poor people in the area. Blacks and whites would live together, work together, eat together, worship together, and share equally in the fruits of their labor. His cousin, Hamilton Jordan, also President Jimmy Carter's campaign manager and chief of staff, wrote in *No Such Thing As A Bad Day*, "Clarence's faith was not a remote, prissy, sanitized doctrine or ritual but a gritty, folksy, in-your-face way of life, based on respect and love for all humanity and applied to every decision and every action."

The bold experiment in interracial communal living was marginally tolerated in the area until the desegregation of schools was ordered. Then, growing hostility quickly turned to threats, intimidation, destruction of property, and gunshots. However, not even an ultimatum from the Ku Klux Klan or a more genteel approach from the "city fathers" could persuade Clarence and the Koinonia community to leave or renounce their lifestyle.

When they could not be defeated by intimidation or persuasion, the surrounding community refused to sell them supplies, and boycotted their products between 1956 and the mid-1960s. During that period, Koinonia found a creative way to continue sustaining itself. A highly successful mail order business was started to sell their pecan and peanut products and garner support from people (partners) all over the country who believed in Koinonia's mission. That business continues to thrive, and faithful partners still contribute regularly to Koinonia.

It was in December of 1965 that Millard and Linda Fuller paid their first visit to Koinonia. In 1968, they would return there to live, helping to implement and guide the partnership housing program after the sudden death of Clarence in 1969.

Following three years of ministering and building homes in Zaire (now the Democratic Republic of Congo) Millard and Linda returned to Americus and founded Habitat for Humanity in 1976.

Getting A Taste

In addition to learning the ropes of our new lifestyle and coming to terms with our freedom, we did the usual things RVers do in our first six months. For us that meant visiting several more of our network campgrounds in North Carolina, Tennessee and Mississippi, and taking excursions to nearby museums, waterfalls and historical attractions. Other than an evening at the Grand Ole Opry, we quickly learned the validity of that old adage "the best things in life are free" or, at most, under five dollars!

Spending the winter in Florida, we discovered it was quite easy to adapt to no snow. We enjoyed the white sand beaches and wildlife refuges of the Gulf Coast, explored the Everglades and indulged in the Sunset Celebration on Mallory Square in Key West. We also secured passes to watch the 4 a.m. launch of the space shuttle Discovery on its mission to service the Hubble Telescope—a truly awesome sight in the darkness.

By the time we headed out of Florida in the spring, we had already plugged into a number of Habitat projects in several states. Each experience had been a satisfying one and whetted our appetite for more. Our work with the Lexington, North Carolina Habitat affiliate helped us to see that building a house is not all that Habitat is about.

We arrived there on a Saturday morning to help put the finishing touches on two homes to be dedicated the next day. Both homeowners were hard working, black, single mothers. The two houses were paid for and built by members of a black Southern Baptist church and a white Presbyterian church. During the course of the several months that it took to build the homes, the parishioners had not only hammered together, but also shared potluck suppers and worship services at each others' churches.

As we all gathered around on Sunday afternoon for the traditional blessing of the homes, presentation of the Bibles to the homeowner families, and the turning over of the keys, the friendships, understanding and mutual respect that had been fostered was evident. Habitat is a unique vehicle for connecting many elements and segments of communities that might otherwise never touch.

What I remember most, however, was the teenage daughter of one of the homeowners who came up to me and exclaimed earnestly, "My mama is so happy, I don't even know what to say to her!"

Pilgrimage To Americus

It had long been our desire to visit the Habitat for Humanity International Headquarters in Americus, so as Larry and I began slowly following spring and the magnificent dogwoods north to our camp in New Hampshire, we called ahead and made arrangements to stay in Habitat's five-site RV park.

We decided to volunteer at Habitat for a few days after touring the Headquarters and area attractions, which included attending Jimmy Carter's Sunday school class at Maranatha Baptist Church in Plains where we had our picture taken with the former President and First Lady.

Larry worked on a home with a group of college students from Minnesota who were participating in the Collegiate Challenge program by spending their spring break building a Habitat home rather than partying on a beach. This program continues to snowball each year as students return to their colleges and relate the satisfying experiences they had. In spring 2002, more than 10,300 students representing over 700 college and university campus chapters in 26 countries worked across the country with 190 HFH affiliates and pledged over one million dollars in donations.

I volunteered in the Global Village Department at Habitat's headquarters, which gave me an opportunity to learn more about the organizational set-up and service opportunities. The Global Village Department, among other responsibilities, arranges short-term Habitat experiences all over the world for volunteers.

Some people have suggested that Habitat should address the housing needs in the United States first or even exclusively, but the vision of Habitat is that we are a global community and that no one's housing need is any more or less important than another's. For this reason, every Habitat affiliate is urged to support the work in another country. "U.S. affiliates last year sent $7.3 million to help with Habitat house-building efforts in other countries," wrote Jill Claflin in the June/July 2000 issue of *Habitat World*. "Many have partnerships, or 'sister affiliate/community' relationships, that go well beyond financial assistance." Notably, most houses in developing countries cost less than one-tenth the amount necessary to build one in the United States. However, Habitat affiliates in those poorer countries are also encouraged to contribute to other affiliates. This mutual support fosters an awareness that one's own destiny is intrinsically connected to their brothers and sisters around the globe.

I was happy to observe the commitment to fiscal responsibility and continuous evaluation and improvement in the entire organization. Unlike government agencies, Habitat has the autonomy to correct mistakes, alter its structure when necessary, continually find more efficient and creative ways to expand its vision, and base everything it does on Christian principles of love, equality, honesty and service.

While other worthwhile movements often lose their focus and eventually wither, Habitat continues to grow its vision of a world free of substandard housing. As of 2002, more than 125,000 homes have been built in 83 countries, housing 625,000 people who otherwise would still be living in undesirable conditions. I believe there are several reasons for Habitat's phenomenal success.

First, the premise is simple and unfettered: *All of God's people deserve a decent place to live.* That premise transcends theological prescriptions; it is one that all people of good will can enthusiastically embrace.

Second, Habitat for Humanity is unabashedly a Christian ministry, providing an avenue by which people can express the love of Christ to others through concrete action. It is a ministry that continues to draw more and more devotees into its fold.

Money Isn't Everything

I was especially impressed with the caliber and commitment of the people who work at Habitat Headquarters. A third of the Habitat for Humanity headquarters staff is comprised of volunteers who receive housing and a stipend ranging from $60/week to $450/month depending on their position and length of stay. Many people have prematurely ended lucrative careers to work full-time in either volunteer or modestly-paid staff positions. What prompts people to do something so flagrantly out of synch with our societal norms? Obviously, they must be receiving something they were not getting from their former occupations. I spoke at length with three volunteers whose stories I would like to share.

A Pact With God

At the age of 50, Jackie Merriman, known to everyone at Habitat as Grandma Jackie, was presented with the opportunity for early retirement, lifetime medical insurance, and a "golden parachute" of almost two-years' salary from General Foods Corporation in Cranbury, New Jersey. At that momentous juncture in her life, Jackie sat down with a legal-sized pad of paper and wrote across the top, "If someone told you you didn't have to work for two years and they would pay you, what would you do?" She proceeded to fill five pages with her desires, but number one was to join the Peace Corps or some other meaningful service organization.

The only impediment to devoting the rest of her life to service work, rather than reestablishing herself in another business as most of her fellow retirees did, was her need for financial security. Raised by her grandmother who had struggled through the Great Depression, Jackie had heard from her earliest years the importance of security and thrift. "So," Jackie relates, "I made a pact with God. I told him 'Make me not to worry about my finances, and I will do your work.'" And God did! Jackie loves to tell how everything fell into place, including the means to purchase a new car *with cash.*

As Jackie began to explore volunteer opportunities, she became aware of the Habitat affiliate in Trenton, New Jersey, near where she lived. She volunteered for a day and later received a copy of the next issue of *Habitat World*. In it, she learned there was a need for volunteers at the headquarters, so in 1989, Jackie came to Americus and worked in finance for three months. Two years later, she returned to take on the assignment of traveling to 15 cities between Key Largo, Florida, and Columbus, Ohio, to help coordinate the teams building houses in each as part of Habitat's celebration of 15 years of service. As a result of that effort, 1500 homes were constructed.

After a brief hiatus, Jackie signed on as an extended volunteer and has served at the Headquarters ever since. Much of her tenure has been in the Global Village Department. Until recently, Jackie served as the Domestic Referral Coordinator, querying affiliates across the country regarding their needs and matching them with people who inquire about working with Habitat during their vacation or a specific time period.

During my few days working in Global Village, Grandma Jackie took me under her wing, as I observed her do with many others. It was obvious that Jackie sees her work at Habitat as a divine mission, not just a job. Jackie contributed significantly to the exceptional cooperation and caring that I witnessed among the Global Village team while I was there.

Though much of her work is done in an office and on a computer, Jackie's assignment in Global Village afforded her opportunities to travel to other countries frequently and thus "keep in touch firsthand with the grassroots' perspective of Habitat." She has never lost sight of the purpose of her work—to give people an opportunity to live in decent housing and to uplift their lives. "If I build a home for someone now," she says, "I won't have to build one for their children."

In the early 1990's, Jackie joined with a group of women to launch WATCH (Women Accepting The Challenge of Housing), which financially sponsored and built seven and a half homes in Sumter County, as well as 10 houses overseas. Their successful efforts were the forerunner of Habitat's Women Build Department.

In the fall of 2001, Jackie moved over to the Tourism Office, where she now solicits and coordinates volunteer teams to construct 40 houses illustrating materials and construction methods used in the 83 countries where Habitat is at work. These homes will be the centerpiece of Habitat's new Global Village and Discovery Center, designed to better educate people about Habitat's worldwide mission.

Grandma Jackie represents the true spirit of Habitat for Humanity—and she passes that spirit on. She is most proud of the fact that her grandson, who was 13 at the time, helped paint a volunteer house when he visited her.

The Crucible

Linda and Paul Mills were highly successful in the hotel business in both northern New Hampshire and near Sturbridge, Massachusetts. However, living on hotel premises gave rise to concerns about raising their children in what they considered an unrealistic setting. They wanted them to know that not everyone enjoyed the privileged lifestyle of their playmates, often children of entrepreneurs, or the wealthy guests they observed.

Linda and Paul decided to look for a more suitable setting in which to work and be of service while raising their family. They had heard about Habitat for Humanity from a friend, but didn't know much about it. However, when they took the children on vacation to an amusement park near Richmond, Virginia, they felt led to "swing by" Americus to visit Habitat's headquarters—a side trip of only 700 miles!

Since they would be arriving on a Saturday, they called ahead to be sure someone could meet with them. Imagine their surprise and delight when the receptionist told them to call back in ten minutes and Millard Fuller would speak with them. When Linda explained to him that they were looking for somewhere to commit themselves long-term, Millard persuasively explained all the reasons why Habitat should be their choice. And so, on October 1, 1989, three months after their visit, the Mills family boldly uprooted and came to Americus with the intention of training to become International Partners and work with affiliates overseas.

An unanticipated medical condition foiled their plans, and after Linda's period of recuperation, they decided it would be best for their children if they worked with Habitat in Americus. After getting settled into a volunteer house, Linda and Paul were asked to take charge of coordinating volunteer housing—assigning volunteers to accommodations, renovating the homes and establishing policies. After serving in that capacity for eighteen months, Paul moved into the paid position of purchasing manager. They bought a house of their own, and Linda taught at Koinonia Partners preschool for a year and a half, after which she stayed home to take care of their family.

Although they weathered financially lean years, Linda says living in the Habitat community "was everything they had hoped for their children. It gave them a global perspective on life, and the interracial environment in Americus schools was good for them." But, for herself, Linda found life in Americus difficult and lonely. Her friends and co-workers in the Habitat community constantly came and went.

Loneliness finally provoked Linda to seek personal satisfaction outside the Habitat circle. In 1992, she began to pursue an interest that had long intrigued her—quilting. When a local quilt shop was opened, Linda worked with the owner and taught classes. A few years later, they also initiated a quilting guild. Subsequently, Linda was happy to discover that a number of Habitat employees were also quilters.

Everything began to come together for Linda in early 1999. She became the full-time tourism director for Habitat, a job which enables her to utilize the people skills developed in the hotel business to introduce visitors to the Habitat story. Around the same time, she was approached by Linda Fuller to coordinate the crafting of a quilt for former President Jimmy Carter's 75th birthday. "Who would have ever thought a quilt I helped design and make would hang in a President's home?" she marveled. "My time here has served as a crucible. Without it, I would never have come into my own as an artist."

31

Actually, Linda believes "the Habitat experience and quilting have a lot in common," as she explained in the February 4, 2000, *Habichat*, Habitat's in-house newsletter. "They both represent grassroots, personal efforts. A quilter sews many pieces of fabric together to create an object of beauty and warmth. In the same way, Habitat's ministry brings many different individuals together, creating warm relationships and community." Beautiful quilts created by Habitat supporters have long graced the walls of the Habitat Headquarters, and the connection between Habitat and quilting is growing. Quilters in Broward County, Florida, for example, pledged to make a quilt for the homeowners of all new Habitat homes built by that county's affiliate in the year 2000.

Linda's next commissioned quilt was one depicting symbols of Habitat's 25-year history, which was unveiled at the anniversary celebration in September, 2001. Linda expressed her thankfulness for the opportunity to feel it was all right to fulfill her creative needs. "I used to be conflicted about doing something artistic when there were so many critical needs in the world. What more could a person ask than to have a job they love, for a cause they are committed to, and to be able to combine it with their artistic expression?" she asked.

"Nothing," I responded. "Your story is indicative of how peoples' lives become ordered when they listen to their hearts and have the courage to respond to their calling."

Linda is now busy overseeing Phase I of the Global Village and Discovery Center slated to open December 3, 2002, which will supplant the present Tourism Office.

Number One

Clive Rainey, who celebrated his 20th anniversary with Habitat on April 1, 1997, has the honor of being the first volunteer at Habitat Headquarters. Clive's story would make an interesting book in itself.

Clive attributes his liberation from the "intolerant and narrow-minded culture of south Georgia" in which he was raised to a stint in the Army during the Vietnam era. Ever since, Clive has been boldly "calling it as he sees it."

Following his tour of duty in Vietnam, Clive was stationed at Ft. Lewis, Washington. While there, he had the opportunity to read widely which, coupled with the climate of social unrest in the country, primed him to return to his native state "to try to make a difference." During the ensuing years, he has worked tirelessly for social change and justice in Sumter County, Georgia.

He attended Georgia Southwestern College in Americus, received a degree in education and history, and later a Masters in teaching reading. His conscience was further piqued by a political science professor who made him repeat the course "until he got it"—"it" being social consciousness. After the student newspaper for which Clive wrote was taken over by the president of the college, he started his own free paper called *The Whirlwind* (printed at Koinonia Farm), which stirred up heated political and social dialogue at the college and in the community, resulting in Clive becoming a local figure to be reckoned with.

Clive taught school for several years, both near Savannah and in nearby Dawson, but began to feel that his efforts would continue to be largely fruitless unless the housing conditions and environment of his students improved. One evening Millard Fuller paid Clive a visit and invited him to Koinonia to view a slide presentation about his house-building work in Zaire. For some time after, Millard tried to convince Clive to oversee the efforts in Africa. Clive resisted, feeling there was immediate work that needed to be done right in Sumter County. A little later, Clive committed himself to the fledgling Habitat for Humanity in Americus and was given charge of selecting the families who would receive the first 12 Habitat homes to be built there.

Clive considers himself privileged that his involvement began so close in time to the original blossoming vision of Habitat, allowing him to receive firsthand training from the Fullers, who themselves had nurtured the budding fruits of the seeds sown by Clarence Jordan.

After two and a half years of doing anything and everything to help launch Habitat in Americus, Clive did work in Africa and later directed the Africa program from headquarters for six years. He has been entrusted with various leadership roles over the years, leading up to his current position as director of the 21st Century Challenge program (I will elaborate on this later.) In each capacity, Clive has endeavored to adhere to the Christian principles upon which Habitat was founded and its mission to serve those in need in a spirit of equality and genuine partnership.

Yes!

It didn't take long for Larry and me to confirm that Habitat for Humanity was, indeed, a ministry we wanted to become more fully engaged with. The opportunity to do so presented itself while we were there in Americus.

II-5. NEWFOUNDLAND BOUND

Ask, and you will receive. . .

John 16:24 (NIV)

The Pied Piper

On the day that the Habitat for Humanity International Board of Directors was to meet in Americus, the then-president of Habitat Canada, Wilmer Martin, came dashing into the Global Village Department waving the brochures he was carrying. He made an urgent announcement to anyone whose eye he could catch: "We need 60 more people for the Ed Schreyer Work Project in St. John's (the capital of Newfoundland) this August" (1997).

The Ed Schreyer Work Project, we would come to learn, is Canada's equivalent of the Jimmy Carter Work Project. Several years before, the former Governor-General of Canada had been challenged by Jimmy Carter to use his name and influence to lend stature and publicity to Canada's growing network of Habitat affiliates.

"It will be an exciting time," Wilmer added, "because this year is the 500th Anniversary of John Cabot's landing, and there will be all kinds of festivals and events going on in Newfoundland!"

This man's zeal was definitely difficult to ignore, and I looked his way long enough for him to fix his gaze on me. It drew me in as surely as if he had been "The Pied Piper." Now he spoke directly to me: "Wouldn't you like to come to Newfoundland and help us build homes in August? I guarantee you'll have a wonderful experience."

Caught up in the sweep of the moment, I responded, "Well, maybe we can. We're going to be at our camp in New Hampshire this summer. I don't think that's too far from Newfoundland." He placed a brochure in my hand and looked directly into my eyes, as if to confirm that we had sealed a contract.

I hurried back to the trailer for lunch and, still caught up in the blush of enthusiasm, told Larry I thought we were supposed to go to Newfoundland. "It's not very far from camp, right?" I added. Larry's dumbfounded look brought me down from my high. "Let's talk about it tonight," he answered.

When I arrived back at the trailer that evening, Larry was sitting with the atlas opened to Newfoundland. "Do you have any idea how far Newfoundland is from camp?" he asked.

"No," I admitted.

"Well, it's almost the equivalent of going across the U.S. I'm not saying I don't want to go, but it's going to take a pretty big financial bite. Besides the $300-per-person registration fee (to cover housing, meals, and other expenses of hosting a blitz build), that's a lot of gasoline, and who knows what it will cost to take the trailer across on the ferry."

Out Of Our Hands

I gave no hint that I hadn't realized we had to get there by ferry. Undaunted, I made a proposal he couldn't refuse: "I will write to some of the churches we've served, as well as a few friends, and ask if they would like to support us financially. We, in turn, will offer to represent them at the build. If we get enough support to make it viable, then we will know that we are supposed to go." That night, I set up our word processor in the common room at the RV park and wrote letters and addressed return postcards until 3 a.m.

Responses came fairly quickly. However, many of the people and churches were already supporting Habitat projects and could offer us only prayer support. We did receive a few donations, and each made me consciously aware of how intrinsically our past is linked to our present—one from the minister who had married us, another from Windham Presbyterian Church, and a generous pledge from our very dear friend Lee Alphen, who has her own unique ministry to migrant workers at the Rockingham Race Track in Salem, New Hampshire. The total of all the donations came to $165. We weren't certain that was enough to tip the scales toward going.

As we left Georgia and headed to Carolina Landing, our decision was still "hanging out there." In South Carolina, we again attended the little Unity Church near Clemson University that we had discovered the previous fall. Larry and I led the music and sang a duet on Easter Sunday and, after the service, the pianist asked what our plans were when we left South Carolina. I told her we were heading up to our camp in New Hampshire and, if we were able to raise enough support, we would go to Newfoundland for a Habitat blitz build. I said this as a matter of fact, with no ulterior motive. The next week, the congregation surprised their "free-spirited vagabonds" with a gift of $250!

In the meantime, I had also been in contact with the registrar of the project in Newfoundland and explained that we wanted very much to come, but that our financial resources were modest. After a number of discussions, we received word that our fee would be significantly reduced by "billeting" us in a private home where we could keep our cat Ross with us. We had also decided that if we went we would not take the trailer, because the cost of the ferry would be prohibitive. Instead, we would "camp" in the bed of our truck. So, along with the donation from the church, everything finally dovetailed—including a favorable monetary exchange rate—to make our trip doable.

Preparations

There was a special feeling of sacredness as we went about our preparations because we truly believed that our desires had been inspired, supported and blessed by God. We had once again seen clearly that when we are responsive to the call of Spirit without being attached to the outcome, we only need do our part and trust that the rest of the details will be worked out.

In New Hampshire, we emptied all the contents of the bed of the truck (which has a slanted shell with windows) and stored them in the big garage on our property. Then we began working on outfitting it to serve as our sleeping quarters. We discovered that the dinette cushions in the trailer (which combine to make a mattress for a full-size bed when the table is lowered) fit perfectly, with enough room on each side to line up our boxes of clothes.

I fashioned window coverings of opaque material, to which I sewed Velcro tabs. The Velcro stuck easily to the fuzzy liner of the shell. Meanwhile, Larry rigged a lean-to that would extend out from the back hatch, so we'd have a little place to maneuver if it was raining. We packed all our Habitat gear and tools into the cargo carrier on top. In the back seat of the cab, we put our food, a small cooler and camp stove.

Since we had already committed ourselves to join Windham Presbyterian Church on the summer work trip to Maine, we decided it would be an ideal opportunity to test our self-styled camper. It worked beautifully. We were ready.

When Does The Tide Come In?

I'm not sure what I was thinking when our son-in-law informed us that we would be able to see the 50-foot tides in Nova Scotia. I guess I was picturing the big waves that used to roll in at night when I walked the beach in southern California. So, on the second evening of our trip, when we arrived at Five Islands Provincial Park on the Minas Basin where the world's highest tides are recorded, I walked into the Ranger Station and asked what time I could see the tide come in. A puzzled look crossed the Ranger's face, but she very graciously explained that it took about twelve hours for it to move in or out.

Walking back to the truck, my face flushed as I realized how foolish I must have sounded. In any case, it is quite a phenomenon to behold (albeit over a period of time) when gradually, almost like time-lapse photography, whole islands and chunks of land quietly appear as the water recedes, leaving a vast expanse of beach unveiled for clamming and collecting multi-colored rocks and shells. The next day, the sea progressively swallowed them all up.

The Longest Day

After spending a day relaxing at the park, we rose early the next morning, broke camp, and headed for North Sydney, from where our ferry would depart the following morning at 7 a.m. We arrived about 3 in the afternoon. Having already decided we would sleep overnight in the ferry line, we passed the interim at the Cape Breton County Exhibition.

We definitely got the maximum for our $2.25 admission—agriculture and animal exhibits, horse shows and barrel racing, an impressive dressage demonstration, and even a live band to dance to. I was delighted when I was given a red pine seedling at the Forestry Department display, believing it would be a fitting memento of our trip when we planted it at our camp. At 11:30 p.m., we headed to the ferry, got our place in line, showered in the facilities there and browsed the gift shops—finally crawling into the truck and falling asleep around 2 a.m.

At exactly 4 a.m., Ross, who had to that point been a patient and model traveler, decided he'd had enough of being cooped up in the truck. He began slamming his body against the back door and beating his paws on the hatch, all the while yelling in the distinctive voice which betrayed his part-Siamese ancestry. After about a half-hour, we managed to quiet him and nod back off, only to be awakened again at 5 a.m. by the loudspeaker announcements instructing incoming cars how to line up in the lanes. Acknowledging that our sleep had come to an end, we got out, walked Ross around on his leash and chatted with fellow sojourners.

It looked like we were driving into the jowls of a whale when we boarded the Joey E. Smallwood ferry, named after Newfoundland's first governor. As soon as the ferry pulled away from the dock, and after saying good-bye to a bewildered Ross who had to remain in the truck, Larry and I quickly found reclining chairs in a dark corner of a passenger room. We immediately fell asleep. We had a 14-hour trip ahead of us.

An hour later, the sound of excited voices awakened us. As we pried ourselves back into consciousness, we saw children jumping up and down in front of the windows, squealing and pointing. Dragging ourselves up, we went to the window to see what the commotion was about, then immediately ran out onto the deck to get a better view of the three pods of whales and dozens of dolphins passing close by the ferry. It was an unanticipated and breathtaking sight!

Of course, with the excitement and the cold misty air, we were now thoroughly awake, so we found a spot to eat a snack and chat with people. For the next several hours we engaged in lively conversations with Newfoundlanders and other Canadians on board. We also enjoyed entertainment in the lounge by the duo Bread and Butter. Their traditional Newfoundland folk songs, interspersed with "Newfie" jokes and tall tales, were great fun and gave us a wonderful feel for the culture and traditions of the country we were about to visit.

We managed to catch a few more winks of sleep before docking at Argentia at 9:30 p.m. Ross was definitely happy to see us. Then, after driving through rain and fog on the 90-mile trip to St. John's, we met up with other Habitat arrivers at a designated McDonald's. Around 11:30, we were led to our housing assignment—a huge, ultra-modern home owned by a vice-president of Petro Canada, one of the major sponsors of the blitz build. His wife greeted us as we stepped inside. The minute we saw their big golden retriever, however, we wondered how it was going to work with Ross in the house. Sure enough, seconds later the phone rang and our would-be hostess was informed that we had been brought to the wrong place and a switch needed to be made.

At 1 a.m., we at length arrived at the old Victorian home of our real hosts, a delightful newlywed couple about our ages. Edna was the steward of all the Provincial Parks in Canada, and Kevin owned a construction business. They showed us a large room and bath just off the kitchen that would be our "headquarters," and after a few minutes of chitchat, Kevin fished a key out of his pocket and handed it to Larry. "The missus and I will be leaving early in the morning to spend the weekend at our cabin. Just make yourselves at home and eat whatever food you find in the refrigerator and cupboards," he informed us. We later learned that such trusting hospitality is a trademark of Newfoundland culture.

We brought in only the necessities, got Ross situated, and gratefully crawled into bed. Thus ended our personal rendition of "The Longest Day."

II-6. HERE COMES THE NEIGHBORHOOD

We can't afford to squander
a big percentage of the next generation.

Millard Fuller, Founder
Habitat for Humanity

Everyone Has A Story

For people who have been fortunate and/or able to provide the "good things in life" for themselves and their families, it is often a temptation to view those who have been unable as somehow deficient or slackers. It is easy to make judgments when we don't know another person's story, even though we assume that our own stories mitigate any shortcomings in our lives. There are countless reasons why a family may find themselves unable to buy a home under the normal conditions—and few of them have to do with unworthiness.

For the most part, we tend to circulate in groups "of our own kind." Our relationships with people whose lives differ markedly from ours are often marginal at best, and nonexistent at worst. For many of us, working side by side with a Habitat homeowner family is the first opportunity we have had to dispel myths, clear up misconceptions, and relate on an equal basis with people whom we soon discover have as much to give to us as we do to them.

Habitat homeowners, we quickly realized, are very much like us. They have dreams and aspirations, they have strengths and weaknesses, they have talents and preferences. They are hardworking people who have overcome abusive marriages, setbacks from illnesses, lack of education, or any number of other obstacles that may have thwarted their financial progress. Perhaps they have even made mistakes along the way. But the dignity and determination with which they often have endured hardships and ill-fortune and still have bounced back to continue striving for a better life for themselves and their families is profoundly moving and inspiring. They are not people to be pitied. They are to be admired, and it is a privilege to offer them a hand up.

You Have Been Selected

The local affiliate's Selection Committee, following carefully prescribed guidelines, does the selection of prospective Habitat homeowners. The first step is to pass a credit check. Then the applicant's income and financial resources are evaluated to see if they fall within the income parameters—usually half the median income of the area. Taking into consideration their income, number of children, and other financial factors, as well as their current housing situation, the committee must be satisfied that the family has a genuine need and that they will be able to comfortably meet their mortgage obligations, for Habitat counts on that money going back into the pool to help finance other homes.

In addition to housing need and ability to repay the zero-interest mortgage, a family also must demonstrate a willingness to partner in the Habitat program through sweat equity and working cooperatively with the affiliate.

Over 150 applications were received after it was announced in St. John's that five houses would be built to celebrate Newfoundland's 500th Anniversary. A little later, the Canadian Housing Authority donated two more lots and challenged the affiliate to build two additional homes. This was the reason for Wilmer Martin's solicitation in Americus—two more crews of volunteers also had to be rounded up.

Only 35 of the applicant families fit all of Habitat's qualifications; that list was then reduced to 12. This is when it gets tough for the committee and where individual circumstances weigh heavily on the decision. At length, they selected the seven fortunate families whom we would shortly come to know. For those families, the news that they had been selected was undoubtedly comparable to having the Readers Digest Prize Patrol knock at their doors. Their lives would soon take a dramatic turn, and the effects would be sweeping and far-reaching. Four of the families agreed to share their stories and what receiving a Habitat home meant to them.

Too Good To Be True

Rick Walsh was skeptical when his sister-in-law informed him and his wife Cindy that Habitat was taking applications. He believed that if something sounds too good to be true, it probably is. When Cindy asked him what they had to lose by applying, Rick couldn't come up with an answer, so he agreed to fill out the application. However, he persisted in maintaining his dubious stance, continually reminding his family that others might be in more need than they. In fact, he refused to let himself believe in the possibility throughout the process until six months later when Cindy called to tell him that Karen Alexander, the chairperson of the Selection Committee, and Shannie Duff, chairperson of the Cabot Habitat affiliate, were coming to meet with them at 10 a.m. the next morning. Rick felt pretty sure they weren't making a personal visit to inform them that they had not been selected.

Rick and Cindy, both high school graduates, had been married 15 years and had three daughters ages 10, 8, and 4 at the time they applied for their Habitat home. With the birth of their first daughter, they made a decision that Cindy should stay home to raise the children. Rick held various management positions in the car rental business, but was only able to afford a three-bedroom townhouse in the provincial housing development for low-income families.

As often happens when a hundred families with very little income are concentrated in one area, the development became rundown and problems associated with discontent and hopelessness surfaced. Rick and Cindy raised their children in the church, teaching them to live by the Golden Rule. Nevertheless, the deteriorating circumstances in the surrounding area were forcing them to spend more and more of their time indoors. As Rick shared, "It was becoming very hard to hold on to our dream of some day moving our family to a better place."

The word "Congratulations" jumped out at them when they opened the envelope Shannie handed them (after their dog had greeted her by jumping up and placing his muddy paws on her skirt). All they could do was yell, "Yes, Yes, Yes, Yes!!!" In the afternoon, they picked up the children from school and together shared the good news with them. "When we told them," Rick related, "it was like informing them we had won a trip to Disney World."

Does Anyone Care Any More?

Jerome Barry grew up in a small fishing village in Newfoundland where everyone helped each other. It was a natural way of life. However, in the big city of St. John's, it seemed that people were more concerned about themselves. He and his wife Elaine worked full-time and lived in rental houses for ten years, often feeling alone and discouraged. It didn't seem that anyone cared. They wanted very much to provide a home for their young daughter Jillian, but never seemed able to save enough for a down payment. All their money went to bills. They even tried living with Elaine's sister, but that wasn't the solution either.

One Sunday, Jerome attended Elaine's church without her. Wilmer Martin spoke about Habitat that morning. Jerome's ears perked up when he learned that Habitat was planning to build five homes in St. John's. He couldn't wait to get home and tell Elaine that maybe there was some hope, after all, that they could own a house.

The application process was long, and the Barrys ended up number eight on the final list of twelve potential recipients. Then it was announced that two more houses would be added, but that news left the Barrys in the precarious position of "runner up!" Their only chance of realizing their dream was dependent on one of the seven recipients withdrawing their application—which is exactly what happened.

"I became discouraged and lost hope, but Jerome never did," Elaine says. When Shannie and Karen came to tell them they would receive the seventh home, Elaine says they "didn't show much excitement or say a whole lot" because their minds couldn't yet believe what they were hearing. Afterwards, they kept saying to each other, "Does this mean we are getting one of the homes for sure?" They never forgot how close they came to not being one of the fortunate ones.

Almost Out of Faith

Cathy Carroll had lost faith in almost everybody. She was wondering where God was in her life. She had been a single mom for five years and didn't know how she could "continue to be enough for my four little angels." After losing her job, she worried about how she was going to support them and also hold up under the constant emotional strain.

At first, Cathy was excited about landing a full-time job as diving coach for the Canadian National Diving Team. However, the time away from her children and having to travel six or seven times a year for competitions began taking its toll on all of them. Cathy became increasingly exhausted, and further strain was added by executive problems within the diving club.

As Cathy relates: "I had had it! It seemed that every effort I made to better my life turned sour. After being laid off, a business venture went sour.

43

Everywhere I turned, it seemed, I fell into the clutches of very mean and untrustworthy people. I wondered what was wrong with me. I was trying so hard not to turn bitter and cynical, but there no longer appeared to be any reason for me to keep trying."

Cathy and her children moved from a government apartment into her parents' home so her rent money could go to them since they had been helping her as much as they could. However, it was neither an ideal nor long-term solution, given her four children and the limited space and privacy. Then, a friend told Cathy that she had seen a notice about applying for a Habitat house and thought she was a perfect candidate. Cathy didn't have much patience with her friend's "lottery-minded help," nor did she have the energy to fill out an application for what she considered a foolish pipe dream. Finally, after her friend's continual insistence, she reluctantly applied, never expecting anything to come of it.

Even when Shannie informed her she had been selected, she refused to allow herself to believe it. "I thought about how cruel it would be to get excited and then to have it taken away. I just didn't believe anything or anybody could be good." It was not until they began having meetings, fund-raisers and get-togethers with other Habitat families and the new "to be" families, and began working off some of their sweat equity preparing the sites, that Cathy accepted it was really true.

To Dream The Impossible Dream

After a failed marriage, Lois Kaulback, a single mom with a young daughter, thought that her life would take a happy turn for the better when she married Lewis in a small town outside of Edmonton, Alberta. However, not long after, a traumatic personal crisis forced them to sell most of their belongings and flee to Nova Scotia, where Lewis was from. The family headed there in a 1962 Comet, hoping to forget the hardships they had endured and praying for a fresh start. Jillian was nine, Becky was six months old, and Lois was pregnant with their third daughter.

Lois stayed at home with the children while Lewis drove transport trucks, being gone for weeks at a time. Isolation, loneliness, and her mother's serious illness spurred them to move once again—this time to St. John's, Newfoundland, where Lois' family lived. There Lewis obtained another truck driving job which kept him away from home 28 days a month, but at least Lois had a loving support system. She baby-sat two small children and did the best she could to manage their single income and provide a loving and cozy home in their two-bedroom apartment, where she shared a bedroom with the two youngest girls since Lewis was home only a few days a year.

At 34 years old and after working since the age of 17, Lois had little to show for her efforts and felt like a failure for not being able to provide a real home for her daughters. Those feelings were inflamed when she overheard Jillian, then 13, tell her friends that she lived in a different apartment, because she was ashamed of hers. At that point, "my dream to have a home seemed virtually unreachable," Lois admitted.

Just two months after her mother's death, Lois' father told her he'd heard about the Habitat project on the radio. Not wishing to leave any stone unturned, Lois applied, even though she felt their chances were one in a million. After being informed that they were in the final twelve, she prayed constantly that they would receive a home if they were the most deserving. During the waiting period she could barely eat or sleep.

The suspense was intense when Shannie arrived and handed her the envelope. Lois could feel her heart skipping, and when she read the first few lines indicating that they had been accepted, she numbly stood reading the rest of the letter as tears streamed down her face. "I wanted to laugh; I wanted to cry. I guess I was in shock. I didn't know how to react. I remember saying, 'I don't know what to say.' I hugged Shannie and said, 'Thank you. I can't believe it. I can't believe it.' Then I called my two little ones from the living room and told them. We did a little dance. I would have to say the joy I felt in my heart at that moment was almost as great and wonderful as giving birth to my children.

"I held my little ones in my arms and, looking up to heaven, thanked God out loud for answering my prayers. Then I remember saying, 'Thank you, mom.'" Lois recalled her mother declaring, "If it's the last thing I do, Lois, I will help get you a home." Lois felt certain her mother had been "pushing pens from heaven" for them. When Lois' father arrived and heard the joyful news, he called Lewis, who was on the road. Lewis had to pull off to the shoulder when his father-in-law told him he would soon be needing a hammer. Jillian "just about hit the roof when she came home from school and heard the news. We felt like the luckiest people in the world!"

Building Community

On April 13th, 1997, the seven families met for the first time. Rick says, "It was very exciting because not many families get to know their neighbors months before moving into their new home. The nicest thing I remember thinking to myself when we met was that we all had been given a new beginning, and we all would be starting it together as neighbors. Oh, what a feeling!"

During the several months before the actual blitz, the seven families put in far more than their 500 hours of sweat equity working on the rebuild. They spent evenings and weekends helping prepare the site and ready the materials. Working side by side, they shared their stories, their hopes, and their dreams.

The total of seventeen children in the families played together or helped, as they were able, alongside their parents. Rick and his children even pitched a tent and slept on their foundation one night. As the families worked together from May until the beginning of the blitz in August, clearing the property and helping put up the foundations and decking, a deep bond was formed. They were already a neighborhood before the houses were erected.

The theme of the blitz build, proudly displayed on our commemorative tee shirts, was "Here Comes The Neighborhood"—a fitting tribute to what had already been taking place on Hillview Drive East!

II-7. THE GROUNDWORK

*Truly, volunteering is a soulful experience
of the highest form.*

Douglas M. Lawson, *Volunteering*

Organization's The Thing

The normal Habitat building process is continually taking place in a few thousand communities around the world as local affiliates build one or two homes at a time over a span of months. Quite the opposite, a blitz build is an intense, accelerated process whereby several hundred people come together to construct a number of houses in four and a half working days, with the last half of the fifth day earmarked for the dedications, closing Habitation worship service and a celebration.

Besides the incredible feat of putting up a large number of houses in such a compact period of time, is the marvel of the organization and preparation that take place prior to such a big event. The completed homes are the manifestation of countless hours of behind-the-scenes work over a period of many months, often an entire year.

The day following our arrival (after catching up on some much-needed sleep), we registered at a warehouse situated about 200 yards from the building site. It would be the hub of the week's activities. Although it was our first blitz build, I knew in one glance that this was a well-organized operation.

In earlier times, the huge warehouse had been used to repair train engines; the government leased it to Habitat for a year at the price of one dollar. The St. John's affiliate had completely cleaned, repaired and renovated it. Offices had been constructed, as well as bathrooms and a large, fully equipped kitchen. There was a stage from which, in addition to announcements and presentations, we would be entertained at each meal by prominent local musicians and dancers, many of whom had participated in the numerous province-wide 500th anniversary celebrations. Behind it, an area was sectioned off to hold supplies for each of the seven houses.

Just outside the kitchen area were serving tables, with the remaining space constituting the dining hall. This layout enabled all the volunteers and families to eat together in one sitting. The room was decorated with streamers of flags, Habitat banners, and large placards in the shape of the Habitat house symbol, each one bearing the name of a corporate sponsor providing funding for one of the homes. The setup worked beautifully, and it took only about three minutes to walk to the work site.

Soul Satisfaction

Shannie Duff, a former mayor of St. John's, headed the organizational extravaganza. It was obvious that she had used her considerable connections and influence to enlist the involvement of a wide sector of the community to support the project. Most of the volunteers agreed that her greatest coup was conscripting the services of the most renowned chef in Newfoundland to oversee the cooking of the food by the volunteers and area church groups.

Shannie invited the chef over for tea with the unabashed intention of "schmoozing" him. She carefully explained the nature of the undertaking and the worthiness of the cause, concluding by saying that the committee could offer him a small honorarium for his services. After listening attentively, he replied, "You cannot afford my services." Shannie's heart sank. "But," he continued, "I think this is a fine project. I will do it for my soul!" The result was a menu and cuisine to rival any in a five-star restaurant.

At the registration table, Larry and I were able to meet the other person whose spirit, heart and efficiency were applauded by everyone involved in every facet of the build. That person was Jackie Caines, the office manager and registrar; she was the one who had personally made our special arrangements. We soon learned that she had made everyone feel special.

The Sponsors

We walked over to take a look at the building site and learned that the Canadian Housing Authority had donated the property for the seven homes and that the City of St. John's had provided the necessary infrastructure.

The placards in front of each foundation indicated that the sponsors—companies that put up the approximately $40,000 per house for the building materials and helped publicize the project—were: Petro Canada, Volkswagen Canada, Newfoundland Power (which also outfitted and financially supported the office operation), Canadian Bankers Association, Emcee Distribution, The Hickman Group (consisting largely of construction-related companies and which donated or sold at cost many of the materials for the homes), and Sobeys (a major Canadian grocery chain which not only donated all the food for the 6000 meals served, but also stocked the pantries and refrigerators of the new homeowners!). As well as their official responsibilities, each sponsor encouraged their own employees to spend time working on the build.

The local Volkswagen dealer donated a Golf GL Harlequin painted in the seven colors corresponding to the colored scarves the volunteers wore to designate which house they were working on. Two-dollar raffle tickets were sold throughout the province and over $90,000 was realized for Habitat. The winning ticket was drawn during lunch on Friday. The car was won by a couple who were volunteers working on the build. Not only were the corporate sponsors an essential component of the blitz, they were also an inspiring one.

The Supplies

In order for seven houses to go up in less than five days, everything must be on hand, readily accessible and in the order that it is needed. That is the job of the volunteers involved in what is called the "prebuild," during which time the homeowners typically accumulate their sweat equity hours.

Because the homes in St. John's were being constructed on a steep hillside, the house plan was a split-entry design. The front entry was on the lower level, comprised of a hallway leading to the staircase and a large basement area for laundry, storage and, in some cases, an additional bedroom. The upper level was the living area, with the kitchen door opening out to a deck that extended onto the back hillside.

Besides the foundations being poured and the decking laid, in this case, the framing for the bottom level was also up when we arrived. Boxes of siding and stacks of 2x4s were in the front yard of each house, and the assembled trusses lay piled in back. Cabinets, sinks, windows, doors, molding, insulation, drywall, paint, nails and other supplies were all parceled out in the seven storage areas in the warehouse, ready to be delivered on demand. Anything that needed painting was given a primer coat there.

The Professionals

On Sunday afternoon, the work crews assigned to each house met briefly with their house captains at the building site. Approximately 35 volunteers with a variety of skills and experience were assigned to each house. The ambitious plan for the next day's work was quickly reviewed, and everyone had an idea of what they would be doing when the build officially began at 8 a.m. the next morning.

Critical to the success of any build is securing qualified building supervisors, almost always professional builders. Shannie garnered the invaluable support of the Eastern Newfoundland Home Builders Association, and a distinguished area builder was the captain for each house. Their responsibility was not limited only to that week, however. They had been involved in the site preparations and prebuilding activities for months before.

Each contractor "encouraged" his sub-contractors to volunteer their time and skills. Thus, professional electricians, plumbers, sheet rockers and siders would be working alongside experienced and inexperienced volunteers and sharing their expertise with them. In addition, skilled and experienced volunteers had been selected to serve as supervisors for specific tasks—framing, roofing, painting, etc.

As we have since observed over several blitz builds, contractors and subcontractors often initially look at a Habitat project as just another house to construct—except they aren't getting paid. Many times they are concerned and skeptical about the quality of workmanship of the volunteers and, thus, a little worried that their reputations might become tarnished. But inevitably, they catch what has been dubbed *Habititus* as the week progresses.

The tradesmen—who initially seem irked and frustrated by all the people in their way, and who are sometimes preoccupied with their other "paying" jobs—are soon swept up by the spirit that infuses a build. They see how swiftly things are accomplished and notice the extra effort and love that go into every swing of the volunteers' hammers. In time, one can see the tension dissipate and a lighthearted demeanor replace it. Before long they are almost indistinguishable from the volunteers who have paid to be there.

The builders form special bonds with the families they work with, and often go out of their way to make small customizations and give the homeowners choices wherever possible. The homeowners, in turn, are undoubtedly the most cooperative that the builders have worked with.

Though they are paying for the homes, they tend to see their builder as a "deliverer," bringing into actuality what had appeared to be an impossibility. Their profound gratitude enables them to take in stride the inevitable problems, delays and disappointments that ordinarily create friction between builder and owner.

One needs only to be observant to grasp that before the week is over, what started out for the professionals as a building project has become transformed into an act of love and pride—not the same pride, however, as at the outset. This pride has to do with knowing that they have used their talents to make one family's dream materialize, and the soul satisfaction is the greatest payment they have ever received.

Ready or not, in about twelve hours all of the groundwork would be put to the test!

II-8. A TIME TO BUILD UP

*Fusion of the **word** of God with the **deed** of God
delivered a message to her heart.*

Millard Fuller, *The Theology of the Hammer*

Day One: Raising The Roof

No one, at least not us first-timers, really believed that we would accomplish what was laid out in the schedule for the first day. Nevertheless, we were all primed and adrenaline-charged as we walked from breakfast to the work site, hard hats and tool bags in hand.

As if orchestrated, an electrifying chorus of 300 hammers simultaneously began resonating along the row of seven houses. We tingled from the sheer thrill of seeing people from four countries and all walks of life bustling about, knowing that all of them had come together for one purpose—to improve the lives of seven families in St. John's, Newfoundland.

If it was overpowering for the volunteers, try to imagine how the families felt. For months they had been working toward and anticipating this day. Now, seeing 300 people descend upon the site, and realizing that they were there solely to build them a home, was utterly overwhelming. Emotions ran strong, and many of the homeowners had difficulty maintaining their equilibrium throughout the week.

Cathy Carroll described her observations and reactions: "The gradual crescendo of hammers every morning at 8 a.m. was music that sounded like hope and peace and love for one another. There was the smell of new wood and the buzz of saws, the hammers banging, measurements for wood cuts being called out to someone out of sight, pieces of plywood being carted through the house, people humming happy tunes, floor plans being discussed and personal changes being considered. Up goes one wall, then another. Then there are four and in no time, before you know it, it looks like a house!

"I went outside through the door that hadn't been there when I'd arrived in the morning, and turned to look at the house. It stood there large as life, as though it was a real house! I felt like it was just as unreal to be called the homeowner.

"I had to leave and have myself an ice-melting cry. I had to accept that I was going to do a lot of crying! I couldn't believe how so many people had God in their hearts enough to travel to Newfoundland to build MY house and to make MY life so happy! My faith was restored; my strength was renewed. I felt so loved inside. I wondered what I could say to all of these people who were loving my family in this Christian way."

Elaine Barry couldn't believe how everyone who worked on her house "just kept working and working, and never once complained that they were tired. Many times we had to make them take a break or go get lunch. It was amazing to see so many people working together, volunteering their time to make someone else's dream come true, and not looking for anything in return except to see us happy."

As Cathy related, many things were going on simultaneously. While people were framing the upper level, windows were being installed in the lower level and siding was being nailed on. Inside, insulation was being cut and stuffed between studs while electricians and plumbers were doing their thing. It immediately became obvious that there was a friendly competition going on between the houses, and now and then a cheer arose as walls were raised or the first trusses were lifted up.

Larry was on the crew of house seven, Jerome and Elaine's, and I worked on house six, Tom and Tammy's. Jerome and Elaine's house was sponsored by Newfoundland Power but, ironically, because it was added on late, it was the only one that wasn't assigned journeymen electricians. Since Larry had indicated on his application that he had at one time been a licensed electrician, he and a biology teacher from Long Island were asked to install all the wiring under the supervision of the electrical inspector who was constantly at the site. (This was the case with all inspectors, as there is no time to "wait for one to arrive" during a blitz build.)

My house was sponsored by Hickman Builders, and Larry still razzes me about the fact that our sponsor brought over a crane to lift our trusses onto the roof (which is usually done by hand). They also lifted trusses onto the other houses that did not yet have theirs up. I helped install windows and insulation, and learned the finer points of putting siding on and keeping it level. By noon, all the walls and trusses were up on our two houses.

As we ate our sumptuous lunch, we had the opportunity to talk with former Governor General Ed Schreyer and his wife Lily, who worked tirelessly throughout the week. Following a presentation of hand-painted mailboxes to each family and several delightful Newfoundland folk songs performed by homeowner Cathy Carroll's trio, we returned to our tasks.

After an intensive afternoon of work, by day's end (I have the pictures to prove it.) the two houses Larry and I worked on had all the windows in, three-quarters of the siding finished, the roof completely shingled, and most of the electrical, plumbing, and heating installed. The other houses were in various stages, but most had the roofs on. Everyone arrived at dinner both tired and satisfied.

Rick Walsh shared how his brother Jim had found a creative way to alleviate a vexing situation during the day. Jim, a professional sider, traveled from Ontario to help side Rick's house and (typical of the professionals I mentioned earlier) was feeling frustrated because Becky, a 16-year-old girl, was taking what seemed like forever to hammer in each nail. Rick was sympathetic to his brother's concern for time, but reminded him that she too had come a long way (from Boston) to help.

Jim decided to ask Becky what she would most like to do, hoping she would choose something other than siding. "Hammering," she replied. Jim thought a moment, and then confirming that the framers still needed help, he approached Becky with a three-inch framing nail in one hand and a one-inch siding nail in the other. "Which would you rather be hammering?" he asked. Looking down at her fingers that already bore bruises from missing the small siding nails, Becky happily chose to help frame.

Day Two: The Men In White

On the second day, Larry continued wiring his house, and I cut insulation all day. The "men in white" arrived to hang the sheetrock. I've never seen anything quite like it. After the ceilings and walls were hung, they climbed onto stilts and, with buckets of premudded tape strapped around their waists, walked through the house looking much like circus performers as they made short work of taping all the seams. Their innovative method sure beat climbing up and down ladders all day. The crews worked through the night and completed every house, thus enabling us to stay on schedule.

We were also able to stay on schedule because of the "elf crews." These are made up of volunteers, who, because they are employed or otherwise engaged during the day, come to the building site at night to deliver the next day's supplies, clean up, or catch up work that is behind in any of the houses. Evidence that the elves had been there was always distinctly noticeable the next morning.

Day 3: The Insulation Queen

Veterans refer to the third day of a blitz build as "hump day." Without a doubt, a blitz is an incredibly exhilarating event, allowing participants to experience the entire building process from beginning to end—almost like fast-forwarding through a video. It is also exhausting and numbing.

For those unaccustomed to it, the cumulative effect of two, long, fast-paced days of physical labor coupled with evening activities or socializing, the emotional drain of continuous, intense relating and the gradual depletion of adrenaline exacted their toll. It was evident that morning in the subdued breakfast conversation and the length of time it took people to walk to the work site.

It was also on Wednesday that I earned the dubious honor of being dubbed "The Insulation Queen." My body protectively covered from head to toe, I cut insulation for three other basements and, in addition, helped clean up our basement, sanded seams, and spackled nail holes in the wood trim. The vinyl flooring was laid in the kitchen and, meanwhile, the steep hillside was dotted with people clearing rocks, raking, and grading in preparation for laying sod. That afternoon a group of volunteers went home for a rest, then returned after dinner and primed walls until almost morning.

Larry and his partner finished wiring, and then helped construct their back deck. Each house was given an allotment of decking, but each crew and homeowner could decide exactly how he or she wanted it configured. It was interesting to see the many variations designed from identical bundles of wood.

Day 4: Oops!

I painted trim (my self-proclaimed specialty) all day, and Larry rolled walls and ceilings. Carpet was laid in ours and several other houses, and cabinets were installed. Outside, the back hillside and front yards were being covered with premium sod that had been donated. A "concrete artist" poured the sidewalks and deftly brushed swirls into them. We began to sense that we were "almost there."

This also was the day that we found a major "boo boo" in the layout of my house. When volunteers began installing the corner kitchen cabinet that was supposed to butt against the window frame, they discovered that it overlapped the window by six inches.

Tammy was in tears, as much a result of emotional exhaustion as disappointment. It only took our house leader Geoff a couple minutes to decide that the window had to come out and be moved so that Tammy's cabinet would fit. "It's my responsibility," he said. "I should have checked it. Tammy deserves to have her house right." So, on Thursday afternoon, the siding was removed, the window slid over, and the sheetrock repaired and mudded. The siding was then replaced, and on Friday it was touch and go waiting for the mud to dry so the wall could be repainted before the dedication.

Despite being worn out, Larry and I stayed after dinner and helped paint trim in one of the other houses until 9:30 p.m. Knowing there was only one day left seemed to give us extra energy.

Day 5: Finishing Touches

There was a festive mood in the air on Friday. Everyone scurried about pitching in wherever they were needed. The goal was to get all of the houses as close as possible to being finished before the afternoon ceremonies commenced. We painted, cleaned, and cleared away the extra materials. Millard and Linda Fuller had arrived the night before and were walking around visiting with people, "oohing" and "ahhing" over what they saw.

Most of the homeowners' eyes were either teared with emotion or glazed with incredulity as it became apparent that the culmination—of their lifetime's dream, their many months of waiting, and their hundreds of hours of work—was close at hand. For all of them, the week of the build was physically and emotionally draining.

Lois says, "I cried every day of the build. Just to look around and watch and work with your family, friends and people who came from all over the world to help turn your dreams into reality was too much for the human heart to contend with. The love and support were beyond comprehension. As our home went up wall-by-wall, doors and windows, it was like standing in the middle of a dream, but when you woke up the volunteers were everywhere buzzing around like bees in their yellow hard hats. You had to keep pinching yourself!"

Following the noon meal, the corporate sponsors were honored. Their enormous contributions and the genuine community spirit they had exhibited had impressed everyone. Millard Fuller, though generous with his praise, shared why it made good sense for corporations to support Habitat. "First," he emphasized, "it's the right thing to do. Second, it helps employees to feel good about their company. Third, it makes the community feel good about the company. And, fourth, it builds company teamwork and spirit. Everyone," he concluded, "comes out a winner."

Returning to the work site, we added the final touches to the landscaping—small trees, shrubs and flowers. Karen Alexander, chairperson of the Family Nurturing Committee, and her husband went to each house and hung on the entry walls "Welcome" signs made of individual wooden letters strung together and lovingly hand-painted in colors to match the decor of each home. The food staff suspended wind chimes from above each door.

As the street sweeper could be heard making its way up the road, the excitement and relief were almost palpable. We had done it!

II-9. THE PERSONAL TOUCH

Christ has no body now but yours,
No hands, no feet on earth but yours.
Yours are the eyes through which he looks
compassion on this world.
Yours are the feet with which he walks to do good.
Yours are the hands with which he blesses all the world.

John Michael Talbot, *"St. Teresa's Prayer"*

United In Love

There were about 300 of us who participated the entire week of the build, and another 150 who plugged in at various times, including Newfoundland's Premier Brian Tobin and his wife, who worked for a full day. Besides the majority from St. John's and other cities in Newfoundland, there were CFA's (short for the Newfie phrase, "Come From Aways") from other Canadian provinces (some as far as British Columbia and Alberta), the United States (several from the West Coast), Jamaica (the Cabot Habitat's sister affiliate), and Great Britain.

We were young and not so young, some many-year veterans of blitz builds, and others, like us, first-timers. We were students, business people, teachers, trades people, bankers, secretaries, store clerks, homemakers and retirees. We were from many different religious persuasions and denominations—but while we were there, we were united in one purpose: we were ambassadors of good will, sharing the eternal good news by writing "sermons of love" with our hammers.

What A Picture

As we stood with our crews and families in front of the houses waiting for the Fullers, Schreyers, Shannie, and Wilmer to join us for our "house

58

pictures," images of the many people and interactions that had taken place over the past five days formed a collage in my mind.

In the forefront was an incident that took place earlier that morning. While I was helping Lois Kaulback complete the second coat of paint in her bedroom, we heard a stir of excitement outside. The employees of Volkswagen, the house sponsor, had just delivered a big wooden swing set. Lois was overcome with emotion as she told me the story behind the generous gift.

On the evening that Shannie Duff and Karen Alexander had come to the Kaulbacks' apartment to talk further with them about their being selected, Karen had asked their four-year-old daughter to draw a picture of her new home. After the business was completed, Shannie went over to look at the drawing. "What is that?" she asked, pointing to something beside the house. "That's a swing set," Becky replied. "Every new house has a swing set." When the incident was reported back to the sponsors—well, you know the rest!

The Kaulbacks were also the recipients of another special treasure. During that busy morning, a young lady who was an architecture student in Montreal slipped quietly across the road and, from that vantage point, quickly produced an exquisite watercolor of the Kaulback house—with the swing set prominently standing beside it. Below the painting, all the crewmembers signed their names, and then framed the masterpiece with molding.

Cathy's crew also presented her with a unique painting. Cathy chose for her wall colors very deep shades of rose, green, yellow, and blue. On a piece of sheetrock the crew artfully painted swatches of the bright colors, signed their names and framed it with baseboard.

More Snapshots

As we had worked together, we learned about and were inspired by each other's stories and experiences. Before this blitz, the Cabot Habitat had built only three other homes. At lunch one day we talked with the son of St. John's first recipients of a Habitat home. He had not been old enough to take part in building his own house but, though he worked nights, he and his friend were not going to miss out on the opportunity to help this time. "We'd just be sleeping, anyway. We can do that next week," he stated emphatically.

Larry worked alongside Merle and Suzie, who have participated in every single Jimmy Carter Work Project as well as many other blitz builds. Based in Arizona, they travel to sites in their fifth wheel trailer whenever possible. Merle is a skilled cabinetmaker by trade and is happy his business affords him the freedom to work with Habitat.

Two young men working on my house had recently started their own successful company. They were participating in the build to learn more about Habitat and to find ways for their company to support its mission. Sherry, who worked for my house's sponsor, took a vacation week to be supportive of her company, but quickly put her heart and soul into what she was doing. She also became an expert at siding under the tutelage of our professional tradesmen. Two teenage girls from New York City, who had asked their parents for air fare to the build as their graduation presents, represented the best in youth. Everyone was impressed by their hard work, maturity and sense of purpose.

A newlywed couple was introduced to us during lunch one day. They had met while hammering on a rooftop in Hungary during the 1996 Jimmy Carter Work Project. Just a month or two earlier, dressed in traditional wedding attire, they had been married on a rooftop during the 1997 Jimmy Carter Work Project in Appalachia.

Then there was Cathy, leader of the Prince Edward Island Habitat, whose hearty laugh and ever-rolling video camera made her presence known to everyone. She not only arrived early to help with the prebuild, but stayed afterward to help families move in and make copies of her personal video diary of the build for anyone who requested one.

We were also surprised to meet a young man, a student at a St. John's college, who was from Aba, Nigeria—the very city Larry and I had lived in! He knew the chief and many of the people we had worked with there. What are the chances of that?

Of course, the media were there, snapping pictures, talking to the homeowners, following the progress of the building, and interviewing volunteers. They, too, were captivated by what was taking place. The daily publicity resulted in people showing up to help or just to watch.

On Thursday afternoon, a couple in a Mercedes pulled up in front of Larry's house, got out, and stood watching. Larry overheard them tell one of the volunteers that they had been considering donating money to Habitat, but had heard the houses were welfare homes and that the workmanship was shoddy. He walked over and asked if they'd like a tour of the house. After introducing them to his house captain, Dieter, and informing them that Dieter was a licensed builder, Larry pointed out the care with which everything was done and explained the thorough inspection process, as well as the requirements for purchasing a Habitat home. The couple was obviously impressed. As they walked back to their car the husband said to Larry, "Yes, we can support this!"

The neighbors up the street caught the spirit, too. About midweek, they began mowing their lawns, washing windows and cleaning up the outsides of their houses. Such is the uplifting and infectious nature of Habitat that spreads wherever it goes.

For The Children

For most of us, the children are what it ultimately comes down to. Though many were clearly overwhelmed by all of the attention and commotion, their obvious wonder and delight as they saw their homes go up and their very own bedrooms take shape were all the reward we needed.

In their own way, the children, too, had made sacrifices for their new homes. Four months of being schlepped from baby-sitter to relative to neighbor while their parents attended meetings and worked night after night and weekend after weekend at the building site or warehouse took its toll on them.

One of Larry's most special moments was when Jerome and Elaine's six-year-old daughter Jillian took him by the hand and guided him to the two smaller bedrooms. She was smiling broadly, a twinkle in her eyes. Then, crossing her arms, her expression changed to one of deliberation. "Mommy said it's my pick which bedroom I have. Which one do you think I should choose?"

Larry looked at both rooms, then called to her attention that she could see the backyard from the rear bedroom, whereas she could only see the next-door house from the side one. "I've been thinking I wanted the back room," she confirmed. "It seems brighter." With that, her decision was made.

Hopefully, in years to come, all the children will carry with them memories of the outpouring of love and generosity that built their homes, and it will encourage and sustain them to know that so many people cared.

What's In It For You?

That people would journey hundreds of miles at their own expense, often on their vacation time, and pay a fee to build a home for a stranger was a complete puzzlement to many of the local people, including Dieter. "I don't get it. What's in it for you?" he had asked Larry earlier in the week. Larry had just smiled and reassured him that he would "get it" when the keys were handed over to Jerome and Elaine.

But, it happened sooner than that. When their crew presented the couple with a beautiful framed print of the Cape Spear Lighthouse (situated at the most northeasterly point in North America), Jerome was so overcome with emotion that he turned and strode to the side of the house to compose himself. Just then, Larry felt a tap on his shoulder and heard his house captain whisper, "Larry, I get it now."

Tears Of Joy

At each house a similar scene was taking place—housewarming gifts were being presented, pictures were being snapped to preserve the memories; hugs and endearments were being exchanged. Larry received a couple gifts himself—a jar of delicious homemade moose stew from Jerome and Elaine and a jar of bake apple (cloud berries) jam made by Bob, a co-worker on his house. Then, a big flatbed truck pulled up and parked in the middle of the street. It was quickly transformed into a stage for the dedication ceremonies.

Bagpipers announced that it was time to convene, and we all found places on the lawn or along the curbs from which to view. As I looked behind and to both sides of me, the poignant scene was indelibly etched in my mind. There were no black ties and tails to signify the importance of the occasion. We were as we had been all week—in jeans, overalls, shorts, tee shirts and our colored neckerchiefs. The air crackled with emotion as we waited expectantly for the big moment. Children, happily playing on the swing set, seemed oblivious.

The homeowners stood with their pastors in front of their respective homes while the house blessing was delivered over the microphone. Each family was presented a Bible. Then, one by one, the leaders on the platform briefly shared their observations and feelings about the week. Ed Schreyer confessed that although he was not a man who readily expressed emotion, tears always came to his eyes when the homeowners were given their keys.

He was certainly with the majority in that regard. It is difficult to hold back the tears of joy when each family, the children often in official tee shirts hanging down to their ankles, stands face to face with their builder who, also overcome with emotion, presents them with the keys to their very own home. It was a proud and personal moment for everyone who had even the smallest role in this drama which will continue to be enacted all over the world until, as Millard Fuller proclaims, "All God's children have a simple decent place to rest their heads at night."

Let The Celebrating Begin

In addition to a special dinner, entertainment and a Habitation Service, there would also be a party—Newfoundland style. During the Habitation Service, Millard Fuller—passionate, eloquent, and inspiring as always—shared the progress that was being made toward fulfilling Habitat's vision and some of the new ideas for involving still more segments of society and increasing awareness of Habitat.

One such novel endeavor involved United Airlines' employees who encouraged passengers to donate their foreign change as they flew in and out of the country. The ticket agents in London wore Habitat hard hats and tool belts. Over $50,000 was collected and donated to Habitat in the first year of the five-year promotion.

Millard also announced the planned Easter Morning Build in Americus the coming spring. The idea of building homes during Holy Week and celebrating an Easter sunrise service with the homeowners captivated me, and I made a mental note to arrange our itinerary so we could be there.

Personally, one of the most moving moments in the Habitation Service was when Cathy's trio sang *St. Teresa's Prayer*, a song by John Michael Talbot. It is a favorite of Larry's and mine, which we have shared at several other work projects. We had let Cathy listen to it, and she agreed it was perfect for the occasion. The words—*Christ has no body now but yours, no hands, no feet on earth but yours*—remind us that we are the embodiment and instruments of the Christ spirit on earth.

Following the service, each family expressed heartfelt appreciation to the volunteers and, in sometimes-shaky voices, shared what their new homes meant to them. Cathy said she'd been "going down white-water rapids for a few years" and all the people there that day had helped to calm the waters. "It is one thing to be a homeowner," she declared, "but it is certainly another to be the owner of a Habitat home with all the memories and love that go into building it."

Lois, their chosen spokesperson, elaborated on the hope that Habitat gives people and, acknowledging their own good fortune, pledged on behalf of the families that the homeowners would all be there to help the next recipients realize their dreams. "Just hang in there," she said. "We're coming. You're next!"

The homeowners made presentations to the special people who had spearheaded the project—Shannie Duff, Karen Alexander, and Jackie Caines. All received well-deserved standing ovations.

It was then time to party. Soft drinks, beer, wine, and snacks were provided as we listened to a few tales recited by Newfoundland's renowned storyteller. A "screeching-in ceremony" followed next, a requirement for those who desire to become an honorary citizen of Newfoundland.

This ritual is taken very seriously, even in regard to people recognized as citizens by the government. Cathy Carroll was born in New York City while her family was visiting there, and was brought back to Newfoundland at the age of three months. Her well-kept secret was eventually discovered, and Cathy was required to be screeched-in before her countrymen considered her citizenship valid!

When they described the foul taste that often caused people to screech, thus giving the ceremonial rum its name, I decided to forego the honor. However, I duly recorded Larry's induction on film. After repeating a pledge, the thirty or so participants were required to down a swig of Screech, eat a piece of bologna and kiss a cold, dead cod! Larry now proudly displays his official certificate of honorary citizenship. It was great fun.

The rest of the evening we danced to a live band and circulated, talking and saying good-bye to homeowners, volunteers and staff. No one wanted to leave. Rick and Cindy finally slipped out, picked up their children from the neighbors, and collected sleeping bags and pillows from their old house. They spent the night sleeping on the soft carpet in their new home.

It's Arrived

On Saturday morning when Rick looked out the living room window, it was very quiet, "too quiet," he says. He wished everyone could be back again, if only for ten minutes. A few individual volunteers did stop by for last minute good-byes, and later a bus with Chinese tourists came up the street. The driver asked if the passengers could walk through Rick's house. "Not blinking an eye, I had a group of strangers going through our house as if it was the first house ever built!" The only bad part was that Rick forgot to check with his wife, who was in the shower.

Cathy also was lonesome for a while. She missed the sounds of the hammers, the fellowship at meals, the jokes and camaraderie. "But I could feel that everyone's spirit was still here, and I knew it would continue to give me happiness as long as I was in this house," she said.

Lois expressed similar feelings. "I guess it was a sense of loss that we felt. There wasn't enough time to personally thank everyone and truly share our feelings with them. They may be gone, but the love and energy they built our home with is nested deep within our walls and will remain there always, as will the memories."

Sunday afternoon we went to visit a few of the families. There was still a steady stream of cars passing by the houses as people came for a look. They had been coming almost continuously since Friday evening and, in fact, we later met people during our travels across Newfoundland who had made a special trip to St. John's just to view the houses. We only encountered one person who had not at least heard of the project.

Parking the truck for a moment midway in the block, we just sat and observed. It was quiet now, but already evident that the families were settling in. Lamps and furniture could be seen through the living room windows, and streamers and popped balloons were strewn in the road, leftovers from the children's first birthday party the previous day. Cars were parked in the driveways, and bicycles lay on the lawn. Several children were playing on the swing set. The neighborhood had definitely arrived.

II-10. BEAUTY AND THE MOOSE

The only way a non-Newfoundlander can understand
how we feel about our island, is to come for a visit
and discover what and who we are.

Lucy FitzPatrick McFarlane, *"Solid as a Rock"*

R & R

One of the definite perks of the RV lifestyle is the opportunity to toggle satisfying service with adventure, and to experience and learn about new environments and cultures. With the build behind us, it was time to have some fun and explore the island of Newfoundland—a place where we had never imagined ourselves.

Since our gracious hosts invited us to stay as long as we wished, we spent several days learning a little of the history of St. John's. We visited Cape Spear and, as evidence that we ourselves had stood at the most northeasterly point in North America, we mailed postcards from the lighthouse gift shop to our grandchildren.

Next we drove over to Signal Hill, the site of the final battle of the Seven Years War between France and England in 1762 that finally established the British in control of Newfoundland after 200 years of rivalry. The Cabot Tower, constructed atop Signal Hill in 1897 to commemorate the 400th Anniversary of John Cabot's landing and the 60th year of Queen Victoria's reign, is where Marconi received the first transatlantic wireless signal in 1901.

We spent one more full day touring the capital city, whose thriving fishing and commerce were its early financial backbone. St. John's also has the dubious distinction of having survived four major fires in 180 years, the Great Fire of 1892 destroying almost two-thirds of the city. As we walked about, I was compelled to take a picture of one of the many streets with row houses, each painted a different bright color. Our hosts informed us that they are referred to as the *jellybean houses*. Because of the long, frigid and dreary winters, Newfoundlanders are cheered by robust colors.

Feeling we had savored much of the flavor of St. John's and its environs, we expressed our appreciation to our hosts and began the 500-mile trek across Newfoundland. We planned to take the shorter ferry ride back, which departed from Port aux Basques at the southwest corner of the island.

The Soul Of Newfoundland

In her article "Solid as a Rock," Lucy FitzPatrick McFarlane states, ". . . two things will be implanted firmly in their [tourists] minds: the lively people and the spectacular scenery." We had already experienced the lively people who are so open and giving and graced with a wonderful sense of humor about themselves and life. Now we were about to be treated to the spectacular scenery of Canada's 10th and newest province.

On almost any main road in Newfoundland, one is seldom without a view of water—the ocean, a bay or pristine lake. Our first destination was Trinity Bay where we wanted to take in the famed walking pageant depicting scenes from four centuries of history in one of Newfoundland's earliest fishing settlements. We followed the players along the rocky coastline of the town, learning about the harshness of the fishermen's lives, touring the company store and watching as women laid fish out to dry. As we walked to the church, fog began rolling in, obscuring our visibility. It was a portent to the sad tale we were about to hear.

The character Mary Moores described what happened on the day of The Great Trinity Sealing Disaster in 1914. On a beautiful sunny morning, the men and boys of the village were attending to their boats and gear when flows of ice bearing hundreds of seals drifted into the bay. The villagers grabbed clubs, sticks and shovels and, wading out into the water, climbed onto the flows and began clubbing the seals, jubilant at such an easy opportunity to harvest furs. Without warning, a cold wind and mist blew in, stranding them in a dense fog. As the names of the 24 townsmen who froze to death were read in the somber memorial service, I was transported back in time and a cold chill ran up my spine.

After a humorous portrayal of bawdy civil court proceedings, a vignette followed that helped us understand the relationship between the merchants (who at the time had functioned as the only government), and the fisherman who were dependent on them for supplies in advance of their next season's catch. We watched as numerous families received the devastating news that they would be given no winter provisions because money was scarce that year. The pageant ended on a hopeful note, however, highlighting the hardiness and endurance that so characterizes Newfoundlanders. For anyone who travels there, The Trinity Pageant is a must-see.

The next morning we headed up to Cape Bonavista where John Cabot first sighted the *new-founde-lande* and was said to exclaim, "O Buena Vista!" ("Oh beautiful sight!") His ship, the *Matthew*, made landfall on June 24, 1497. Oh beautiful sight, indeed! After touring the lighthouse, we spent most of the day sitting on or strolling along the immense craggy cliffs and watching porpoises playing and puffins bobbing in the water below. We ate our lunch at the base of the statue of John Cabot, which looks out over the beautiful new land he found.

Two months earlier, an exact replica of the *Matthew* had sailed from England and landed at Cape Bonavista on June 24, beginning 46 days of celebrations during which the historic landfall was reenacted at Cape Bonavista and sixteen other ports of call in both Newfoundland and Labrador. At each stop, the arrival of the *Matthew* touched off elaborate local anniversary festivities. One of the things that impressed us was that, despite the recent hoopla, there were few visible vestiges. The island remains unspoiled by artificial tourist come-ons, enabling one to view life as it is and always has been, amid the backdrop of the ever-present sea that is so much a part of Newfoundland's soul.

We finally wrested ourselves from our reverie and began making our way to Terra Nova National Park. As nightfall approached, we were given directions to a municipal park on a small lake where we could camp free. One of the bonuses of RVing in Newfoundland is that, unless posted, travelers can park almost anywhere. All around the island motor homes can be spotted nestled among the trees and on the beaches. We greatly appreciated the sense of freedom and personal responsibility we felt there.

Remains Of The Day

At 5 a.m., we were abruptly awakened by Ross reprising his tantrum in the ferry line. No amount of coaxing would settle him down. Acknowledging his protest, we got up and were on our way by 6:30 a.m.—a first for us! Two hours later, we were hiking the two-mile loop around Sandy Pond—with Ross. If it was supposed to be a retributive forced march, he didn't know it. He pranced along, keeping a steady pace on the boardwalks and soft sheltered path, stopping only when we halted to pick a

68

handful of blueberries. We did accomplish our objective, however. Ross slept soundly the rest of the day and night, and never again threw one of his fits.

That afternoon we hiked part of the Coastal Trail in Terra Nova National Park. The lushness created the illusion of being in a rain forest. Our destination was Pissing Mare Falls. Someone had a sense of humor, we thought. When we found it, we agreed that the moderate trickle splaying over the rocks was aptly named, and decided to climb up the rocky terrain to the top. Larry got a little ahead of me and suddenly yelled down, "I found one!"

I must digress a little here. Before we left New Hampshire, where every year there are a goodly number of moose-car accidents, we were warned that moose were an infinitely greater hazard in Canada. All along the Trans-Canada Highway there are foreboding signs about moose. However, thus far in our adventure, we had not even caught a glimpse of one, let alone been near enough to be endangered.

Larry would not give a clue what he had found. He waited for me to scramble up to where he was, then with a mischievous twinkle in his eyes ceremoniously pointed to a big flat rock. Looking closer, I recognized the bones of a moose, which had undoubtedly crashed down the falls to its demise. We memorialized our find by taking a picture of the dearly departed, chuckling about it all the way back to camp.

A World-Class Beauty

The steady rain the next day did not dampen the beauty of the 250-mile drive to Gros Morne National Park. All along the way were views of distant mountains or picturesque coves and bays lined with sleepy fishing villages. In the late afternoon we arrived at the park, selected as a UNESCO World Heritage Site. Everyone recommended we spend several days there.

As part of the restroom and shower complexes at Gros Morne, there are "kitchen shelters"—pavilions with wood stoves, a supply of wood, picnic tables and sinks with hot water. That amenity makes it very convenient for tenters (or truck-campers, in our case) to cook and clean up when it is raining. It is also a great place to get to know the other hardy souls who seek its refuge. We all decided the prudent thing to do on that cold, wet night was to attend the lecture at the Visitors Center. The subject was glaciers, which account for a large portion of the park's topography.

The following day, since the light drizzly rain wasn't prohibitive, we leisurely drove north up the 50-mile length of that section of the park, taking several hikes and tours along the way. Once again we attended the evening lecture, and on our way witnessed one of the most blazing red and pink sunsets we have ever seen.

That evening's topic was the area in the southern section of the park called the Tablelands, where some 600 million years ago Europe and Africa collided with North America, forcing a portion of the earth's interior to be pushed above the surface. Due to the density of heavy metals that constitute its make-up, the mountains that were formed are devoid of any vegetation. The summer ranger, who in his "other life" is a fifth-grade teacher, treated us to a Robin Williams-like performance, complete with music and props, the *coup de grace* being a costumed demonstration of how Newfoundland's floral emblem, the insect-eating Pitcher Plant, works. I could only hope he made his students' lessons nearly as memorable.

The weather the next day was spectacular for hiking the two miles of marshland in order to catch the boat tour of Western Brook Pond (anything not an ocean is called a "pond" in Newfoundland), a huge fresh water fjord formed when the earth snapped back up after the pressure of the receding glaciers was released, trapping salt water from which the salt evaporated after hundreds of years. Our captain guided the boat so close to the 100-foot Denim Falls that the spray washed over us. We were surprised to find that there, too, was a Pissing Mare Falls. Perhaps every National Park in Canada has one.

That evening after dinner, we made the steep climb up Berry Hill in the campground, hoping for a clear view of another stunning sunset, but it was too cloudy. However, as Larry was scanning the lush panorama with his binoculars, he spotted a massive bull moose grazing in a distant field below. It was definitely animate and, even at that distance, impressive. The score was now one dead and one alive.

The next day we hiked the trail in the Tablelands. There was almost a surreal look to the brown, lifeless terrain. Many people say it resembles a moonscape. If nothing else, it certainly was a strange feeling to know we were treading on the interior of the earth.

The Potato Patrol

Beginning to feel that our senses were supersaturated from the sights and experiences of the past two weeks, we turned the truck toward home, planning to catch the 11:30 p.m. ferry that would dock in Nova Scotia early the following morning. Battling heavy rain and strong winds, we arrived at the ferry at 9 p.m. This time we knew what to expect—or so we thought.

As we moved forward in the line of cars to board the ferry, we were directed into a large garage. Two men in white jumpsuits appeared from nowhere, yanked open the front doors of the truck, thrust vacuum hoses inside, and began vacuuming the floor around our feet. If you think we were startled, it was nothing compared to Ross's reaction. His claws were clamped in a death-grip on my shoulder. Noticing my plight, one of the men signaled the other to turn off the vacuum.

"Do you have any potatoes or plants with you?" we were asked.

Remember the little red fir I was so happy to receive at the County Exposition? During the previous several weeks, I had carefully tended and cared for it, and was eagerly anticipating setting it into the soil at our camp. "Just this little red fir," I naively volunteered, showing it to the man, "but I got it in Nova Scotia, not Newfoundland."

"That makes no difference once it's been here," he replied, as he reached in and plucked it from my hand.

"What's this all about?" Larry asked. I knew by the tone of his voice that his self-control was close to disintegrating.

The attendant thrust a brochure into Larry's hand. "This will explain it," he said, closing the door. A moment later, the underbody of the truck was being sprayed with high-pressure hoses. "Would you mind washing the bikes while you're at it?" Larry said sarcastically. Of course, no one could hear him except me.

The brochure explained that Newfoundland is home to a particularly virulent potato beetle, and no potatoes or anything else grown in the earth are allowed to leave the island. Well, there you have it. Nice of them to vacuum first and explain later.

On the ferry we wound down a little by listening to Air Canada's Flying Fiddler perform in the lounge. After his well-received impromptu performance on a flight, Air Canada (as well as other transportation companies) gives him free passage to any destination in exchange for his entertaining the passengers. We later found a dark corner and curled up on the floor in the passenger's room to sleep away the crossing. The ferry was buffeted by winds and rain most of the night, which only served to lull us into a deeper slumber. Debarking in North Sydney at 6:30 a.m., we began retracing our route home.

71

The Elusive Moose

Every time we passed a moose-warning sign on our return, we guffawed and talked back to it. "Sure," we quipped, "we wouldn't want to let down our guard. A moose might charge out of that field at any time!" Then, we began fantasizing about pulling into our driveway and finding three moose grazing in our yard. Actually, that was not out of the realm of possibility—well, maybe not *three*.

As it turned out, our vision was quite prophetic. A few minutes after crossing into New Hampshire, we approached a small bridge with cars parked along either side and dozens of people milling around. Curious, we pulled over—and then we spied her. About 50 feet away, standing up to her belly in the small pond, was a big cow moose munching on moss, apparently unperturbed by her gallery of spectators. Since I had no film left, you'll have to take my word for it.

II-11. THE EASTER MORNING COMMUNITY

Life's inmost secret is the divine pattern in you
which you can only really know
when you are giving yourself in service.

Eric Butterworth, *Spiritual Economics*

Our Plans

At the beginning of 1998, we received enough financial support from friends to consider doing several blitz builds that year. First, we planned to participate in both the Holy Week Build in Americus, Georgia, and the Habitat RV Care-A-Vanner Conference being held there several days prior. Knowing that we would be ready for a little R&R afterwards, we made reservations at a state campground on the Gulf Shores of Alabama, looking forward to visiting nearby natural and historic sights.

Meanwhile, we applied to participate in the Jimmy Carter Work Project that would take place in Houston that June. An ambitious goal had been set to build 100 homes in a week. As Lily Schreyer said when she heard the announcement in St. John's, "Only in America!" From there, our intention was to attend the Ed Schreyer Work Project in Regina, Saskatchewan, in mid-July, then head to the West Coast for the rest of the summer and following winter. We were soon to learn that if we truly let Spirit be our guide, we would be wise not to plan so far ahead!

From Gypsies To Care-A-Vanners

We did, however, make it to Americus. With our trailer parked in the Sumter County Fairgrounds, we attended the RV Care-A-Vanners' meetings and learned about its history, growth and current reorganization. The group, which originally called themselves the RV Gypsies, was the brainchild of Lois and Jack Wolters. For ten years, they successfully coordinated the ever-increasing number of RVers who travel by invitation to Habitat affiliates all over the country, spending a couple of weeks at each to build homes and help foster and promote awareness of Habitat in the local community.

By the time of the conference, the need had become apparent for the informally affiliated group of RVers to be coordinated from Habitat headquarters. Over the years, their mailing list had grown to more than 4000. In 1998, the RV ministry was incorporated into the Global Village Department's outreach, and the program has continued to rapidly expand. (In the fiscal year 2001, ending June 30, 2002, 969 Care-A-Vanners in 634 rigs built with 92 affiliates across the country. They put in 75,232 volunteer hours!)

Hosanna Circle

On a drive-through one evening, we got our first glimpse at what would soon become the only known *Easter Morning Community*. It was being developed on 65 acres of wooded land and, in counsel with the National Wildlife Federation, the homes were situated to preserve as much of the natural setting as possible. Two things stood out almost immediately—the bright red color of the clay and the incessant singing of the birds. Eventually, 142 homes would comprise the community. We were to build the first 20, all of which were located on Hosanna Circle.

A large canvas tent was erected near the entrance to serve as our eating center and meeting place. We would eat in three shifts. Area churches would prepare lunches, and local restaurants would cater dinners. It would be a totally different arrangement than Newfoundland, but the purpose and result would be the same.

We were psyched as we headed to dinner and orientation on Friday evening. The twenty families were introduced, and our homeowner, Margo Mitchell, stood out of the crowd with her bright red Western-style outfit and a white Western hat. She stepped forward as her name was called, flashed a big smile, and waved to everyone. We had a feeling we were in for a delightful time working with her.

Small But Mighty

The building week went much the way it had in Newfoundland with the exception of a torrential downpour on Wednesday morning during breakfast that turned the ground into a sea of mucky red. We had an unusually small crew on our house, but it was a fairly experienced and energetic group that quickly became a cooperative, congenial team. Two of the couples were veterans of several RV caravans. George, our house leader, was a local resident who worked full-time for Habitat. His work ethic and amiable leadership style encouraged everyone to want to give their best.

Larry and I helped with framing and installed all the windows. I again worked on siding and insulation, this time crawling underneath the house to insulate between the floor joists. Most of the job had to be done lying on our backs, and having to wear long-sleeved shirts, safety goggles and nose masks to protect ourselves from the fiberglass made the cramped quarters almost unbearable. I was thankful when we were finished and I was assigned to trim paint all the windows and oversee the rest of the paint crew. Meanwhile, Larry helped install doors and learned the fine art of hanging kitchen cabinets under the tutelage of a master shipbuilder.

For us, now that the process of a blitz build was no longer a novelty, the people captivated our attention most—1207, representing 42 states and four countries outside the U.S., congregated in Americus that week. Larry worked closely on several projects with Don from Toronto, a service strategy manager for Xerox of Canada who had spent one of his vacation weeks every year since 1993 working at a Habitat blitz build.

Greg (who headed up the siding crew) and Sue brought their 18-year-old daughter Becky with them so she could experience the satisfaction that they received from working with Habitat. Greg was also responsible for a first-time couple being there. When he had shared with his friends about the last blitz he had attended, they had all told him to "let us know the next time you're going to a build." He did, and one couple followed through and became enthusiastic participants.

Crystal and Jeremy, both of whom are employed by Habitat headquarters in other capacities, decided they should experience the fun so they could understand what motivated everyone else to participate. Hank and Susan, recently retired RVers, had come to Americus to attend the RV conference and ended up staying for the build. They, too, became hooked, as did Linda, a lady about my age from California, who shared the dubious honor of working under the house with Margo and me. One young woman who worked tirelessly on the roof was ecstatic when she received news of her acceptance to help lead an all-female build. As before, our ages, lifestyles, talents and skills, even our reasons for being there, were highly diverse, but we shared one common purpose—to build a home with Margo and her family.

People often ask if they have to have special skills to work with Habitat, and it's sometimes difficult to convince them that they don't. We point out that they can receive on-the-job training for any aspect of building they desire to learn, but the only thing *really* necessary to have is an open heart and a willingness to pitch in wherever and however they can. The person who keeps the floors swept and the "droppings" picked up is as important to the process as the person who hammers.

I think warmly of Nancy, who was assigned to security at our site. For every two houses, there was a tractor-trailer full of the required supplies. A person was assigned to each one to make sure only authorized people from the designated houses were taking the supplies and to report if anything was missing or needed replenishing.

Nancy, who lamented that she didn't feel she was contributing enough, turned her assignment into a mission of love. She encouraged and praised us as we came to get a drink of water from the cooler, brought coffee and Cokes to the caffeine addicts, provided bandages and TLC for minor wounds, cleaned up the scraps around the premises, and every so often walked through the house to marvel at our progress and give her approval and support. She was a shining example of the principle that any task performed with love is a divine one.

Faith Produces Perseverance

In one way or another, each participant made their own special contribution, not only to the erection of the house but also to the spirit of the endeavor. And when it came to spirit, Margo, our homeowner, set the tone. She greeted us Saturday morning decked out in a brown and beige camouflage jump suit and a white net cap—her "uniform" throughout the build. Obviously charged with excitement, with a hammer in one hand and a measuring tape in the other, she struck poses for us on the ramp leading to the deck of her home. She was ready to begin.

Throughout the long hard week, Margo's spirits never flagged, and though she was often in discomfort due to injuries from an automobile accident, she crawled under the house to insulate, lifted heavy sheetrock, and contributed to every aspect of the building of her home. As she worked alongside us, she shared about the faith that had carried her through thirteen long years of trying to obtain a Habitat home. During nine of those years, she took classes and worked two and three jobs to support herself and her son Nakia after leaving a trouble-filled, seventeen-year marriage.

In 1994, Margo was in a serious car accident and spent three weeks in intensive care and a year in rehabilitation. Nakia, who was 10 years old at the time, was her constant nurse and caretaker. After getting back on her feet and to work again, Margo applied twice more for a Habitat house and was turned down. At times, she became discouraged and bitter, but she never gave up.

"I knew that maybe there were some things I needed to change in my life to earn the reward of a home, but at other times I didn't understand why I was being passed over. However, I am a child of God," she said, "and I knew there was a house out there for me. So I kept praying, and my mother (who is a radio evangelist) also prayed for me. Then one day in early 1998, I saw Millard Fuller walking down the street. I stopped him, and asked him what I was doing wrong. 'Why haven't I received my home?' I asked. 'If you check the Habitat files, you will see that I have been applying since 1985.'" A month later, Margo was informed that her long wait was over. "I am a living witness to what can come about through faith and some assertiveness," Margo attested.

Those virtues were backed up with intense physical labor. During the prebuild, Margo was working the third shift sanitizing equipment at Tyson Foods. She would return home in the morning, freshen up and grab a bite to eat, then spend the rest of the day putting in her sweat equity. She kept up that grueling schedule for three long months and, by the week of the blitz, had satisfied more than the required 300 hours of sweat equity entirely on her own.

Margo said she was "simply in awe seeing all the people who have come together, not even knowing who I am, to work as a family and build me a home. The way life is these days," she continued, "you don't always think of people being so sincere and caring, but there are many wonderful people out there. It is such a blessing to have all these people here on my behalf, dedicating their time, their energy, and their money out of the willingness of their hearts to help me get something that will bring joy to my family, enable me to reach another level of society, and help me gain respect in the business world and everyday life."

What a joyous time we had on Friday as we attended to the finishing touches, put in the landscaping, gathered round while Margo opened housewarming gifts and entertained us with her antics, took the traditional group pictures, and shared hugs and tears of parting. Expressing her appreciation, Margo told us, "It seems like I have known you all my life. You have become like parents to me. I know this house will stand through flood, hurricane or tornado because it was built with love. It is a blessed home—it is our home! There is always a room for you at 147 Hosanna Circle."

Teach Your Children Well

Without a doubt, there is a very special place in Margo's heart, also, for the young family who sponsored her house (i.e., donated the money for all the materials). The Taylors—Kirk and Jo, their young son Kyle, and baby Claire—were an inspiration to all of us.

When I asked how their sponsorship had come about, Jo explained that she and Kirk, who came from modest backgrounds, had had the good fortune to do well financially. When they moved to Atlanta and bought themselves a new home, they agreed that someone else should have one as well. They called the Atlanta Habitat office and asked about sponsoring a house. However, they were referred to Americus where sponsors were still needed for homes in the Easter Morning Community, and they agreed to sponsor one of them.

Though the Taylors were uncomfortable with having their generosity spotlighted, when I shared how deeply touched I was, Jo elaborated on their motives. "We have been blessed. God has provided abundantly for us. We believe that the obedient response to our faith is to share our resources with others. We want our children to understand not just the *idea* of sharing with others, but the *emotional impact*. If we simply write a check and send it to a faraway address, there is little impact on our children. But, when we see the tangible results of sharing, and when they can participate in giving and sharing, we believe they begin to understand more about what it means to follow Christ's teaching."

The Taylors chose Habitat as their vehicle for sharing because they "believe that the family unit is central to teaching values. Kids need a consistent place to 'go home to.' We believe that when a family has a house that they own and are responsible to take care of, they have a better chance to communicate and model the values of respect, resourcefulness and responsibility. Participating in Habitat is a tangible investment in a family— today and into the future."

Probably the highlight of the week for all of us who worked on house eighteen, was watching four-year-old Kyle and his father put together a birdhouse for Margo. As he held a grown-up screwdriver in his small hands and concentrated on turning a screw, the man filming the official Easter Morning Build video asked, "What are you doing, Kyle?"

"Building a bird house," he replied, barely turning his head as he maintained focus on managing the screwdriver.

"Who is it for?"

"For Margo," he answered, his sparkling eyes conveying his excitement and delight.

"What kind of bird house is it?" the videographer asked.

He looked up. "A bluebird house," he politely explained, then turned back to his task.

When it was completed, we gathered around as Kyle presented the product of his efforts. "This is for you, Margo," he said proudly, "to hang in a tree for the birds."

In Their Footsteps

One of the construction supervisors on Margo's house was a young woman named Sarah. Larry and I were impressed with her determination to do things well and her gentle, supportive manner with the volunteers. As we walked to lunch one day, I asked her how she had ended up in Americus. I was fascinated by the story she related.

Sarah had thought that her parents would be thrilled when she announced she had decided to volunteer at Habitat headquarters for a year after graduating from college. After all, it was they who had instilled in all eight of their children a heart for service. As a family, they had often taken clothing into the poor neighborhoods of Chicago and worked in soup kitchens together. Sarah had also volunteered in various capacities during high school and college. At DePaul University in Chicago, Sarah and her friend Erin took leadership roles in the Community Service Department and together founded the Habitat for Humanity Campus Chapter there. It seemed a great idea to head for Americus to do something different and challenging like construction.

However, Sarah did not get the response that she anticipated from her father. Instead, her "dad was livid at this turn of events and convinced that I would never get a job nor be self-supporting." After spending $60,000 on her education, he had an expectation that she would seek a secure job—and volunteering did not qualify as such. That was an after-work and weekend activity. Furthermore, if she wanted to volunteer, she didn't need to move to Georgia to do it. There was plenty of help needed right in Chicago.

Nevertheless, with the quiet backing and encouragement of her mother and siblings, Sarah held fast to her decision and pursued her calling. Over the course of the next couple years as Sarah worked with Habitat under the umbrella of the AmeriCorps program, her father gradually became fully supportive of her choice, and both her parents are now involved with their local Habitat affiliate in the Chicago suburbs. We had an opportunity to meet them when they came to Americus to visit Sarah during the build, and they told us how very proud they are of what their daughter is doing.

I was touched by this young woman's resolve and the strength of her convictions. It made me wonder how often parents are confronted by the seriousness with which their children live out the messages they learn at home—both good and bad.

The Homeowners

All of the homeowners were African-American and the majority of the volunteers where white, offering an interesting and sometimes humorous interplay between the two cultures. One of the most obvious differences was our worship styles. The white ministers who led the morning devotions gave messages that stimulated our thinking; the black ministers woke us up!

At the Habitation Service on Good Friday evening, held at a beautiful large Methodist church, the proceedings were fairly formal until Tony Campolo stepped up to the podium. A well-known white American Baptist minister and sought-after speaker who is on the staff of a predominantly black church, Tony poked fun at our racial differences in a way that had us all laughing uproariously. As his trademark Good Friday sermon, "Today is Friday, But Sunday's Coming," reached a fiery crescendo, we loosened-up (*dehonkitized* was the term he used), normally staid worshippers rose to our feet shouting on cue, "But Sunday's coming!" I'm not sure we'll ever again look at the Easter story in quite the same way.

The most stirring and memorable words were delivered at the Easter morning sunrise service by Anthony, also a minister, who had been chosen by his fellow homeowners as their spokesperson. We all listened with hushed attentiveness as he spoke from his heart about the choices and responsibilities facing the homeowners.

"This community will be known by what we homeowners make of it," he said. "If we sit out here every weekend and have a party, then people in Americus and Sumter County will call this a partying community. If we decide to let drug dealers come into this community and sell drugs, then we will be known as a drug community. But, if we get together from time to time and reason together in God's word, then the people of Americus and Sumter County will feel the presence of God out here, and we will be able to say that somewhere in America there is a community that worships and believes in a risen Lord."

Then, he implored the homeowners to give as much time and attention to nurturing their spiritual homes as they had given to building and furnishing their new earthly homes, "because, in the end, your spiritual home is all you will have."

Following the service, we all walked in silence from the tent and gathered round as Millard Fuller pulled away a sheet and unveiled the dramatic entrance sign mounted on an arched and pillared brick wall. Against the white background of the sign, the rays of a blazing gold sun reached out from behind a bright red house. Written across the sun in blue letters were the words *Easter Morning* (the *T* in Easter was a large red cross) and below the house the word *Community*. Across the bottom in red lettering it read, *"Every house a sermon of God's love."* The silence was then broken and the week culminated as Millard led us in three loud cheers of "Oyee!"(an African chant used to rally a crowd). I looked at his exuberant face and wondered what it must feel like for him and his wife to see yet another phase of their ever-expanding vision become reality.

Change Of Plans

Following lunch on Good Friday, Millard asked for everyone's attention and announced that he had just received a call from Jan Bell, executive director of the Birmingham, Alabama affiliate. On Wednesday evening, shortly after returning from her visit at the blitz, a devastating tornado had struck five communities in the Greater Birmingham area. There had been significant loss of life and the destruction was extensive. Jan knew their affiliate would be needing help down the road to respond to the housing needs created by the tragedy.

Millard and the International Board immediately committed $1 million to the Birmingham affiliate for the rebuilding. Shortly after, fundraising letters were sent out appealing to supporters to double their regular pledges for a month or two. We were all reminded that Habitat is not a disaster response organization and were asked not to rush to Birmingham and descend upon Jan before she was ready. All those who wanted to be contacted to help at the appropriate time were asked to leave their names and phone numbers on a sign-up sheet.

When Larry and I later had a moment to discuss the news, I saw immediately by the look on his face that he was thinking what I was. We both sensed that this was the moment we had dreamed about for years. We knew we must go to Birmingham immediately on our own. Without the slightest hesitation, we called and canceled our reservations at the Gulf Shores.

III. DISASTROUS ENCOUNTERS

. . . volunteers achieve a stunning impact on an
almost endless number of problems and dreams.
The composite of all their individual acts
of kindness and courage moves mountains of pain,
hopelessness, neglect, and indifference and,
with each success, provides hope and
examples for all the rest of us.

Brian O'Connell, *Voices From The Heart*

III-12. A TIME TO TEAR DOWN

Great perils have this beauty,
that they bring to light the fraternity of strangers.

Victor Hugo, *Les Miserables*

Making Arrangements

Larry and I moved our trailer over to the Habitat RV park to clean, catch up on laundry, and get a little rest while we went about the process of figuring out how to make arrangements to help in Birmingham. We were advised to contact an Alabama Baptist Association, which would most likely be responding to the disaster.

On Monday, I called the local Baptist Association and obtained the number of one in the Rock Creek area of Alabama, but they were so inundated with pleas for immediate help that they were unable to handle my request for assistance in finding a place to park. I was referred to the Birmingham Baptist Association (BBA) and, when I called there, Peggy answered—a lady who qualifies as a saint! Despite the fact that her phone had been ringing incessantly for five days, there was no hint of hurry or frenzy in her voice.

I explained that we were full-time RVers who wanted to come help but could not afford to pay private campground fees; therefore, we needed to set up at a church or some other free facility. Ideally, I added, we'd like water and electric hook-ups and would need access to a shower. She asked when we planned to arrive, then assured me that arrangements would be made; all we needed to do was show up at the registration tent.

Getting Settled In Tornado Country

On Thursday morning, eight days after the tornado had struck, we headed out of Americus and arrived in mid-afternoon at the registration tent in Jefferson County. As promised, one of the volunteers recognized our names and directed us to Westwood Baptist Church, which would become our home for the next several weeks.

The Church, with a membership of 2400, was an impressive, sprawling, brick complex. Watson, the facilities manager, greeted us with gracious Southern hospitality and helped us get situated behind the gym. Then he gave us a tour of the building, indicating where we should go in the event of a tornado warning. In fact, he informed us, one was predicted for that evening.

One of the Church's ministries was an all-encompassing child and youth program, which included a fully equipped nursery and day care, and early-morning drop-off and after-school pick-up service. The full-sized gymnasium had two shower rooms that we could use.

After settling in and eating dinner, we turned on the evening news. Nashville, Tennessee, had been hit by a tornado that afternoon in the Centennial Park area where we had visited the previous year. Our reaction made us realize that, as a result of our travels, frequently the daily news now touches us personally. The places we have visited are no longer simply names or images on the screen. It is as though we are hearing reports about our hometown.

Early in the evening, as a storm began moving in our direction, all of the stations preempted their programming to carry continuous storm tracking and monitoring reports. In the following weeks, we became accustomed to such episodes (which are a regular occurrence in the Southeast's version of Tornado Alley) and well acquainted with "storm watch" vocabulary: *cells, hooks, microbursts, straight-line winds, tornadic action*. Moreover, weather forecasters are often local heroes. We later saw banners all over the stricken area proclaiming, "James Spann is Our Man!" Many credited him with saving their lives by convincing them that the April 8 storm was one they must take seriously.

On our first night in Birmingham, though, it all was new to us. We anxiously followed our atlas closely, trying to locate the counties that were highlighted on the tiny map in the corner of the TV screen. One thing that is vital to know in the South is the county you are in and the names of the surrounding ones. People generally reference locations by county unless they are talking about a large, well-known city. Thus, if you ask someone where they are from, they most likely will say Jackson County or Franklin County instead of the name of a town or city.

Having caught just a glimpse of minor storm damage on our way to the church, we were wide awake and on edge until midnight, when it finally appeared that the storm would pass us by. Even then, as we lay wondering what we would encounter the next day, it was difficult to fall asleep.

In the early morning hours, I was awakened by a roaring noise that thundered right over the trailer. I bolted upright in bed, saying "Oh, no," as I thought for sure a tornado was upon us. By the time I roused Larry (who acquired the ability to sleep through the sound of artillery bombardment in Vietnam), I realized it was only a low-flying jet. I shuddered at the thought of how the real thing must have sounded. I was unable to get back to sleep.

On Our Way

We checked in at the Birmingham Baptist Association registration tent at 8 a.m. the next morning. Inside the tent were boxes of gloves, mini-pouches with Band-Aids and aspirin, fruit, drinks, donuts, snacks and jugs of water for the volunteers to take with them. We were given a strip of blue cloth to tie to our wrist or belt loops and asked to register the time we left. We would also be required to check back in and record the time we returned. Everyone had to be accounted for, both for safety and security purposes.

All of the ladies conducting registration displayed the same calm demeanor that I had encountered over the phone with Peggy, despite the fact that they had worked non-stop since the storm, barely grabbing a few hours of sleep each night. Their patience and equanimity were admired by all the volunteers. National Guardsmen and FEMA (Federal Emergency Management Agency) personnel were on hand outside the tent, as well as a bearded gentleman who had staked out a corner on the grass. Next to him was a big hand-lettered sign: "Free Chain Saw Sharpening."

When there were enough volunteers to fill the van, we climbed in and headed for McDonald Chapel. Though I had long anticipated that moment, I suddenly felt my stomach knot up. It struck me that I'd never projected how I might feel if and when I encountered the scene of a major disaster. How was I going to react when I came face to face with it? Perhaps others in the van were experiencing similar anxieties, because the only one doing much talking was the driver.

Stark Contrast

The van stopped at an intersection at the bottom of the bowl-shaped community of McDonald Chapel, and we all stepped out. We were to help the volunteers who were already working on a corner site clearing and sorting debris and taking apart the remains of a house by hand. This was necessary in a large number of cases in "Mac's Chapel" because the weight of the bulldozers would crush the old septic systems.

Setting our backpack and water down, we just stood there for a few minutes. The damage had looked terrible enough through the window of the van, but standing eye-to-eye with it, it became almost incomprehensible. As I slowly turned 360 degrees, I realized that we were positioned at the center of the full force of the tornado. It looked like a giant Mixmaster had been turned on high speed and churned everything. It was almost impossible to imagine the power of something that could wreak such havoc in a minute or two, and it was equally difficult to believe that anyone had survived; yet incredibly, there had been only two deaths in McDonald Chapel.

I could see the remains of the Open Door Church up on the hill by the highway. It had received a great deal of media attention. The cars in the parking lot had been flung down into a ravine. Inside, people had crouched in a hallway singing hymns while the building crumbled around them. Miraculously, everyone survived.

On a vacant corner across from the property we were to work on, lay a perfectly intact roof from someone's house. On another corner was only a foundation with debris piled on top. Before beginning work, I grabbed my camera and took panoramic shots of the devastation all around us. When the photos were developed, we discovered that they could not capture the enormity of the destruction.

It was hard to know where to begin on our house. The roof was gone, and two exterior walls were collapsed. They and all the interior walls, furniture, appliances, cabinets, food and clothing were intertwined in a gnarled heap on the foundation. Wiring, insulation, fencing and clothes were tangled and scattered everywhere. There was a constant crunching sound as volunteers walked about on broken glass. As on a Habitat build, everyone just picked a spot and started doing what they could do. Doing something helped us realize that we weren't simply enmeshed in a bad dream.

What a stark contrast this was to the joy we had felt only a week before as we had built homes for twenty happy families. It was a harsh outpicturing of the truth about the temporary nature of possessions, in which we invest so much of ourselves. In a half-minute they were gone! The scene brought back Anthony's prophetic words: "Your physical home can be taken from you any time. It is your spiritual home which will save you."

Sobering Work

Our assignment was to completely dismantle the house and haul it to the curbside, while sorting out anything that the family might want to salvage. What made the work even more arduous was that we had no rakes or wheelbarrows. It gave new meaning to the expression "working with your hands." We used pieces of walls or doors on which to transport debris to the curb. It was strange how the things you would least expect survived unscathed—a punch bowl and cups or dozens of home-canned preserves.

We quickly discovered that there is a reverence about this work. As we picked up knickknacks, toys, souvenirs, Bibles and, in this case, Seventh Day Adventist leaflets, we began to piece together a picture of the people who lived in the house. Every so often a cluster of volunteers would stop and gather around to look and shake their heads when pictures of the family (or at least someone's family) were found. We put them inside the their car to protect them from further rain, although all of the windows were shattered or blown out.

By midday, when members of the Birmingham Baptist Association came by with a hot chicken dinner, the curbside heap was beginning to sprawl. Larry and I took our lunches and sat on the steps of the foundation across the road. A camera crew from the Red Cross saw a picture in that and asked us to share with them how we had come to be there and why. Shortly after, a photographer from Peace Project also snapped our picture. Everyone was fascinated by the variety and numbers of volunteers—especially those from out of town—and extremely appreciative. An Allstate agent came over to our house and, when he realized we weren't from the area, thanked us on behalf of the family for being there.

Life Gives And Life Takes Away

As I was taking a moment to have a sip of water, I noticed an elderly, stooped, black gentleman standing by the foundation that we had sat on during lunch. His grandson stood by his side with his arm around his grandfather's shoulder as they both quietly surveyed the wreckage. I walked across the road, stood with them a moment, then asked if it had been his home. He answered that it was. "I'm so sorry," I offered. The old man shrugged his shoulders. Without rancor, and with the acceptance of one made wise by time, he replied, "That's life. Things are given and things are taken."

Actually, for him and numerous other residents of the racially mixed community of McDonald Chapel, it wasn't the first time that life had taken away. Forty-two years earlier, a powerful tornado had touched down in exactly the same spot, killing 22 people. Those who survived had had to rebuild from nothing. For some, the second time was once too many, and they would choose not to return.

The old man matter-of-factly described his ordeal of the week before. He had been sitting on his porch watching the strange lightning zigzagging horizontally across the black sky. He could hear the weather reports coming from the TV inside, but they were not forecasting that the storm would hit Mac's Chapel. He no sooner went inside and closed the door than he heard what sounded like a train on his front porch. He and his wife dropped to the floor in the middle of the living room as it hit, tearing away all of the house but leaving them unscathed.

Miracle In The Rubble

After lunch the van returned with rakes and wheelbarrows purchased by the Salvation Army. They definitely helped speed up the operation. More volunteers arrived in the afternoon, and we observed them struggling to adjust to what they were seeing, just as we had. Slowly, but surely, the floor of the house began coming into view.

As Larry walked across it, one foot slipped through a hole in the flooring. Steadying himself, he pulled his foot out and noticed a shoebox beneath the boards. He caught a glimpse of something moving. Reaching down and lifting out the box, Larry smiled and tilted it for everyone to see. Inside were three plump kittens, approximately two weeks old, who had obviously been well cared for by their mother in the midst of all the havoc. A few days later, I would see her crossing the road to the then-barren site looking for them.

Two of the young women immediately scooped the kittens up and took them to the corner of the lot to feed them water from bottle caps. One woman took two of them (which she immediately named Tornado and Survivor), and the other claimed the third. They both left to take their new

90

charges home. Such are the little miracles that are encountered in the midst of a monumental catastrophe.

After most of the debris was cleared away from our house, we all stood watching as the remaining wall was knocked down. In this case, there was no cheer of accomplishment. It was a sobering task to raze someone's home.

The van picked us up about 3:30 and, after we checked out, we returned to the church, showered, ate a quick meal and went to bed early. We were physically and emotionally spent.

Stormy Weather

On Saturday, approximately 1000 volunteers (half of them Mormons) converged on the area to clean up. Unfortunately, halfway through the day, another severe thunderstorm came through, and everyone had to be evacuated.

Back at the church we changed out of our drenched clothes and spent time talking with some of the young parents who were decorating for the children's "50's party." It included pizza and root beer floats and roller-skating to music from the fifties. For parents who were obviously not around during that era, they did a pretty authentic job. Everyone was having a great time until the tornado siren sounded around 8 p.m. We put Ross's harness on him and joined the crowd in the music room that was below ground level. Most of the children were so intrigued by Ross they were distracted from concern about the weather. The storm passed without incident and, more accustomed to the scenario than we, everyone partied on. We went to bed.

Where Have All The Trees Gone?

Sunday afternoon following church, we decided to drive the 30-mile length of the storm track out to the community of Oak Grove, where the area all-grades school had been demolished. We were not the only ones who had that idea; but the slow line of traffic enabled us to take everything in.

The Rock Creek and Oak Grove areas had been heavily wooded, and almost all the trees had been downed, many of which were already cut up and stacked in piles along the roadside. It was difficult to distinguish where homes had been amidst the wasted landscape. Now and then we would see a wreathe staked in front of a foundation, and a chill would run through us.

When we arrived at the school, we parked and got out so I could take a picture. We talked awhile with members of an area Baptist church who were serving food and offering supplies to victims and volunteers. One man, a life-long resident, told us that coming home from work along the road a few days after the storm, he had become completely disoriented because of the missing trees, houses and other landmarks.

It was a story we would hear again and again. Besides the deaths of relatives and friends and the destruction of their homes, among the things most mourned by the victims and area residents was the loss of the trees. As we would see a year later when we returned, the newly rebuilt houses looked forlorn and lost on the barren land and, because of that, the communities would never look the same. Many people remarked that after the storm they were able to see houses and other landmarks that they never knew existed.

Side By Side

On Monday we were asked to help take apart one of two homes that had literally been sucked together. They belonged to elderly sisters, aged 82 and 90, who had lived next door to each other for 64 years. Most of what had been their homes was gone, except for the facing side walls, which now stood side by side, and the back hall and bathroom of the house we were working on, where one sister had cowered during the storm. The other one had been out of town.

We would hear numerous tales of people being saved by lying in their bathtubs with a mattress or blanket over them. Indeed, as we saw for ourselves, in most cases what remained of a house, if anything, were the interior hall and the bathroom, which is exactly where the weathermen advise people to go if they do not have a basement or shelter.

Turn Off The Gas

This was the first day we worked with Clay, an area resident who had been there almost every day for two weeks, using vacation time or volunteering during the day while holding down his night job. His motivation was simple: "I just love people, and these people need help." He was seldom seen without his chain saw in hand and a cigarette dangling from his mouth. We also worked with a woman, and a couple who later invited us to share Mother's Day with them. All three had taken the day off work because they felt they "had to be there."

Clay was happily chain-sawing sections of the main wall when I walked by and caught a whiff of gas. "I smell gas!" I yelled. Almost immediately Larry smelled it, too. We all decided we should move across the street. Larry stopped a passing car and asked the driver to tell the gas company workers up the street to come to our site.

Clay walked across to his brand new truck, sat down in the street behind it (a lit cigarette still in his mouth), and began sharpening his chain saw. Suddenly, there was a loud whooshing sound. Gas was blowing out of a pipe in the ground right in front of his truck. We all yelled at Clay to put out his cigarette, but before he understood what we were saying, the gas shut off. The company foreman informed us they had turned on the gas to check for leaks. Brilliant move!

The next day a van full of Methodists arrived from Fort Payne, North Carolina (about 90 miles away), to work on the other house. Each day for a week, the pastor had been shuttling a fresh crew to help with the clean-up. This group included several women in their early thirties who worked at an aerobics gym, and there was no doubt that they were in excellent physical condition. They carried beams and cement blocks like they were pieces of molding or a briefcase, and they only stopped for lunch or to take a sip of water. They even brought their own healthy food to eat instead of the more carbohydrate-rich Red Cross and Salvation Army meals.

The gas company foreman stopped by to say he had been observing the Methodist women working and he'd informed two of his crew that if they didn't step up their pace, he was going to fire them and hire one of the women in their place. His safety awareness may not have been the sharpest, but he did have a keen sense of humor.

A Glimmer Of Hope

The sisters had owned beautiful china and many knickknacks and keepsakes accumulated over their lifetimes. When we found things that were unbroken, we set them aside and cleaned them off as best we could. One afternoon, the 82-year-old sister came by and just stood for a while with an expressionless face as she watched us work. One of the volunteers took her by the arm and proudly showed her some of the items that had been salvaged. The woman shook her head sadly and said, "It's so hard to lose everything." There was nothing to say or do except hug her.

As our pile by the road grew and the remains of the two houses diminished, we observed that a new roof and porch were already being constructed on a damaged house across the road. We were told that the owner was a builder by trade. After several days of tearing down, it was a hopeful sight to see something once again going up.

Order Out Of Chaos

The next day, we were assigned to begin working on the properties on the hillside along Xavier, the main road into McDonald Chapel. It was actually pretty amazing how quickly an orderly system evolved in the chaos.

Ricky Thacker, a Baptist minister whose church was close to Pratt City (the last community in Jefferson County to be hit) had been one of the first on the scene there, helping to cover roofs and take other stop-gap measures to minimize further damage. Because there had been no loss of life in Pratt City and the area was not as heavily wooded as others, volunteers were able to go in immediately. After coordinating that effort, Ricky was asked by Emergency Management to do the same thing the next day in Edgewater (after emergency crews had cleared the roads of trees and fallen wires), and the following day in Mac's Chapel where he then stayed for the duration of the clean-up phase.

Damage assessment and needs had to be determined for each property and a permit for demolition signed by the owners. Once that was procured, the property could be assigned to volunteers to follow through with whatever was necessary. In some areas of Mac's Chapel, many of the small, former mining-camp homes were rentals owned by absentee landlords. In a number of cases, it took months to contact them and secure permission. Meanwhile, there was plenty to keep all of us busy.

Up Hill, Down Hill

The first area to be cleared was adjacent to a corner lot where a man's brand new doublewide trailer had been sitting, ready to be mounted onto a foundation. The tornado blew it over to the next-door property—not in one piece, of course. The long black metal frame was looped around a shorn-off tree like a horseshoe around a stake. Large, downed trees were added into the mix of insulation, trailer materials and debris from other houses.

Two factors made the job particularly tedious—one was that the owner wanted us to try to determine what was reusable and stack it in a separate pile. The other was that the logs and rubble had to be hauled down a steep hill about 50-60 yards long. Then, of course, we had to walk back up and

94

start all over again. Where were those Methodist ladies when we really needed them?

Those with chain saws cut up trees, while the rest of us picked up litter, raked, and loaded wheelbarrows, then took turns transporting them down and up the hill. I was embarrassed to even give the appearance of being tired when 72-year-old Helen, a full-time worker for the Baptist Association Medical Assistance Office, arrived and kept pace with us—with a constant smile and good humor!

We did receive a little comic relief from an elderly gentleman who showed up with a large flatbed truck outfitted with a winch. He instructed us to take the large pieces of debris only halfway down the hill and stack them on top of his cable. After a sufficient pile accumulated, he secured the cable and pulled the load down to the road. Unfortunately, more than half of it fell out along the way, therefore requiring us to collect it all again and carry it to the curb. Undaunted, he tried once more. However, when the cable snapped, without a word to anyone, he rolled it up, threw it on the bed of the truck and drove off—leaving us with yet another scattered mess to pick up.

In the late afternoon, just about the time we were all feeling like we would not accomplish our mission for the day, 30 University of Alabama students arrived and began bounding up and down the hill, making short work of the remains. Three cheers for youth!

Earlier in the day, Larry had helped knock down the walls of a house. Later, a bulldozer came and, in a few minutes, crunched and shoved the foundation down to the street. As I stood watching, tears welled up in my eyes because it didn't seem right; it was too impersonal. Somehow it seemed more respectful to take someone's home apart by hand.

Curbside Service

We waited for the Red Cross truck to come by with chicken dinners to take back to the trailer. Cooking was definitely not an option for that evening. The lunches, dinners and snacks provided by the Salvation Army and Red Cross were greatly appreciated. It would have been very difficult to put in those grueling hours in the increasingly hot weather (the end of April in Alabama) and have to worry about shopping for and preparing food.

It was our feeling, though, that it was somewhat inefficient for both services to come by within minutes of each other at every location. It would have made more sense for them to divide up the various sites. But since they didn't, we quickly learned to pick and choose between them according to our preference or need: one had the better lunch and the other the better dinner. One gave us bags of fruit, and the other munchies. One had coffee and soda, the other had water and juice. In addition to the Salvation Army and Red Cross, church groups and individuals circulated with food and drinks, and we could also stock up at the registration tent. Suffice it to say, we were well fed.

Reality Check

The next day we continued working our way along the houses on the hill. We got our first look at the interior of one that hadn't appeared too bad from the outside. The couch was standing on end. Part of the ceiling was hanging down. Insulation, broken glass, books, window shades and curtains were strewn all over the floor. We became aware that the days of seeing nothing but litter and mess had gradually dulled our senses. We were beginning to see it as the norm. As other volunteers would confirm, it was hard to shake the feeling that the owners were messy housekeepers, or to imagine that their houses were ever neat and orderly.

The same was true in regard to the victims. We only saw them in poorly fitting donated clothes, with their hair unkempt, bags under their eyes, looking tired and bedraggled. It was difficult to picture them bright-eyed, dressed up for work or church, with a suit or makeup on. It was hard to imagine them living normal lives before the tornado, sitting in front of a TV or working in their yards. Only when we saw a picture of them or their house from an earlier time did it truly register that everything had looked entirely different just a couple weeks before.

The victims themselves had to be reminded that ordinary life was taking place beyond the rubble. I remember comforting and consoling an older woman whose husband wanted her to accompany him to their grandson's ball game. She was feeling guilty about going because people were there working on her property. Strain and exhaustion were written all over her. I assured her it was very important that she go.

"Not only that," I added, "but you need to get away from here for awhile and allow yourself to do something normal."

"So, you really think it's okay?" she asked, seeking permission.

"Absolutely," I reiterated.

"Thank you," she said with obvious relief, as tears trickled down her face.

Another manifestation of this phenomenon was rather humorous. I was sitting on a log in front of a ten-foot pile of rubbish, finishing up my lunch that had been packed in a Styrofoam covered tray. After carefully placing my napkins and wrappers inside the tray so they wouldn't blow away, I stood up with my empty soda can and tray in hand and automatically looked around for a trash barrel. When I realized what I was doing, the incongruity between my actions and the fact that I was literally surrounded by garbage struck my funny bone. I lifted the soda can up high and loudly inquired, "Are we recycling?" This brought laughter from everyone around as they, too, saw the picture. Each day thereafter, I took special delight in watching new volunteers check their impulse to find a proper place to dispose of their trash.

The Ice Cream Angel

It was a long hot day, and everyone was beginning to wilt. Suddenly, we heard a sound reminiscent of our childhoods—the familiar jingle of an ice cream truck. A local volunteer knew the owner and had challenged him to do his part. He pulled up alongside the curb and pointed to the sign on the side of his truck, indicating which ice cream bars were free. Like little children, our faces broke out into wide grins as we all crowded around to make our selections. Reaching up to take a creamsicle (my childhood favorite) from his hand was like seeing myself in a snapshot from the past. What is it about an ice cream bar that can so magically lift our spirits and melt away our weariness? It was just what the doctor ordered. That ice cream man looked very much like an angel!

Still Smiling

While we were working next door to a forlorn-looking brick house missing its roof, I noticed a woman standing in front of it with a broad smile on her face as she talked with a volunteer. I walked over and introduced myself and asked if she owned the house behind her. Mariesha nodded affirmatively. "How can you smile?" I queried.

She responded quickly. "We're here, aren't we? The things can be replaced! I'm not going to whine and wring my hands. It doesn't change anything."

Mariesha survived the tornado in the bathroom; her son David was in a closet, and her husband crouched under the pool table in their front room.

97

They were waiting for the insurance company to decide whether their house could be salvaged or would need to be demolished. I talked with Mariesha awhile longer and learned that her greatest sorrow was not over her house, but rather her next door neighbors "who didn't make it."

"I'd have gladly lost all I had in exchange for them," she added. Mariesha had frequently come home from her job at the bank to spend the lunch hour with her neighbor, Joy. She had recently given Joy a book of inspirational readings, and they often shared together about their faith. Joy and Woodrow Pratt had retired early the night of the storm, because they had plans for the next day. As they lay in bed, their house was swept under Mariesha's garage.

Mariesha, her husband, and their 17-year-old son David all searched for the Pratts for three hours in the dark and rain until they were forced to evacuate. The next morning, David found their neighbors' bodies. "It was God's grace and mercy not to leave just one of them," Mariesha remarked gratefully.

When Mariesha was able to call the bank where she worked, she asked for someone to contact her parents to let them know she was all right, and to have them come and get David. She felt he needed relief for awhile from the oppressive scene of destruction which was not only a constant reminder of finding the bodies of his neighbors, but also that his life had once again been turned upside down. Two Aprils prior, David had almost died from a brain abscess, the result of a bike accident that drove his nose through his brain. Mariesha had taken five months off from work to nurse him back to health, during which time the bank generously continued to pay her salary.

I was aware that David was in deep emotional pain as I worked alongside him. We talked quietly. "Maybe something good will come of this, do you think?" he asked.

I touched his arm and told him I believed it would, but that it might take a long time to see and understand it. "For now," I said, "you need to concentrate on taking one day at a time."

Feeling compelled to leave a symbol of my caring for this family that had so touched me, I returned a few days later with a jar of my blueberry jam. Finding no one home, I placed it with a note in the clearest spot I could find amid the shambles in the kitchen, never knowing until a year later whether Mariesha found it.

New Assignments

Work continued for a couple more days in Mac's Chapel, after which it was closed to volunteers so that the cranes and dump trucks could come in to remove the mountainous piles along the roads. The Baptist Association temporarily suspended their involvement, and the members who had worked for three weeks straight took time for much-needed rest and to regroup for the recovery phase.

We took a few days to regroup, also, catching up on rest and household business. We had received word that we were accepted to both the Jimmy Carter and Ed Schreyer Work Projects. Since we weren't sure how long we would be in Alabama, we forestalled our response. Realizing we, too, needed some normalcy, we indulged ourselves in an evening of square dancing.

Then, hoping we could be of further use, we contacted the Sylvan Springs Methodist Church situated midway along the storm track. It had sustained some damage to its sanctuary, but was operating a relief center from the fellowship hall. Ironically, the pastor and a large contingent of the congregation had left the day after the storm for a planned mission trip out of the country. Consequently, the youth leader found himself in charge of organizing response efforts in that area.

The first day, he assigned us to clear a piece of property on Rock Creek Road. The house, the basement and foundation of which were constructed of concrete blocks, had been picked up and slammed against a huge tree about ten feet away. Because the tree stopped it, the owner was able to salvage much of his furniture. He planned to have the rest of the house bulldozed to the road. Above ground level, the foundation was faced with bricks. Part of our job involved collecting and stacking good bricks and blocks.

That day we worked with Ron, a flight controller in the Air Force who was stationed in Montgomery and had driven up on his day off. Over lunch, he told us that he was in a transition period in his life, looking for something to give him a sense of purpose. When he heard about the tornado, he felt compelled to come. He had never done anything like that before, and he was deeply moved. It helped put his own pain in perspective, he confided.

The man who owned the house stopped by on his lunch hour and talked with us. Because he worked nights, he had not been home when the storm hit. His wife and son had sought refuge in a storage closet in the basement and both survived, though his wife had been injured when a concrete block fell on her head. They were extremely blessed.

99

On their street, only the house next door remained standing. On my way back from a trip to the "blue room" (one of the omnipresent portable toilets), I stopped to talk with the owner who was outside making repairs. He indicated where every home in the area had been—where now there was almost no trace of their existence. For one reason or another, almost no one had been home that night. "I probably wouldn't be alive if I had been home," he said. Pointing to the side of his house, he explained that shafts of splintered trees and wood from the other houses had been shot through it like spears.

When we were finished for the day, we drove up onto the ridge of Edgewater B, which looked down over Edgewater A (both former mining camps). The tornado had completely stripped the ridge. Neatly laid out where houses had once stood were the household items salvaged from each. Several men sat in chairs chatting, as though they were around a campfire. To protect their property from being stolen, they had been alternating nights sleeping in the van parked nearby. We thought we had become used to the sights and stories, but as we stood there we could only shake our heads in disbelief.

That evening there was a message on our voice mail informing us that the worst flood in 50 years had made a complete mess of the garage on our camp property in New Hampshire. Unable to entertain any more thoughts of disasters, we shrugged our shoulders. We'll deal with it when we have to, we decided. At least by then, we reasoned, it will be dry. Tomorrow there will be more for us to do here.

III-13. PUTTING A FACE ON TRAGEDY

The real beauty of nature and of persons
is often revealed
within the ugliness of pain and suffering.

Thomas Moore, *Voices From The Heart*

Community Ties

Brenda and Lonnie Calvert's two-story house and deck, as well as the storage building for their plumbing business supplies, sat on the top of a steep hill overlooking the east end of Warrior River Road, the main road through Rock Creek. The property of the couple in their early fifties was part of a large tract of land on the hillside owned by Brenda's 70-year-old mother, Dorothy Mitchell. Her home was just beyond and below theirs. Earlier that year, Brenda's thirty-year-old son Greg, his wife Becky, 21, and their two young sons, Scott, 4, and Jonathan, 2, had moved in with her because of Greg's debilitating heart condition.

Rock Creek, 20 miles southwest of McDonald Chapel, is an all-white, closely knit community, the foundation of which is its two main churches—Union Hill Baptist and the Church of God. Everyone knows each other or is related to one another. They are hard working, faith-filled, self-reliant people who pull together in adversity. Many of the properties had been in family hands for several generations.

Though the damage was just as severe in some of the other communities, Rock Creek was considered to be the most impacted by the tornado because of the great loss of life and the large percentage of displaced households. The Church of God was the most profoundly touched—6 of the 10 people who died in Rock Creek were members of the congregation. Also, the Church's Family Life Center was demolished (30 people survived the storm in the women's rest room—the only thing left standing), the church and parsonage required extensive repairs, and 80% of their families' homes were destroyed or severely damaged.

Narrow Escape

Minutes before the storm arrived, Lonnie stopped at Holden's Food Mart down the hill, a few blocks from their home, to pick up the tomatoes Brenda had asked him to get. After Greg, Becky and Scott had left to attend a friend's party, Brenda took a shower and began preparing supper. She could see a dark cloud in the direction of Oak Grove to the west, but it looked like smoke from a fire. Then the siren sounded at the nearby elementary school. When it sounded a second time, Brenda tried to call her mother and her Aunt May, who lived nearby. She was unable to reach either.

When the siren sounded again, Brenda looked out the door. Her heart pounded wildly as she saw shingles, trash and tree limbs swirling around in the wind; trees were whipping back and forth. Grabbing her purse, keys and medicine, she ran out to one of their plumbing vans, but a water heater had been flung and lodged against the door. She jumped into her car and headed down Mitchell Drive toward Holden's, momentarily stopping halfway to stare at a horse that had been impaled by a piece of wood or aluminum. She knew she couldn't do anything to help it.

In front of her, flames were shooting up as the power station transformers at the bottom of the hill began exploding. It looked like a fireworks show. She could hear the loud, steady "bing, bing" of the power lines snapping. As she turned left onto Warrior River Road and approached the local Texaco, in her rear view mirror Brenda could see power poles and trees toppling every which way, like giant dominoes.

When she pulled into Holden's parking lot, Lonnie opened the market door and yanked Brenda inside. In her scramble for safety, she tripped on a rug and fell to the floor, breaking a tooth. The power went out as they reached the back of the store where they hovered along with the owner behind a large heavy cooler.

Several times Lonnie ventured to the front to watch what was happening outside. The windows were shaking, and through the flashes of lightening he could see all the store's signs blowing away, trash and branches flying by, and Brenda's car sliding across the parking lot. The heavy backhoe hitched behind Lonnie's van held it in place, although the van was bucking up and down. The store itself sustained almost no damage.

It's Not There

When they were certain the tornado had passed over, Brenda and Lonnie cautiously emerged from the store and looked up toward the hill, from which their house was always clearly visible. Through the intermittent flashes of lightening, they could see that nothing was there. Later, the realization would hit that had Brenda lingered a few minutes longer, she would not have been there either. But then, their most immediate concern was to get the rented backhoe to safety, so Lonnie, with Brenda following in her car, drove 5 miles out of Rock Creek to leave the van and backhoe at a friend's.

By the time they returned, emergency vehicles and news media had gathered at the edge of town. The downed trees and wires made it impossible for vehicles to get through. With Channel 42 news cameras accompanying them, Brenda and Lonnie made their way up the hill on foot, climbing over trees and limbs, power poles and other debris. Brenda was barefooted—in her haste, she had neglected to put on shoes.

Once there, Brenda could only wail, "It's all gone, it's all gone. Everything is gone!" Their home had been flung down the steep ravine behind their house. Two of their plumbing vans, Greg's Volkswagen, and Lonnie's truck were suspended in the trees. Their boat was nowhere to be seen.

With the cameras still following, they made their way to her mother's house. The air conditioner in Dorothy's kitchen window had been propelled the length of the house, the force of it helping to knock down most of the side wall. The wind had sheered off the roof and all the siding. The propane tank had been overturned, and Lonnie was fearful the house might explode. Borrowing a flashlight from the camera crew, he managed to get the gas turned off.

Dorothy

Dorothy worked several evenings a week cleaning offices in Birmingham. She had left work earlier than usual that evening at the encouragement of co-workers who had heard that a bad storm was headed toward Rock Creek. When she approached, it was pitch dark except for the lights of emergency vehicles. No one was allowed in except rescue workers. Dorothy drove to her daughter Charlene's house in nearby Sylvan Springs, which itself narrowly missed being hit, and waited anxiously for news of her family.

Dorothy eventually received a call from Brenda informing her that her house was badly damaged. Brenda still didn't know if Greg and Becky and the grandsons were all right. Dorothy told her to concentrate on finding them. She'd worry about her house in the morning.

Night of Terror

Earlier that day, Becky had dropped off her youngest son Jonathan at her parents' home on Hillview Drive, just a couple blocks away, then was gone for several hours helping a friend with an errand. When she returned to Brenda's, she immediately became concerned about the way the sky looked. "The clouds were rolling like waves of smoke in the sky," she recalls. She was a little irked that Greg was playing Nintendo with friends and hadn't showered nor gotten their son Scott ready to attend their friend Michael's birthday party down the hill. They both showered quickly, and although Greg said they could ride out the storm at Brenda's, Becky insisted they leave. Somehow, she felt this one was different.

They arrived at Michael's in time to watch the end of "Twister" with the six or seven other people there. Outside they could see lightening flashing. When the credits ended, Becky suggested they turn to the weather channel. The weatherman had just announced that a tornado had touched down in Tuscaloosa, when they heard a loud crash and the lights went out. Michael's house was old, and the floors sagged badly. As he opened the door to see what was happening, the lights flickered back on dimly, enough for them to see the floors rise up and bow.

Fearful that the house was going to explode or be pulled apart, Greg jerked Scott out of Becky's arms, and Jamie, a friend of Michael's, grabbed Becky's hand so hard that her rings and watch fell off. They all raced across the street to take cover at their neighbor's brick house. Jamie and Becky made it to the back of the house, but by the time Greg and Scott got across the road the full force of the wind was upon them. Greg pushed Scott down into the ditch along the roadside and covered him with his body. It was deep enough that he felt very little of the sucking force.

Becky crouched against the back of the house screaming, "Where are my babies?" She prayed that if she could have her children and husband, she would try to never sin again. Jamie shielded Becky with his body and stuck his hand up to protect them from the falling bricks. A number of them landed on his hand, which later required reconstructive surgery. When the storm passed over, Greg jumped up, exclaiming jubilantly, "Yeah, we made it! We made it!" Scott, who had been shrieking with fright as they lay in the ditch, relaxed a little when he saw his daddy's happy face. Across the street, Michael's house was still standing, though 2x4s were sticking through the walls where they had all been sitting.

Greg's happiness was short-lived as he suddenly remembered Jonathan. Leaving Becky and Scott with his friends, he jumped into his car, but realized he could go nowhere. Although he'd had a heart attack just two months before, pumped with adrenaline, Greg ran toward his in-law's house, passing by Union Hill Baptist Church. A deputy sheriff was trapped in his accordianed car—a huge tree had fallen in front of it and a fireman had rammed into the back of it. Greg found his in-laws' home intact, but their car was gone. He later learned they had made a trip to Tuscaloosa and were not back home yet when the tornado struck.

Greg then asked a neighbor to drive him up the road behind his parents' house. As a bolt of lightning lit up the sky, he realized that nothing was there. Frantic, they scrambled up the hill and began digging through debris looking for Brenda. About a half hour later someone arrived with a flashlight, and Greg saw that his mother's car was gone. Figuring she must have gotten away, he ran down the road to the Texaco.

Meanwhile, Becky, worried that Greg had been gone so long, left Scott with their friends and followed the same route Greg had taken, finally meeting up with him at the Texaco station. They both went down to Holden's where they knew Brenda and Lonnie would eventually come.

Reunited

Brenda and Lonnie were frantically trying to learn if Greg and Becky and the grandchildren were all right. Believing that they had all gone to Becky's parents, they were assured that no one had been injured in the area where they lived. Still, they kept asking everyone who came by if they had seen them. They would not be able to rest that night until they knew they were all safe.

Finally, someone told Brenda that Greg and Becky were at Holden's Food Mart. They rushed over and, shrieking hysterically, fell into each other's arms. Everyone was wet, muddy, disheveled and in shock—it would take Becky days to get the pine straw, leaves, dirt and mud disentangled from her long, thick, curly red hair—but they were all alive.

The Longest Mile

In the dark and rain, Greg and his in-law's neighbor trudged back through the path of destruction to Michael's house to retrieve Scott. It was the longest walk of Greg's life as they climbed over and around downed trees, power lines and the twisted wreckage of buildings and cars, checking friends' and relatives' homes along the way. Stunned by the sight of dead bodies, Greg was, nevertheless, relieved to find that his Aunt May and her husband survived the storm in their bathtub, though eight houses on either side of them had been obliterated.

After finally retrieving Scott, he made his way back to Holden's and called a friend in nearby Hueytown who came and brought Scott, Becky and him to their home. From there, they contacted Becky's parents to assure themselves that Jonathan was safe and to let them know they were all right. Brenda and Lonnie also spent the night at the home of friends in Hueytown. Since the rain and thunder continued throughout the night, no one slept.

Rapid Response

Ignoring the fact that the Concord Fire Station in Rock Creek was blown away, the fire fighters stuffed their clothing with bandages and anything else they might need and began making their way through the wreckage, conducting a methodical search in the rain, street by street, house by house, determining who had survived, who was unaccounted for, and tagging homes where fatalities had occurred. The injured had to be carried out on doors or anything else available to the waiting ambulances on the edge of the destruction. By 7 a.m., everyone had been accounted for and all the bodies removed.

The Morning After

Dorothy Mitchell, normally a very polite and deferential woman, glared out her car window at the policewoman who tried to prevent her from entering Rock Creek. "You will have to lock me up! Otherwise, I'm going through," she announced emphatically to the officer. "That's my home up there. You're letting all those news people in." At that, the policewoman let her slip past.

Even as Dorothy tells it today, some of the details are fuzzy. "It was a very confusing time," she says. When Dorothy is faced with a calamity, she feels better if she can work. That is exactly what she told the news reporters who came up and found her shoveling the mud and debris out of her house and asked why she was doing it, since it appeared her house was destroyed. "And, I need to be by myself," she added, to no avail. They hung around asking more questions and taking pictures.

Brenda and Lonnie were picking through the wreckage scattered around their property that morning while several men from Alabama Power worked on clearing the fallen lines and poles. When one noticed that Brenda was barefooted, he pulled a pair of men's shoes out of his truck and gave them to her. A little later the men also shared their sub sandwiches.

Brenda and Lonnie discussed whether or not to stay at his parents who lived an hour away. Brenda did not want to have to commute back and forth that far when she knew there was so much to do. "I'll just sleep here in the car, if I have to," she said adamantly. Overhearing their conversation, the same man who had given her the shoes came over and handed them $100. "Take this and get yourselves a motel room and something to eat," he said.

Greg did not go back up to the house until the third day after the storm. The stress of that harrowing night had caught up with him.

Taking Charge

The next day, Brenda went to the Calvary Church where the Jefferson County Housing Authority was set up and applied for free housing for six months. Brenda, Lonnie, and Dorothy stayed in one house, and Becky and Greg and the children in another next door. Brenda and Lonnie moved in that night, armed with Red Cross air bags, and pillows and blankets given to them by one of the churches. The house was furnished with only a stove and refrigerator.

They covered the windows with trash bags and, using plastic utensils and bowls, ate their first meal—cereal—in their temporary home. Gradually, they furnished and stocked the place with donated household goods and food, most of which was disseminated by the area churches. Becky's family gathered enough furnishings to make their house livable for the children.

Over the next week, Dorothy worked at her house almost non-stop, shoveling out all the heavy muck and debris, and with the help of Brenda and volunteers, carried salvageable items out to the driveway to dry. Fortunately, the weather turned beautiful after the storm. She bought big tarps and covered her custom-built kitchen cabinets until they moved everything that could be saved from both Brenda's house and hers into rented storage sheds. Looking back, she has no idea how she had the strength to do what she did.

Without waiting for help from agencies, Dorothy found a carpenter who made a materials list for replacing the roof. She purchased them with money from her savings. The second Saturday after the storm, Pastor Steve Garland from Faith Baptist Church, which was serving as the volunteer check-in and coordination center, sent over a crew of volunteers—5 Baptists and 5 Methodists from Jacksonville, Alabama—who built a new roof. Meanwhile, the side wall had to be completely taken down, as well as all the wet sheetrock throughout the house. The next week Dorothy was ready for another volunteer crew to reconstruct the wall.

The two major concerns taken care of, Dorothy allowed herself to collapse for a while. Her blood pressure had skyrocketed, and she was totally exhausted. Then another group from Jacksonville came and worked for a day getting the sheetrock started. That was when we arrived on the scene.

The Ravine

On Friday, May 1st, we had our first look into the ravine. Countless volunteer hours had been spent clearing Brenda's property—extracting the vehicles from trees and retrieving their belongings from the ravine—before we were sent there to help. After hearing her story and spending a few minutes staring in disbelief at the remains of her house below, we and a group of students from University of Alabama sororities and fraternities cleared up the remainder of the junk around the foundation and hauled it to the road.

There were a number of personal belongings Brenda was especially eager to locate in the tangle of appliances, trees, walls and furniture: canceled checks and business receipts gathered for an appointment she was to have had with an IRS representative the day after the storm, her jewelry box, her daddy's military burial flag, and 24 albums of family photos. I could completely empathize with Brenda's despair over her pictures, because they are my earthly treasures, also. I always used to say, "In case of emergency, the kids and pets first, the photos second."

Brenda's plight touched our hearts. Larry and I decided we would like to help her as much as we were able. We had already inquired about moving the trailer to a place closer to where we were working and had been informed that Faith Baptist Church, just three miles up the road from

Brenda's, had full hook-ups along the front of their parking lot, installed 30 years earlier for missionary conferees. We went over to talk with Pastor Garland (called Brother Steve by most), a tall, well-built man with a booming voice. He was more than happy for us to use their facilities. No one had hooked up in the last 14 years. We told him we'd hold off until we were sure we were going to be around awhile.

Returning to Brenda's late Saturday morning, we continued cleaning up. Two of the sorority girls stopped back with plants for her. She was deeply moved by their caring gesture and, as she did with everyone who worked on her property, Brenda took a picture of them and asked them to sign their names and addresses in her Bible. When her house was rebuilt, she promised she would send everyone a picture of it.

After going down the hill to eat lunch at Union Hill Baptist, which had been serving three meals a day since the disaster struck, we returned in time to join forces with two vans full of people from a Birmingham-area Methodist church. For the next several hours, we began the daunting job of trying to untangle the jumble in the ravine and locate anything of value to Brenda. Larry was intent on trying to find her picture albums. Very little of any significance, however, was retrieved, and barely a dent was made in the formidable mess.

Then they all climbed into the vans and left—leaving Larry and me alone, hot and tired, standing on the edge looking down into the ravine. Totally overwhelmed and discouraged, we looked at each other and agreed that there was not much the two of us could do. Perhaps it was time for us to move on.

Not Yet

However, we had promised Brenda we would return on Monday, so we did. She asked if we would mind painting sealer on her mother's basement walls. Brenda was concerned about her mother and anxious to get her home in livable condition as quickly as possible. She knew there was not much more we could do at her own place. We were more than happy to take on something manageable and, besides, it was cool in the basement. The heat and humidity were steadily increasing each day.

As we looked around Dorothy's house, it was obvious that we could put our Habitat skills to use right there. The sheetrock crew had only completed half of the kitchen; the rest of the house needed to be finished. Deciding we would stay at least another week, we called Brother Steve and let him know we would move our trailer over the next day. Thus began our relationship with Dorothy, the gracious matriarch of the Mitchell family. Over the course of the next month, we would become strongly attached to all of them.

Sheer Force Of Will

In a few days after a disaster, except in the local area, the news media move on to new news, conveying the unspoken message that everything is over and done with. Nothing could be further from the truth. Until you are there, it is difficult to conceive of how long and grueling the recovery period is. There is so much to do and there is no let-up. In the first weeks, mental numbness and adrenaline keep the victims going, but as reality begins to set in and it becomes clear that things are not going to be back to normal for a very long time, they must keep themselves going by sheer force of will.

Larry and I funneled all of our energies into Dorothy's house, freeing Brenda as much as possible to attend to the myriad other issues she had to deal with. Dorothy qualified for a FEMA grant, which helped purchase some of the supplies she needed. She was also the recipient of money and materials from her church and Old Rock Creek Baptist Church, whose pastor was her brother-in-law. Each day or two, Larry would make up a list of needed supplies and Dorothy or Brenda or one of the handymen who did odd jobs would purchase them.

While we worked on Dorothy's house, Brenda's husband Lonnie was putting in long hours trying to keep his plumbing business alive, and Brenda, who until recently had also coordinated all the clean-up crews that were sent to their property, was dividing herself between helping with the business, overseeing her mother's situation, watching over her son's health, and taking care of the grandsons.

Because they had let their insurance lapse one month before the tornado hit and did not qualify for a FEMA loan or grant, Brenda and Lonnie faced having to reconstruct their home, and one for Greg and Becky, by themselves. Having many business connections, Brenda ran all over striking deals with people and salvaging materials. She and her faithful hired hand Gary spent two days in the scorching heat cleaning and loading bricks from a house across Warrior River Road and hauling them up the hill to be stored for future use. We were impressed by Brenda's resourcefulness and stamina, and especially her heart.

On The Alert

A few days after we began working at Dorothy's, the ALERT team returned. We first saw them on the news in the early days after the tornado, and our ears had perked up when we heard they were from our native state of Michigan. The ALERT (Air Land Emergency Resource Team) program trains Christian young men in the areas of disaster relief, aerial search, land search and rescue, underwater search and recovery, community service, and humanitarian aid. Government leaders may request their free services.

These young men exemplified what can be accomplished when faith is expressed in action and when hearts and energies are steered in the right direction. Sitting at one long table during lunch at Union Hill Baptist Church in their uniforms of dark navy tee shirts and work pants, they were an impressive sight—even more so was the manner in which they conducted themselves. Before each meal, they stood and sang a hymn for grace, and before leaving, cleared their plates, wiped the tables, and pushed in their chairs. They were friendly and outgoing, happy to talk with people and respond to questions, and always answered with "Yes, sir," or "Yes, ma'am."

The ALERT team spent two extremely hot days tackling the ravine that we had abandoned. By the end of the second day, incredibly, they had hauled everything up by means of human chains and ropes. Larry went over one afternoon to dig around and see if he could find any of the things Brenda was still looking for. She was ecstatic when he found two of her photo albums with pictures of Greg when he was in grammar school.

The top of Brenda's jewelry box was later found about 20 miles away by one of the power company workers who had been at her house the day after the storm. He recognized Brenda's picture inside, and brought it to her. Eventually, she received a call from a man in Adamsville, about 20 minutes away, who had located their boat. It was a twisted ball of aluminum. Neither her tax records nor her daddy's burial flag was ever found.

As though it were a carefree summer weekend, Brenda prepared and hosted a steak barbecue for the ALERT team the first day they worked, and grilled chicken the next. I finally convinced her to let me make my Armenian rice pilaf and a big fruit salad on the second day. The guys sang grace, as usual, let Scott and Jonathan wear their hard hats during lunch, shared about their varied backgrounds, and entertained us with a few more songs before returning to work.

Anniversary Warnings

Saturday, after the ALERT team had retired for the day, we went back to the trailer, showered, popped a tape into the VCR, and settled down to record the hour-long one-month anniversary special about the tornado. During a break halfway through the show, the meteorologist indicated that we were going to be in for some severe weather that night. A few minutes later, the program was interrupted again as the National Weather Advisory Service began issuing tornado watches and warnings and, sure enough, they were headed our way. There was a knock on our trailer door. Brother Steve had come down from his house to be sure we had heard the news. He said he would tell the cleaning people to leave the door nearest our trailer unlocked.

The weather warnings continued and the station announced they would rebroadcast the special in its entirety the following week. A little later, there was another knock on the door. Brother Steve said he had heard that this storm could be a duplicate of the April 8 storm, and it appeared to be following exactly the same track. He took us into the church where he opened the door to a storage closet and showed us the concrete crawl space under the baptismal font. It didn't look terribly inviting. For more than one reason, we hoped we wouldn't have to use it.

Back in the trailer, I gathered together the two things I had observed were most valuable to the tornado survivors—our photo albums and our file of business papers. Larry grabbed his short wave radio, a flashlight, blanket and Ross, and we headed across the parking lot into the church just as the skies opened up. Sitting in the hallway for over an hour, we listened to the radio and occasionally peered out the door. Finally, we heard that the storm had weakened and veered away from us. Leaving our things in the closet in case we had to make a quick return, we retired to the trailer. The driving rain pelted the trailer until 1 a.m., after which we finally drifted off to sleep.

I imagined that as bad as the night had been for us, it must have been horrific for the people who had suffered a few weeks earlier. I was right. The whole Mitchell family had spent much of the night cowered under the porches of their rental houses. That scenario had been played out all over the Greater Birmingham area. One definite aftermath of the storm was that no one would ever again take a tornado warning lightly.

III-14. FOR OUR SAKE AND THEIRS

We are strong when we stand with another soul.
When we are with another, we cannot be broken.

Kathleen Brehony, *Ordinary Grace*

More Than Work

Although the work we were accomplishing at Dorothy and Brenda's was critical to their physical recovery, we also knew that our personal interactions with the members of the family were equally vital. It was important for them to learn that people outside their own family and community cared about and loved them. But as anyone involved in service work will attest, we were learning much, as well. This family was showing us how ordinary people can meet overwhelming adversity and still maintain their dignity and concern for others. We are forever grateful for their tutelage.

One Fine Lady

Dorothy was amazing. She never let her physical appearance belie her weariness. Each day she arrived at the house neatly dressed, her hair done up and make-up on. She assisted us wherever possible, insisted on providing lunch every day and, in the evening after we left, stayed to clean up and make sure everything was in order for the following day. Only occasionally did Dorothy arrive after we did in the mornings; and only rarely, when fatigue finally overtook her, did she stay home for a day in her temporary housing.

It was soon obvious that her Christian faith was deeply ingrained and something she put into practice in her everyday life. Dorothy never complained about problems or setbacks that might well have been irksome under the best of circumstances. She was always more concerned with other people's needs than her own, often refusing things that were offered because "others needed it more." She was genuinely grateful for even the smallest tasks that were performed for her. If we weren't able to accomplish what we had hoped to on a particular day, she would dismiss our apologies by saying, "You just don't worry. It will get done. I just appreciate every little thing that y'all do to help me." She never let us leave without expressing her gratitude.

It became apparent that over the years, in her own small way, Dorothy had helped and nurtured dozens of people, giving them odd jobs and a warm meal, slipping them cigarette money as they went out the door, and even putting up bail money. "I just like to help people and make them feel like they're cared about," she would say to us. "I have a soft spot in my heart for underdogs who haven't had much of a chance."

The money she so freely shared had not come easily, nor had Dorothy's life been a cakewalk. As she became comfortable with us, she gradually divulged some of her history and heartaches. These confidences were the product of trust, "because you've stood by us," she said.

Dorothy had worked alongside her husband on their sweet potato farm and, in fact, the house we were now restoring was originally the building in which they had sorted and stored the potatoes. However, after enduring the extremely difficult marriage for almost 30 years, Dorothy divorced her husband and finished raising her three girls alone, supporting them by working various manual labor jobs. Some mornings Dorothy would have to give herself a pep talk when she got out of bed in order to face another long day. She would look in the mirror and say, "I'm going to have a great day. Everything is going to be fine." Then she would ask God to help her through it. Dorothy had recently retired after working 23 years as a school custodian, but was still cleaning offices part-time up to the night of the storm.

Years earlier, Dorothy had learned to cope with major loss when another home and most of her possessions were destroyed as a result of arson. When she had gone to her daddy for sympathy, he had responded by giving her a healthy dose of tough love, which she recalled as she faced her current situation. He said, "I'm gonna tell you one thing. See that ditch out there?" After Dorothy acknowledged it, he continued, "You can wallow in that ditch from now on or you can pick your life up and move on." Though it was not what she had wanted to hear at the time, she chose the latter option.

Dorothy was constantly overwhelmed by how many people had helped her and how much others had given her. Some nights she had difficulty getting to sleep because of it. But it was obvious to us that she was simply reaping what she had sown. "What you have given has come back to you," we would tell her. Who wouldn't want to help this gracious lady? We certainly did. It was a joy just being around her.

To Love Again

On occasion, Brenda stopped by our trailer to talk. Those times gave her respite and comfort from the constant sight of her ruins. Brenda, also, was no stranger to hard work. She had labored seven years in the mines shoveling coal onto conveyor belts. She also shared with us some of the lifelong struggles and challenges she had faced. She had endured more than her share of anguish—the loss of two husbands and a long, painful recovery from first and second-degree burns sustained over sixty percent of her body as a result of a house explosion. She was both physically and emotionally scarred.

"Before the storm," she confessed, "my heart was stone cold." But after the tornado, largely due to the outpouring of love from others and, in particular, the ministering of Brother Steve who was "always there" for her, Brenda had finally begun to find peace in her heart. "You showed me how to love again," she told him. It was an edifying reminder that even what we consider the worst of circumstances can be used to help heal and strip away the painful illusions of the world.

We were especially touched when Brenda and her friend Dana took an afternoon to weed a small plot of earth in Dorothy's yard and plant a variety of flowers as a Mother's Day surprise. Dana then read me the poetic letter of love and appreciation that she was going to present to her own mother. In the midst of all that mess and the press of work before them, these two women had not lost sight of the importance of focusing on a little bit of beauty and love.

A Lesson On Receiving

On Mother's Day, Brenda arrived with Scott to attend church with us. Scott thrust a bright red geranium plant toward me. "This is for you, Carol," he said proudly. After church Larry and I left to spend the afternoon with the couple we had met in Mac's Chapel, enjoying a wonderful meal and fellowship with them and their family. When we returned in the evening, Brother Steve stopped by with two small packages and a card for me. They were from Dorothy. The gifts were a heart-shaped pin decorated with tiny, jeweled red roses and a pair of crystal candlestick holders. Inside a card that expressed her love, a $50 bill was folded into a square smaller than a postage stamp and taped to it. I was moved to tears by the acts of caring and generosity from these people who had lost so much. I determined, however, to return the money.

The next day while I was writing letters in one of the Sunday school classrooms, Brother Steve stopped by to chat. I discussed with him the gift I had received from Dorothy. He reminded me that I needed to graciously accept it.

"The people in this community are very self-reliant and proud," he explained. "It is important for them to be able to give back. FEMA and the Salvation Army pulled out of Rock Creek sooner than normal because so many people here refused help. They told the agencies to help someone who needed it more. And besides that," he added, "God has already repaid Dorothy. I just delivered a substantial gift to her from the ladies of an area Elks Lodge."

Trying To Cope

Greg and Becky had also had plenty to cope with before the storm. Greg had had three serious heart attacks, yet had been denied disability or any other kind of aid. For a while, family members had helped subsidize their apartment and his $400-a-month medications. Finally, a month before the storm hit, they had moved in with Brenda. Since Brenda liked running the plumbing business from her in-house office, she was happy to have Becky as "go-fer," running errands and doing the shopping. The children would play by Brenda's side while she worked, and Greg could rest quietly when he needed to.

Now, all that had been blown apart, and the stress had exacerbated Greg's condition. Greg and Becky had a good relationship, but they were completely overwhelmed. The Red Cross replenished Greg's medications that were lost in the storm, and when Becky contacted the Dept. of Human Resources for assistance, Mrs. Gyvaghn not only immediately gave them food stamps but, also, upon learning of their long-term plight, set Greg up with Medicaid and helped him re-file for disability. They believed she was truly an angel sent to look after them.

Feeling it was worth a try, Larry and I encouraged Greg and Becky to apply for a Habitat home. I helped them fill out the application and write a cover letter, then added my own letter of support, explaining some of their extenuating circumstances. They gave their consent for me to share their story with Brother Steve.

True to form, Brother Steve was aroused by their need, and I could almost see the wheels turning in his head. With Greg and Becky's permission, he made copies of the letters to circulate among the area Baptist churches with the aim of raising enough money to help buy supplies to build them a house on Dorothy's property. I had no doubt that he would follow through. Greg and Becky were clearly relieved to have some hope that they might eventually restore order and stability to their family.

What About The Children?

"But, Your Majesty, what about the children?" Anna says to the King of Siam after rebuking him for his stern rules and protocol in the wonderful musical "The King and I." One could only guess what images Scott carried with him of that frightful night or how the aftermath was affecting him and Jonathan. Any feeling of normalcy had disappeared from their young lives.

For sure, they missed waking up in the morning and having Brenda cook them breakfast. It was difficult for them to adjust to not living in the same house with her. Most of their toys were gone and their familiar routines disrupted. Despite an occasional tantrum or outburst of anger, however, I was amazed at how well they held up.

Jonathan was only two, and generally Becky kept him with her. But four-year-old Scott was often with us as we worked, doing his best to assist or keep himself occupied. He and I became buddies when he "helped" me paint the outside of Dorothy's foundation. At the end of the day, covered with more white than was on the wall, he confided, "I like you 'cause we paint together." Once in awhile, the confusion and disruption would catch up with him, and he'd protest that he wanted to go home because "I'm tired of working."

It helped the children, as well as the rest of us, to do something special, and celebrating Dorothy's 71st birthday fit the bill. In the basement of her house, which was our official lunch and break room, we sang "Happy Birthday" as she blew out the candles on the chocolate zucchini cake I had baked. Scott and Jonathan's eyes danced with delight. Our gifts to her were a jar of my handpicked, homemade wild blueberry jam and a small plaque with a verse about friendship to hang in her home once it was restored. We devoured the cake and peach ice cream and, of course, took pictures to commemorate the occasion. No one paid attention to the cans of paint and other materials piled around us.

Shopping Spree

The first time the nearby Church of Christ announced that they had received money to buy appliances and furniture for people, Dorothy refused to go. The second time, I insisted on taking her. She signed up for a stove, washer and dryer. Her own large double-door refrigerator was repairable. The minister's wife, Mrs. Pilgrim, told us to go to the B and L Catalog Outlet Store where they had arranged for storm survivors to pick out any furniture they needed. The next day, Mrs. Pilgrim would pay the bill with the money sent to their church from sister congregations all over the country.

First, Dorothy came home with me for lunch. After we ate, since I had agreed to help her "put into proper words" her heartfelt "thank yous" to the people who had given her money and supplies, I jotted down what she wanted to say to each. Then, we left for our shopping date.

We walked into the store and the effusive owner asked Dorothy's name, then took her by the arm and spirited her into the showroom. "Oh, Miss Dorothy," she gushed, "I am so happy to do my part to help you." As we walked into the showroom, she indicated with a sweeping gesture of her arm the three living room suites that she could choose from. "However, Miss Dorothy, if you don't like any of these, you can look through the catalog and choose something else."

I knew of course, that Dorothy wasn't going to reject what was being offered. "Do you see one you like, Miss Dorothy?" the owner was asking as Dorothy stood there looking from one to another, her eyes wide open in disbelief.

Her answer was barely audible. "I kind of like the blue set."

"Well, you just sit right down and try it out and make sure it's comfortable," the owner instructed.

After Dorothy confirmed that it was, indeed, very comfortable, the owner helped her select which color lamps she wanted to go with the two-piece set, as well as the end and coffee tables she preferred. Then she guided her into the back rooms to choose the size and style of bed and dressers she would like. Leading her back up front by the register, the owner verified Dorothy's selections as she wrote them on the sales slip. Dorothy nodded her head in affirmation while her eyes watered with tears. "I've never been given anything like this," she managed to say.

"Think nothing of it, Miss Dorothy," the owner assured her. "We all feel so badly that so many of y'all have suffered. It's the least we can do. You have a nice day now."

As we walked out and got into the car, Dorothy's face lit up like an excited child's. "That's going to look so nice in my house," she bubbled. "Let's go back to your trailer and celebrate with a cup of coffee!"

I'm really not sure who was happier, Dorothy or me. I can't recall anything that has given me such pleasure.

The next morning, Dorothy knocked on our trailer door at 7:30 a.m. She had a bag of sausage and biscuits in her hand, so I put on a pot of coffee. She had barely slept the night before, and she was obviously still reeling from the thrill of the previous day's excursion. I read her the letters I had written, and her eyes teared up in grateful remembrance as she listened to the one to Brother Steve. "That's just what I wanted to say," she nodded approvingly.

Oh, For A Little Electricity

We completed two major tasks in Dorothy's house—taping and mudding the sheetrock that had already been put up in the kitchen and hanging sheetrock in the small living area, bedroom and bathroom. While I taped and mudded the new walls, Larry helped upgrade the electrical service.

In order to conform to current codes, extensive rewiring needed to be done on Dorothy's house. She was taken aback by the high estimates for the work. Remembering that he had been an electrician prior to becoming a preacher, we approached Brother Steve one evening about Dorothy's situation.

By then, we knew that Brother Steve was not reticent in determining what people's needs were and coming up with quick and direct ways to meet them. Even so, we were amazed when at 10 a.m. the next morning he showed up at Dorothy's house with Bob, a retired master electrician who offered to do the wiring for free and also arranged for the materials to be donated by Home Depot.

Once the wiring was installed and inspected, we all thought we would soon have power. However, Alabama Power, which had worked many other miracles in response to the tornado, ran into some major snags in Dorothy's case. Almost two months after the storm, Dorothy still did not have power. With the sheetrock hung and the walls painted, we'd gone about as far as we could without electricity. We began making plans to leave, knowing good-byes would be wrenching.

Change Of Plans

By that time, Larry and I had decided to opt out of the Jimmy Carter build. After sampling the Alabama heat, we weren't sure we would hold up well in Houston. (We later learned that 300 people were taken to the hospital the first day from heat sickness.) Comparing the two previous blitzes we had been on, we realized we preferred the smaller, more intimate one in Newfoundland. One hundred houses were scheduled to be built in Houston; six would be built during the Ed Schreyer Project in Regina, Saskatchewan. Reminding ourselves that no one house or location is any more important than another, we chose to go where we fit best.

Since it would be too late in the summer to head west afterwards, we decided, instead, to meet Larry's brother and sister-in-law at the Wisconsin border following the Regina build and camp across the Upper Peninsula of Michigan with them. The ALERT team had invited us to visit their training center in Watersmeet, Michigan, and we promised that we would.

As we began preparing for our trip north, we made reservations at one of our campgrounds in Indiana for a two-week stay, hoping to escape the heat and get rested and caught up on ourselves before heading to Regina. That's what we thought, anyway.

On Sunday, May 31st, there was news on TV that a tornado had completely leveled the little town of Spencer, South Dakota—population 320—the previous evening. When the camera zoomed in on the damage and reporters spoke to stunned survivors, we had a gut reaction. We could not dismiss this as another passing story, because we now knew what those people were going through and what lay ahead for them. Pulling out our atlas, we located Spencer. It was directly on our route to Regina! It couldn't be any clearer where we were headed next.

We made phone calls to South Dakota to see if we could be of help and to arrange a place to stay, then said our good-byes to the congregation of Faith Baptist, telling them what a marvelous witness they had been in the community and what a special pastor they had.

We also touched base with Jan Bell, the director of the Greater Birmingham Habitat affiliate. Although we had done our best to spread the word about Habitat, we had hoped to be of more direct assistance to her. We promised we would come back in the fall to help with the rebuilding. Thanksgiving would be a particularly significant time to return, not only to help Habitat, but also to celebrate with Dorothy and her family. There we were, naively making plans again.

You've Made A Difference In My Life

Brenda, Dorothy, and the boys came to see us the night before we left. It was one of those awkward times when there is so much you want to say to each other, but words are not adequate—when you all want to convey how much you mean to each other and acknowledge that something special has taken place that has bonded you in spirit. Dorothy gave us a beautiful plant she had potted in an antique vase. Brenda, wanting to make sure we remembered Alabama, gave me a "Bama" work scarf and Larry a "Bama" cap.

Later in the evening Greg and Becky stopped by. They had framed portraits of Scott and Jonathan for us. They were sending us off with pictures of their most prized treasures. Becky left a note for us to read later. It expressed their love and gratitude, and their prayers that we would always have everything we needed as we traveled to help others.

After they departed, I opened Brenda's card. On the front it said, "You've Made a Difference in My Life." The verse inside, by Emily Matthews, expressed the sentiment that if we are caring and supportive of others, especially those who are suffering pain and strife, we can make a difference in the world.

Though it was given to us as Brenda's expression of the difference we had made in *her* life, we were well aware that they all had made a huge impact on *ours*. Without a doubt, we had been guided to this family for a reason—for their sakes *and* ours. All of us were immeasurably enriched and blessed by our time together.

III-15. IT'S GONE!

Angels have tread here. . .

Minnehaha County Commissioner Tom Dempster,
observing 8000 volunteers searching for victims' valuables

A Miracle

The day after the tornado leveled Spencer, the front page headline of the June 1, 1998, Sioux Falls *Argus Leader* read: **THE TOWN IS GONE**. That was the pronouncement of South Dakota Gov. Bill Janklow as he spoke with journalists on Sunday, the morning after the storm. Six people were dead (a seventh died from a storm-related heart attack a few weeks later), half of the town's 320 people were injured, and 14 were still hospitalized as a result of the deadliest twister in the state's almost 50 years of record keeping.

Actually, that news was much better than the Governor thought it would be when he got his first glimpse of the town on Saturday night just an hour after the F-4 tornado, which was 4800 feet wide at its strongest point, ripped through Spencer at 8:44 p.m. on May 31st. He had sped there from his home east of Sioux Falls (some 50 miles away) after hearing that a tornado would likely hit Spencer, and was himself blown off the road into a ditch as he ran into the edge of the powerful storm. The warning sirens had not sounded because the electricity had been knocked out. However, most people were aware of the tornado warning for McCook County issued at 8:32 by the National Weather Service. "A siren wouldn't have made a difference," the Governor said. "The fact is, we are lucky we didn't have 200 killed in this devastation. That was a miracle."

Immediate Response

Twelve miles to the east, in the next-door town of Salem (population 1300), people were arriving at the National Guard Armory from all over the area within an hour after Spencer had been hit. With all of Spencer's town offices and infrastructure gone, including the post office, much of the relief effort would be shifted to the Salem Armory, and that night it was used for second-line triage.

Bev Christensen, a young mother and former Army nurse, heard the news at her home in Marion, 30 miles south of Salem, as she and her husband Jim relaxed with Bev's visiting aunt and uncle. Bev and Jim immediately called their close friends in Kansas, natives of Spencer whose parents and other family members still lived there, to inform them. They wanted to fly out right away, but Bev convinced them to stay put because the Governor had already made it clear the area would be sealed off. She promised she would go to Spencer that night and attempt to locate their family.

Try as she might, Bev could not talk her way past the police, despite offering her assistance as a nurse. She was told that lists of survivors were being compiled in Salem and that her nursing skills would be greatly needed there. That was definitely true. No one with any medical training was at the armory, and the only medical supplies there consisted of a small box of bandages.

Bev and a handful of volunteers set up tents and cots, though no victims had yet arrived. Instead, around midnight the big overhead doors at the back of the armory lifted up and loads of clothing and blankets were dumped on the floor. "Well," Bev suggested, "we may as well put up some tables and sort and lay these things out so they'll be ready when the victims arrive."

Finally, around 2 a.m. a woman in her mid-sixties was brought in. She had a displaced fracture of the forearm. Recalling emergency first aid tricks, Bev used a towel for a sling and secured it with her shoelace until the lady could be taken to a hospital. A few more victims arrived—including a woman experiencing kidney dysfunction who was taken to a nearby hospital, and a man whose face was cut open and lacerated. He was transported to the town of Mitchell where he later underwent reconstructive surgery.

None of the victims spent the night at the armory. Those few who did not have friends or family to stay with were taken into the homes of nearby Salem residents. At 4 a.m., after putting more things away, Bev and the other volunteers went home.

It was almost two days before Bev learned that her friends' family had been out of town at the time of the storm. They had contacted their children and informed them that they were safe.

Phenomenal Outpouring

The outpouring of assistance from all over the state was phenomenal. South Dakota is comprised mainly of rural communities, and South Dakotans are accustomed to supporting each other to cope with the harsh circumstances that often characterize life in that plains state. By Tuesday, after emergency crews had cleared the major debris and hazards, and families had had an opportunity to survey their loss, the Governor began making appeals for help with sifting through the mess for personal belongings and valuables. The National Guard and inmates from the trusty unit of one of the nearby correctional facilities had already begun the daunting task.

The rotting household perishables were beginning to present a health problem, and authorities were anxious to get in quickly with heavy equipment to bulldoze the unsalvageable homes and bury the unwanted debris. The rats that frequented the premises of the grain elevator on the edge of town were moving in for easy pickings. The Governor put out a call for 1000 volunteers to arrive at 9 a.m. on Thursday, June 4, to make a major effort to complete the salvaging phase. One young woman bet her friend that 2000 would respond. Neither was right. In all, 8000 volunteers arrived from five states, the majority from South Dakota.

By 8 a.m., there was a line of cars, vans and trucks stretched a half-mile along the highway leading into Spencer from the south. By 9 a.m., it extended 3 1/2 miles, and another line of traffic stretched a mile to the east. People were asked to sign a waiver as they checked in, and by 8:30 a.m. when 3000 waivers had already been filled out, it became obvious to officials that they were not prepared to feed that many people. The Governor made an appeal for help on the radio stations. Food came from everywhere and, although the lines were long, everyone was fed.

Surveying the incredible scene, the Governor explained the unprecedented response: "We fight each other at times, but when we need each other, we are one big family, all brothers and sisters." Vice-President Gore was also moved by the tremendous outpouring of support. "As powerful as this tornado was, it's not as powerful as the force of human compassion at work in this town," he asserted.

The volunteers were instructed to collect all the clothing, photographs, keepsakes, toys, jewelry, cash and other valuables and put them in 55 gallon bags, which by day's end "lined every street in the 25-square block area." The clothing would be cleaned at the State Penitentiary and the Human Services Center in Yankton, and displayed at the armory and County Courthouse in Salem for people to claim.

Taking Charge

The morning after the tornado, Bev was awakened at 10 a.m. by her aunt. "Come on, let's go to Salem," she said. "I have to do something to help before I go home." When they arrived at the armory, Bev could not believe the amount of donations that had been delivered since she had left only a few hours before. Someone ran up to her and said, "Oh, you're the woman who was here last night. What should we do?" Drawing on her Army training which had taught her to do whatever needs to be done, Bev began assigning the volunteers tasks to try to get a handle on the incredible volume of stuff that just kept coming and coming.

She and her aunt made a list of what was and wasn't needed and contacted local radio stations to disseminate the information. All through the day and night people continued bringing things to the armory, including almost $3000 in cash, which Bev and a local volunteer stuffed into a bag. To accommodate people who wanted to write checks, they named the growing cache the Spencer Relief Fund.

Uncomfortable with being responsible for that large an amount of money, Bev contacted the Salem Pastoral Association at 7 a.m. on Monday morning and asked if they would take charge of the fund. They decided to set up an account at the bank. Bev again went on radio informing people who wanted their donations to go directly to the victims to address them to the Spencer Relief Fund. A few days later, that fund became the seed money for the Governor's Tornado Relief Fund.

When Bev arrived at the armory on Monday morning, volunteers again approached her. "Thank God you're here. What should we do?" By then, everyone agreed that Bev should be in charge until she was told otherwise. Later that day, the first of what would eventually total 15 used vehicles was donated. In consultation with the Civil Defense Coordinator Arden Rapp, they were offered free to Spencer victims on the basis of need and first come, first served.

On Tuesday, the Pastoral Association decided to approach the Dept. of Civil Defense about the need to have someone officially in charge at the armory. Already on a five-day absence from her current job, Bev decided to quit. She felt it was God's calling that she be at the armory. On Friday, she was officially hired as the Donations Management/Volunteer Coordinator for the duration of the relief effort there.

Meanwhile, donations continued pouring in and needed to be sorted and shelved. A core of faithful volunteers (ages 4 to 92) worked indefatigably trying to keep up with the flow. Arnold, a construction worker from Humboldt, in addition to collecting donations and delivering them to the armory, built shelves and racks to display shoes and other items. Local residents Teresa and Carol headed up the front desk operation—answering phones, enlisting volunteers, generating flyers, etc. After the first week, fast food contributions began to dwindle, but substantial stores of food had arrived at the armory. Bev asked her good friend Brenda to head up a kitchen crew and, along with area residents LaVonne and Phyllis, they prepared and served three meals a day for both survivors and volunteers.

Spencer Bound

I initially attempted to contact the Lutheran Association near Spencer, since I had determined they were one of the predominant denominations in the area. As fate would have it, all the area ministers were away on a retreat when the tornado struck. Because the clean-up was taking place so rapidly, I was advised to keep checking on whether we would be needed. We headed to our campground in Indiana to rest while we continued trying to make arrangements.

After several unsuccessful contacts, I was put in touch with Bev. She listened carefully as I told her we had just finished helping with the relief effort in Birmingham, were heading in her direction, and would like to help if we were needed. I explained that it was necessary to know how long we might be useful, because it was almost a month before we were scheduled to arrive in Regina and we had no campgrounds in our system between Salem and there.

Bev said she would check everything out. When I called back in two hours, she spelled out the arrangements. We would plug in at the armory, use its shower facilities and, if and when the operation there closed down, we could help at the Salvation Army warehouse in Mitchell, 40 miles west of Spencer.

Around noon on June 11, we pulled up to the armory and with the help of Jim, the local Sheriff (a caring and supportive presence throughout the relief effort), we situated the trailer and took our first look inside the armory.

We were dismayed by the sea of used clothing piled high on rows of tables extending the length and width of the armory gymnasium. Along the side and back walls, household goods, small furniture and appliances, toys and books, and toiletries were arranged. Half a row, four shelves high, was overflowing with stuffed animals. In the front of the armory were several tables of new items, which were most sought-after by the survivors. With everything in their lives in shambles, it gave them a boost to receive something that was new.

Samples of the Family Food Boxes and Infant Care Kits sent by the Church of Christ were on display. Stacked in one of the hallways were banana boxes filled with assorted canned and packaged food delivered by the Nebraska-based Orphan Grain Train, an international ministry begun in 1993 by members of the Lutheran Hour Ministries. The organization collects and transports food, clothing and medical supplies to people in need around the world. (We would learn much more about the outreach of this organization at our next destination.) Shelves stocked with food and household supplies covered half the kitchen area, and tables were set up for eating in the remainder.

Behind the kitchen counter preparing lunch were the three smiling cooks. On the serving table sat a large plastic storage container full of the biggest chocolate chip cookies we had ever seen. Schwans had donated a tractor-trailer load of frozen foods, including dozens of boxes containing balls of cookie dough just waiting to be popped into the oven. The aroma of baking cookies constantly wafted in the air the whole while we were there.

We ate lunch and met some of the volunteers, then Bev made arrangements for us to drive over and see what was left of Spencer. We felt we needed to make a connection with it.

It Wasn't There

Just like the headline had said, the town was no longer there except for a couple streets of houses on the perimeter. We had seen the full-color newspaper pictures of the destruction, and now, the only evidence of it was a mountainous wall of debris piled along the south end of the town in the distance. There were a few National Guardsmen and prisoners in orange suits raking and shoveling, but as we drove up and down what had been neighborhoods less than two weeks before, it was almost impossible to distinguish where individual properties had existed. Everything had been bulldozed and leveled, as though in preparation for planting.

We got out, walked around a little and took several pictures. Only the front wall of the granary was left standing, the roof and other walls lay collapsed around it. Where the gas station had been, a few tires were lined up and two lonely light posts jutted up out of the pavement. All that remained of the bank were the foundation walls and the safe vault. I guess that's why it's called a safe. Every church, school and store was gone. We didn't stay long because there really wasn't much to see.

It Keeps Coming

The amount of donated goods arriving at the armory was plain mind-boggling. Three days after the storm, there had been enough to outfit a city of 3000, instead of 300. And it kept coming, despite appeals to the public to send only money. We soon learned that we had seen only the tip of the iceberg on our first walk-through. Every room in the armory was stacked with clothing, blankets or boxes of food.

People all over the country were touched by the plight of the little town. It was difficult to turn someone away who had driven several hundred miles to deliver the clothes they had gathered. One lady came all the way from Michigan with a carload of clothes and $200 her church had collected. "I just had a need to bring it personally," she said. She refused repeated offers to stay for lunch, and immediately turned around and headed back. Another woman drove from Arkansas. And two sisters who were moving their household goods across country, upon hearing of the disaster, diverted to Salem and donated all their furnishings (thousands of dollars worth) except for a few family heirlooms.

Every day the *Argus Leader* listed the donations of people and organizations. Individuals, large and small businesses, discount chains, pizza places, banks, hospitals, churches, service groups, gas stations—indeed, every segment of the community in the environs of Spencer, as well as distant cities and towns—found ways to contribute to their neighbors in need. When people's hearts are touched, they have the capacity to be extremely generous.

The means were varied and sometimes unique: offering a dog, donating 30 dozen eggs, contributing band instruments and school supplies, providing storage in basements and garages, hosting fund-raisers, donating portions of sales receipts, collecting food, clothing and toys, offering periods of free housing or nursing care, doing laundry for survivors, and contributing hundreds of thousands of dollars.

Donna Ruden, a town board member at the time, made her home (which was left untouched) available to residents for more than a week after the tornado to conduct insurance and banking business. The Security State Bank and fire department phone calls were forwarded to her house—her phone rang from 8 a.m. to 10 p.m. Offering her home as a central gathering place for adjusters and survivors was an invaluable service.

Our Assignment

We met with Bev to learn about what had taken place before we arrived, her assessment of the current situation, and what she expected of us. Since she had been commuting 60 miles round trip for over 10 days, arriving at the armory by 6 a.m. and leaving near midnight, she was exhausted. She looked to us to spell her at times and to share some of the decision-making and leadership. We offered her use of our trailer for occasional respite and invited her to sleep over any night she needed to.

Our highest priority was to assist survivors any way we could when they came in for supplies. They sometimes needed help deciding what to take or assistance loading items into their car, and they readily welcomed a listening ear and a supportive arm around the shoulder.

The Toy Store

The first order of business was a major reorganization of the armory to maximize the available space. After consolidating the contents of two trailers into one, I was put in charge of turning the other into a "toy store." Gathering plastic crates and cardboard boxes, I stacked them at one end to make cubby holes for displaying as many stuffed animals as possible. The remainder filled a huge cargo box. A few tables were brought in, and on them we displayed books, games, puzzles, sports equipment, etc. Meanwhile, Larry kept the pantry stocked and did a lot of hauling and moving of things. In the evening we helped put together a quick hot dog meal for a large group of teens who had come to help.

One of our greatest delights was informing a child of the existence of the toy trailer and bringing them to "shop." Larry asked one little girl if she had any toys. "No, sir," she said very seriously, "the wind took them." He led her by the hand to the toy trailer. "You may take anything you'd like," he told her.

Though the children had lost almost all that was special to them, we were fascinated to watch as they browsed through the trailer. We would have guessed that they would scoop up as much as they could, but just the opposite was the case. They very methodically sifted through everything, selecting just the right stuffed animal or picking out a particular book or game. One 10-year-old girl had lost her entire collection of Berenstain Bear books. She reminisced, "I sometimes alphabetized them, but not always." Each day she checked the supply of books at the armory and succeeded in finding three or four replacements.

A True Public Servant

It was well known that Gov. Janklow was a tough, straightforward man. But through this disaster, many would see a different side of their 58-year-old Governor, who had only been out of the hospital a few days following major surgery when he personally took charge of the disaster response. His mother wasn't surprised, however. "He has a genuine concern for people. I saw it from the time he was little," she proudly told a reporter in the June 6 *Argus Leader*.

The Governor "served as chief executive officer, laborer, minister, doctor, lawyer, building inspector, media representative, and mediator," following the storm, and could be seen one moment barking out orders and during the next consoling or hugging a resident. Though it was an election year, few would suggest that his actions were politically motivated for he had been just as visibly involved in previous South Dakota disasters.

Larry and I were happy to see that the Governor had taken charge of the Tornado Relief Fund, thereby assuring that money donated would be used strictly for the South Dakota disaster and that there would be greater flexibility in dispensing it than would be the case through other agencies. In addition, there would be no administrative costs since the Community Development Foundation would manage the fund absolutely free.

We were also impressed by the way the state put its prison population to productive use. At the Spencer site, we walked through a model of a simple, well-built two-bedroom home constructed by inmates. These homes were normally available to elderly low-income people in rural areas, and were sold and installed anywhere in the state for $20,000. The Governor had announced that they would be made available to any survivors who wished to purchase one. Besides the service to those who needed homes, the prisoners were learning useful skills, rotating each month as framers, carpenters, sheet rockers, painters, etc. The Governor told me that a high percentage of the inmates became employed in the building trades after they were released.

The "trusty program" gave prisoners an opportunity to perform various kinds of public service around the state. Inmates played a highly visible and significant role in the clean-up after the storm. Many of them remarked that it made them feel good "to come out and help." One prisoner added that "maybe in some ways, it will make people understand that we're not so bad." Unlike Alabama prisoners we observed at McDonald Chapel who accomplished almost nothing, their South Dakota counterparts knew that if they didn't work, they would not be given the privilege again. Inmates were entrusted with the responsibility of looking for people's valuables right along with other volunteers, and recovered $1,600, which had apparently blown out of the bank.

On the evening of June 15, I saw the Governor in action myself at a meeting of all the Spencer residents held at McCook High School in Salem to discuss the town's future.

To Rebuild Or Not To Rebuild

Everyone who was able was at the meeting, including FEMA members, the Red Cross, Salvation Army, church leaders, media, and anyone interested in being involved in the recovery effort. The Governor had previously voiced his clear displeasure with financial and government advisors who had suggested that rebuilding was economically unviable. To be sure, there were a number of unfavorable factors—the high proportion of elderly population (1/3 of Spencer residents were over 65), the fact that the town (like many small rural towns) had already been struggling before the storm to remain vital, and the formidable prospect of building a completely new community virtually from scratch.

These arguments did not impress the Governor in the least. From day one, he repeatedly affirmed that Spencer would be rebuilt with the help of government programs and relief efforts. "I'm not going to play God and decide which towns live and die," he proclaimed. "We're going to rebuild Spencer to the extent they want it rebuilt."

The Governor began the meeting by assuring anyone who wanted to rebuild that there would be help for them. "Your age and health are not factors," he said. "If you want to come back, we will help you come back with dignity." He proceeded to explain much of what had been done and the reasons behind decisions, and announced that the Governor's Fund had reached $661,000, though donors to agencies and churches had designated a portion of it. Initially, every resident family would receive $1000. The rest of the money would be put to use on an individual-need basis in coordination with the Unmet Needs Committee. In distributing the funds, "people will come first," the Governor promised.

He then spoke about the opportunity that was before them to design a brand new community that would be modern, functional, and economically efficient. After unveiling a drawing of how all the major community services might be combined in one complex, he briefly discussed the architect's conception.

Afterward, everyone was asked to indicate on lists displayed on easels whether they were going to rebuild, or if they were undecided. The Governor did not want anyone to feel pressured to make a decision, but explained that the information would be helpful in planning future infrastructure. Perhaps, he said, if the properties of people who planned to rebuild were widely scattered, they might want to look at swapping land so that the cost of infrastructure could be reduced and there would not be big gaps in between houses. I'm sure at that moment the residents could not understand the significance of the latter concern, but as we had seen with the little bit of rebuilding that had already begun in Alabama, the large plots of barren land in between houses made the communities look incomplete, desolate, and disjointed.

There was ample opportunity for asking questions and, as in any large mix of people, there were a few who aired gripes, a few who were skeptical, and many who wanted to do whatever it took to pull together and get the job done. Considering the amount of stress the residents were under, I was impressed by their responses. I also admired the Governor's patience and the deliberation he put into his answers.

As I waited to speak with him at the conclusion of the meeting, I heard the man in front of me explaining that he only needed $2500 to get his business rolling again. The Governor listened intently, then gave the man his secretary's phone number and told him to call the next day and they would take care of it as quickly as possible. That's what I call personal service.

The Antique Lady

One afternoon, I saw a frail, elderly lady come into the armory. One of the local volunteers immediately joined her. After a time, the lady left with a small bag in her arms.

"That was Mrs. Bartholow, the 'antique lady,'" the volunteer explained, though it didn't mean anything to me. "She came to look for some dresses. She told me the wind took all of hers." But what moved the volunteer was that, despite the vast array of clothing, Mrs. Bartholow would take only three dresses. "I don't want to take more than my share," she insisted.

I later saw a story in the June 3, 1998, *Argus Leader* about Evelyn Bartholow, the tiny 85-year-old "antique lady," who for twenty years was proprietor of the antique store on a Main Street corner in Spencer. Evelyn was sitting in her chair having a cup of coffee when a window began rattling and blew in. She got up to see what was happening, and another window blew in. In that brief moment, a 2x4 was driven through the chair she had been sitting in. Her couch stood on end, objects flew about the room, the ceiling gave way and mud began raining down on her. The next thing she knew, she was standing in her doorway calling for help.

Two teen-age brothers, who had accompanied their electrician father to the area to see if they could be of assistance, cleared away rubble to get to Evelyn and found a chair for her to sit down on while awaiting an ambulance. Exhibiting the same sense of fairness she had displayed at the armory, Evelyn refused to get into an ambulance for over an hour, insisting that she would wait until the more seriously injured were taken care of.

No wonder the "antique lady" was an endearment to the entire community. Townspeople made a great effort to salvage anything they could from the ruins of her shop and, later, a benefit lunch was held at a local cafe to raise money for her.

More Migrant Workers

Leonard, who would turn 78 that October, had called the armory several times expressing his desire to help. Bev offered to put him up in someone's home, but he insisted on "camping" in the armory. When we learned that Leonard was on his way from Rapid City, Bev asked Larry and a couple of volunteers to fix a place for him to sleep in one of the back rooms. They found a bed and a small table in the furniture trailer, then rummaged around for sheets, pillows, a bed spread, throw rug, chair, lamp and clock. After everything was set up, they sectioned off the area with portable dividers. Larry commissioned me to make a sign that read, *Habitat for Humanity Blitz Build*. When Leonard was escorted into his "suite," he was as delighted as a child walking into the toy trailer.

After the long drive from Rapid City, Leonard barely threw his things down when he volunteered to operate a forklift to unload one of the semis. He continued in the hot sun, smiling from ear to ear, until someone insisted he stop to eat. Leonard charmed everyone, and worked extremely hard. He would occasionally disappear for an hour or two for a nap, then come out refreshed to begin again.

On Monday, our "camping area" grew as a pop-up trailer and a small motor home pulled in behind us. Wray, Sandy, and Phyllis, all Seventh Day Adventist mission volunteers from Rapid City, arrived to help with preparations for the rummage sale that would be held Friday through Sunday. Very few survivors were coming through the armory any more; most had already taken the clothing they needed and had stocked up on food and household supplies.

We all met with Bev to establish a game plan and delegate responsibilities. The goal was to unload as much as possible at the rummage sale and sell the rest to a used clothing company, donating all the proceeds to the Governor's Tornado Relief Fund. Wray and Sandy were experienced at flea markets and helped devise a system to presort and label items in the back rooms so that the tables could be quickly replenished. Leonard was assigned to be the official "counter" when the people entered.

Larry, besides keeping the kitchen stocked and boxing the food to send over to the local food pantry, was the official mover and hauler. His biceps were visibly enlarged by the time we left! I was in charge of reorganizing the clothing room one last time. Besides the dozen or so volunteers who had been working at the armory since the night of the disaster, many others contributed countless hours transforming the armory until, on the night before the rummage sale, it looked like a well-ordered department store.

Ready Or Not

Thursday night, after everything was tagged and the signs hung, we all stood back and surveyed the armory. We had that good feeling you get when you have prepared for a big event and all that is left is for it to happen. Everyone gathered in the kitchen as we brought in a beautiful *Thank You* cake for Bev, presented her with flowers, and expressed our appreciation for her leadership. She had done a bang-up job.

In the morning the volunteers were allowed to rummage from 7 to 11 a.m., after which they enjoyed a pizza lunch. Already throngs of people were lined up outside waiting for the doors to open at noon. For $5 each, individuals purchased plastic bags donated by area merchants that they could stuff with clothes, toys, and small household goods. Furniture and larger items were price-tagged. About 15 big-ticket items had been donated, and raffle tickets were sold for those. The winning numbers were to be drawn on Sunday afternoon.

Leonard, whom we quickly dubbed "Count Count," sat by the door clicking a counter as six hundred people poured through in the first hour—1300 by the end of the afternoon. Within fifteen minutes, all the carefully sized and stacked clothes were disheveled as people filled the aisles body-to-body rummaging through them. By day's end, $8000 was collected. We straightened up and replenished the stock, then braced ourselves for round two. The doors would be open for twelve hours on Saturday.

Another 1000-plus people passed through the next day, leaving with their bags bulging. The Tornado Relief Fund gained another $3500. And on Sunday, 550 people spent $1100 on purchases. When the doors were at last closed, Bev presented all the volunteers with small gifts of appreciation while we waited to hear the total from the sale and raffle. Our efforts had produced almost $13,000! (The money received for the salvage would later bring the total to $14,000.) All that remained to be done was to dismantle the operation and clean up the armory.

Letting Down

With the help of a contingent of young men from the Dept. of Corrections, we completed the job by noon on Monday. During lunch, the realization began to sink in that the purpose which had consumed most of the volunteers for 22 days had come to an end. Many lingered for a long while, putting off leaving. They would have a few days of adjustment after their intense involvement, but undoubtedly their families would be happy to have them back.

In the afternoon, Larry and I accepted the invitation of a young Hutterite woman, with whom I had spoken during the rummage sale, to visit her Hutterian community. Hutterites are identical in religious beliefs to the Amish, except that they live communally (about 85-100 to a colony), each family in a separate home. The communities build their own houses, furnishing them with items purchased from Hutterite groups that specialize in furniture making. The meals, financial resources and work of the farm are equitably shared.

It was our first visit to an "intentional community," and our host, the daughter of the community's leader, gave us a thorough tour of the farm, turkey barns, machine shop, child care center, kitchen and dining areas, and church (the service is conducted in high German). She also took us through every room of her house, including the sewing room downstairs where the women make the traditional garb worn by all members after the age of five. Our questions were all answered forthrightly, and we learned that even in a tightly controlled setting such as theirs, there is a tug of war between the generations. We left with a freshly slaughtered chicken, a gift of appreciation for our service to Spencer.

The next day we gave ourselves a quick tour of the City of Sioux Falls and ate lunch by the waters that cascade over the pink granite, of which many of the old buildings in the downtown are constructed. Such local excursions are our way of rewarding ourselves and adding to our growing appreciation for the history and diversity of our marvelous country.

We, too, needed a few days to let down, process what had taken place, and to prepare ourselves for our next mission. One thing we both agreed on—we didn't want to see any used clothing for a very long time!

III-16. HOME ON THE RANGE

We bring the face of hope.

Jeannie Peercy, LDR missionary

Another Diversion

Our plan when we arrived at the Salem Armory was to spend the remainder of our time either there or at the Salvation Army facility in Mitchell before leaving for Regina. As the end of the Salem operation approached, we were unable to come to an agreeable arrangement with the Salvation Army. However, before we had time to begin contemplating an alternative, Bev introduced us to Rose Kormann, Director of Lutheran Disaster Response (LDR) in South Dakota. She was there to evaluate the situation in Spencer and determine if LDR might be of any assistance.

Rose gave us a quick sketch of the predicament of the northwestern South Dakota farmers and ranchers resulting from the harsh winter blizzards in 1996-97, and LDR's role in trying to respond to the very complex aftermath that was still having a deleterious effect on the people of that area. Though a year and a half later, many were still immobilized by their plight and in need of help to pull themselves out of the downward physical, mental and financial spiral the disastrous winter had precipitated.

LDR had hired leaders in two of the hardest hit areas to assess the extent of the need and find ways to bring practical and uplifting aid to the victims. A call went out to Lutherans all over the country for groups to come to the affected areas to do the actual physical work.

In the Selby area, about 300 miles northwest of Salem, Ramona Yohe, wife of the pastor of St. John's Lutheran Church, had been hired to evaluate the needs in that area and organize recovery efforts. In the next couple weeks, she was expecting two large groups of out-of-town volunteers back-to-back and was feeling a little overwhelmed by all that needed to be done.

Rose gave us Ramona's phone number and suggested we call and offer our services. Ramona accepted on the spot.

Weather, Weather Everywhere

On June 25, we headed toward Selby, stopping on the way to see the Corn Palace in Mitchell, the brainchild of three businessmen who wanted to put the town on the map during the dust bowl era. The entire exterior of the famed performing arts center is decorated with specially grown colored corn, some of which is used to create intricate murals that are changed every year.

At night we camped at the Big Bend Corps of Engineers Park on the Missouri River. We hoped to spend some time in the Visitors' Center that was advertised in their brochures as giving an excellent overview of the Lewis and Clark Expedition. After wandering back and forth for an hour looking for it and almost getting the trailer stuck in mud trying to turn around, we inquired at the administrative office and learned that the center had been blown away by a tornado in 1992! Seems like we just couldn't get away from the aftermath of tornadoes.

The next day we toured the Capitol in Pierre, a simple edifice made of cream-colored sandstone that seemed an appropriate reflection of South Dakota. There we observed the omnipresent state prisoners in their orange jumpsuits grooming the grounds, and spent awhile at the quietly beautiful site of the impressive "Fighting Mustang" memorial to the late Governor George Michaelson and his cabinet, all of whom were killed in a plane crash in 1993.

After eating lunch at Oahe Dam, another Corps of Engineers project, we headed up route 83 toward Selby. All the way, severe storm and tornado warnings were being reported on the radio for the area we were driving into. The skies became menacing and the wind picked up as weather forecasters advised people on the road to pull behind buildings or, if necessary, abandon their vehicles and head for a ditch. As we looked in every direction and saw nothing but flat open space, all we could hope was that the storm was well enough ahead of us that we wouldn't run into it.

Around 2:30 p.m. we arrived in Selby, a small town of about 700 people, relieved that all we had encountered was some heavy rain. After pulling into the parking lot and finding that Ramona wasn't at home, we decided to take a walk around the area to get our bearings. The main drag of town was a block and a half long. Stopping in at Beren's Hotel Cafe to have a cup of coffee, we were surprised to find the place full in mid-afternoon. Then we made the delightful discovery that free coffee and dessert was being served in celebration of the Hotel's 20th anniversary. That was the best news we'd heard all day.

Returning to the trailer, we tried to wind down a little by playing a game of Yahtzee (our favorite relaxation pastime), but barely got started when the sky suddenly turned black and the increasingly strong wind gusts began buffeting the trailer broadside. As the rain began to come down hard, Larry scurried out to the truck and turned our rig around to face into the wind. For almost an hour we watched sheets of rain driving past us horizontally. Then, everything stopped, almost as abruptly as it had begun. Another tense episode in our growing list of weather encounters had passed.

A little later, Ramona arrived, introduced herself, showed us where we could set up the trailer and gave us a quick tour of the church. We agreed to accompany her the next day as she visited several ranchers to determine what help they might need.

For Amber Waves Of Grain

All the times throughout my life that I sang "Oh, beautiful, for spacious skies, for amber waves of grain," those words had no real meaning to me. On that day, however, I saw with my own eyes fields of golden grain bending in the wind like ocean waves against the backdrop of the unending clear blue sky. The intensity of the sight and the excitement of experiencing the imagery of those words firsthand are indelibly imprinted in my mind.

As we drove over 200 miles to visit four ranches, we gained a new appreciation for the word *isolation*. Some of the people lived 50 miles down a series of dirt roads with only one or two other homesteads along the way. Directions to the places were very specific: Go 3.5 miles to the first dirt road on the left. Proceed 6.2 miles to the red mailbox and turn right. Proceed 5.8 miles to the fork in the road. Take the left hand fork and proceed 10.2 miles to the end of the fence, etc.

Cycle Of Woe

While we drove, Ramona briefed us on what had happened that terrible winter, and schooled us in how such disastrous events create a vicious cycle of far-reaching effects that can all but cripple individuals and an entire area.

The facts of the winter of 1996-97 are outlined in the March and April 1998 issues of the LDR newsletter *Recovery*. The winter began early with "a major ice storm in late October. Then the first of a dozen blizzards struck before the ground had a chance to freeze. By winter's end, a dozen feet of concrete-hard, wind-scoured snow blanketed much of the western Dakotas. . . . The weight of the snow drove fence posts deep into the soggy ground. Some 480,000 cattle and other livestock froze to death or were smothered in the storms.

"Farm buildings were destroyed under the weight of ten ponderous feet of snow. . . Hundreds of miles of cattle fences were demolished. . . Windbreaks . . . were simply crushed by dunes of snow that sometimes reached to the tops of full-grown trees.

"Spring brought even greater pain. Melted snow with nowhere to go formed a vast inland sea. Farms were cut off by dissolving roads. The pressure of saturated soil squeezed foundations and caused basements to collapse. . . Hail storms battered shingles and punched through roofs and windows with softball-sized chunks of ice."

Finally, the three-day blizzard in April that hit during calving, coupled with the quick thaw that flooded the barns, forced many dairy farmers to capitulate. Many of them had to sell what was left of their herds for almost nothing—if they could find a way to get them to market! One farmer described having to use "a tractor to pull horse trailers to the farmyard, then haul them out that way."

Those were the facts. Then Ramona described the human toll, helping us to visualize beleaguered farmers having to shovel or plow their way to their barns all winter to feed their animals; to understand the extraordinary costs for high-energy feed which the animals required to survive the cold, as well as the increased fuel needed to heat their farm houses; to empathize with the heartbreak of farmers and ranchers having to watch their animals die, see their livelihoods disappear, and to face the possibility of losing their land; and to understand that these people were so exhausted and numbed that many were left helpless and hopeless.

Because a great many were elderly whose children were grown and gone, they were left to face the aftermath alone. When the barrage finally ended, they had all they could handle just to carry on with the necessary spring chores and planting. There was no time, money, energy or will to begin dealing with the monumental clean-up and repairs, and there had been little substantial help from federal insurance or emergency agencies. Many people became victims of accidents or developed serious ailments as a result of their extreme physical exertion and stress, many others became severely depressed, and there was an alarming number of suicides.

Quiet Desperation

When Lutheran Social Services (LSS) and LDR first became involved, they dispensed some of the $300,000 in donations where it could be most beneficial in assuaging immediate needs—paying off overdue grocery, fuel or medical bills and underwriting the most urgent repairs, all done on the basis of need without regard to the denomination or faith of the recipients. One single, working mother owed a $400 grocery bill. The court was going to auction off her only car (her means of transportation to work), until LSS paid the debt. Because there were so many outstanding debts to local businesses, they, too, were in jeopardy of folding; consequently, they refused to grant any more credit.

Although Orphan Grain Train already had sent 20 semi-loads of food and other emergency supplies into South Dakota, Ramona explained that most of the government and relief agencies had left quickly, or had not followed up after victims had filled out paper work. Only when LDR embarked on a systematic search to ferret out the people who were suffering, did the extent of the disaster come into focus. Many victims were at first reluctant to speak with Ramona. It often took several contacts to build up trust and convince them that LSS/LDR was sincerely committed to helping and would follow through. Ramona spoke with such compassion and empathy that we couldn't help feeling a great sense of mission in what we were about to do in the next couple weeks.

At the first house we visited, a couple who appeared to be in their late 40's or early 50's showed us their pole barn that had been destroyed by a micro-burst of wind, pieces of which had been hurtled through the walls of their house. Shingles and siding had been stripped off the side facing into the wind. The husband apologized that he was not able to accept help at that time because he was in the middle of haying and would not feel comfortable having people work on his home when he couldn't work alongside them. It was agreed that if LDR could help furnish the materials, he would later be able to manage the repairs himself with help from neighbors. Both he and his wife expressed concern that others were more in need than they were.

At the second house we visited, the elderly couple were both recuperating from cancer. They had problems with their foundation being undermined from the water and needed cracks sealed in the basement. Then we visited a farmer who needed help repairing fencing. Standing by the bullpen, he pointed to where the snow had drifted so high that the bulls had been able to walk out, but with nowhere to go, they had simply returned.

The last couple, who had a young boy and lived in an extremely isolated area, was also in need of help to repair livestock pens and fencing. The wife still wore a brace after having her neck fused as a result of injuries sustained from a fall off a horse, and the husband was recuperating from hip replacement surgery. Both were in continual pain and able to take care of little more than the daily household necessities.

These homes and situations were just a small representative sampling of the quiet desperation that existed all over the area and which, until LDR made a commitment to address it, had been all but ignored. In this phase of the recovery, LDR determined what needed to be done at each location, the urgency or extenuating circumstances, what materials were required, whether LDR would furnish all or part of them, and if volunteers were needed.

Of all the ongoing needs, mending fences was the most critical. Without fences to contain their livestock, farmers could not rebuild their herds. Orphan Grain Train spent $86,000 on posts and wire purchased at less than wholesale cost, and arranged for donated trucking to transport the materials from other states to South Dakota. In the summer of 1998, over 130 miles of fencing was replaced. Their enormous contribution, which supplemented the normal LSS/ LDR support, enabled substantial help to get to the most remote and isolated areas of South Dakota. For their outstanding service, Orphan Grain Train was presented the Distinguished Corporate Partner Award for 1998 in Sioux Falls, South Dakota, on January 28, 1999.

Getting Organized

Ramona, Larry, and I left for the Timber Lake Community Center, 60 miles west of Selby, at 9 a.m. on Monday morning. We unloaded boxes of food from Orphan Grain Train, as well as cots and sleeping mats, and began organizing the kitchen and preparing lunch for the busload of 53 adults and youth from the St. John's Lutheran Church in Fremont, Ohio, who would be arriving later that morning. The group would be quartered at the Center because most of the initial jobs were in that area.

After lunch, Ramona briefed everyone about the situation and the kinds of work they would be doing, gave them time to get set up, and divided

142

them into work teams. Though it was mid-afternoon by then, each work team went out to visit their job—some as far as 30 miles away. Larry's group, because of the skilled people available, was assigned to a job back in Selby, then had to return to Timber Lake for dinner, devotions, and finalizing of the next day's schedule. By 9:30 p.m., the three of us headed back to Selby—again!

An interesting and pertinent side note is that to get to Timber Lake (a small Western town right out of the movies) we had to cross the Missouri River at the city of Mobridge and, in so doing, moved from the Central Time Zone into the Western Time Zone. That meant that after an hour's drive, we arrived each morning at the same time we had left (which the rest of the week was 6 a.m.), and when we returned home at night it was an extra hour later. This fact alone made it one long and exhausting week—before adding in the work factor.

Giving A Jump Start

The next day Larry and I joined several of the other men at Verna's ranch in Selby. Verna had a beautiful large spread. The lean-to attached to the big barn, which was used to shelter farm machinery and sometimes cattle, was sagging badly, the sides were bowed out, and the foundation was rotted. It took quite a bit of time to agree on how to safely attack the job, but before the day ended, jacking it up with posts until the side swung in, then pouring concrete footings around the posts completed half of it.

I spent some time talking with Verna, a lovely and gracious lady who had been divorced for 22 years and had run the ranch with her three sons, two of whom had since moved away. One son still lived with her, but worked long hours at the local power company and was hard pressed just to accomplish the necessary chores. They had been totally stymied about how to deal with the lean-to themselves.

The next day, when the job was completed, Verna's son took one of the teen-age workers for his first horseback ride while she showed Larry and the other volunteers around the ranch, which included a large barn housing a collection of antique automobiles belonging to her sons, as well as two new Corvettes (one belonged to her grown daughter) and two Harley Davidson motorcycles which had been won and never driven. As a consequence, some people questioned whether Verna (who had assisted Ramona in many ways over the past year) "deserved" help.

I had been assigned to a different job that day, and Larry linked up with me in the late afternoon. Joining Pastor John Bull, nicknamed JB, and several farm youth from his congregation, we pulled up mangled posts, sheep fencing and barbed wire, then pounded in new posts and strung new barbed wire for George and Josephine, both in their 70's. Although they no longer raised sheep, they had lost a year's rent on the pastureland because they had been unable to repair the fencing themselves.

George, a POW in Germany for nine months during World War II, had sustained back injuries when his B24 was hit by anti-aircraft fire and he was forced to bail out. He was always in a great deal of pain. For 33 years, Josephine had handled most of the chores of their sheep ranch and raised their two sons while George was on the road truck driving. Years of hard physical work had taken its toll on Josephine also, and she suffered from painful arthritis in her back. However, both insisted on working right alongside us, too proud to stand by and let someone else do their work.

In fact, it was obvious that they were having difficulty accepting our help. As Josephine explained, "We've always helped others. We never had to have anyone help us before." I tried to make her feel more comfortable by maintaining that that was part of the cycle of life—they had helped others, now it was their turn to be helped, and someday someone would help us.

George tried pounding a few fence posts, but his body quickly made him stop. "If I could do this," he said wistfully, "I'd do it all day long." I tried my hand at pounding in a few, but soon deferred to the youth. Instead, Josephine and I rolled up the old sheep fencing, and I soon became adept at clipping the barbed wire to the posts after George laid the wire with the tractor and the boys tightened it.

The youth delighted George and Josephine and lifted their spirits. Josephine even called the local newspaper to come out and take a picture of them. George and Josephine's mood visibly improved as each day they could see that more and more had been accomplished. By the end of the week, we had completed three quarters of the job. Buoyed, Josephine and George felt confident they could finish the rest themselves.

On Friday, they could barely contain their joy as we sat around their table for lunch and celebrated with cake and ice cream. George shared a little about his World War II experience and proudly showed us his Purple Heart, which he had received just a few years before. Josephine unveiled the numerous quilts she had created from squares of hand-embroidered flowers, each a stunning combination of colors. Then we all went out to the garage to view George's hobby, a collection of Farm-all tractors he had restored. He let the young people pile onto one and drive it around the yard, and all the while Josephine snapped pictures. Our good-byes were tearful as George and Josephine entreated us to come back some day for a visit.

Meanwhile, the other groups had completed a variety of jobs at other locations—tearing down collapsed sheds, repairing barn roofs, mending corrals and other fencing, and clearing shelter belts (strategically planted stands of trees of varying heights which act as barriers against the strong prairie winds and shelter for the animals from the heat and snow). Many of them had been demolished and needed to be cleaned out to make way for new growth or plantings.

Each group observed the same progression of reactions from the families they worked with. At first, the family seemed listless, at a loss to know where to start, and expressed difficulty in accepting help. But when the volunteers began digging in, suddenly they became enlivened, offering tools and machinery and pitching in themselves. Their mood shifted visibly as they were given the jump-start they needed to get going, as well as a healthy dose of hope. At the end of the week, all of them felt ready to carry on by themselves.

Not Judging By Appearances

It is quite easy for most of us to feel good about mobilizing to help people who appear completely devastated and destitute as a result of a disaster such as a tornado. However, a number of the volunteers were experiencing some difficulty when they saw well-kept farmhouses and new vehicles, questioning why we were spending our time helping people who appeared relatively well off.

We discussed this with Ramona as we drove home one evening. "Just because people aren't destitute doesn't mean they don't need help," she responded fervently. "Do we want them to sell off everything they have and become paupers before we feel they are worthy of compassion and aid?" she asked. Then she shared an incident that had taught her to never again judge people's need by their outward appearance.

When her family first moved to Selby, Ramona worked as a kindergarten teacher's aide. Whenever there was a special event or performance, one particular little boy would always be dressed for the occasion in a beautiful suit. Ramona assumed for a long time that he came from a wealthy family. She later learned that his grandmother was raising him and another grandchild and that her only income came from sewing clothes for people. During the evenings, she made special little outfits for her grandchildren.

In one short but very intense week, we had learned invaluable lessons about the dynamics of working with proud people, the critical role of hope in the healing process as well as financial and physical support, and the true nature of compassion. The families and Ramona were excellent instructors.

Mission of Might

The group from Grace Lutheran Church in Westminster, Maryland, arrived on Saturday, wearing specially made tee shirts featuring two figures reaching out to each other against the background of a cross and shining sun, and which read: "Mission of Might—Grace Lutheran and St. John's Lutheran." There was only a handful of teens in the group of 24, most of whom were members of the youth folk choir. This mission team would bunk at the local high school in Selby and eat their meals at the church—a logistically superior arrangement for us.

The Grace Lutheran people were keenly attuned to each other and their mission, guided by the thoughtful leadership of Carol Arbaugh, head of the church's Social Ministry Committee, and her husband Mel. Social ministry has been an important part of both Mel and Carol's lives from an early age. Mel's love for service was fostered by his Brethren upbringing, and Carol was actively involved in two vital ministries during her years at Western Maryland College, a Methodist school in Westminster.

Following college, Carol ministered to Sioux Indians in Nebraska as a VISTA volunteer, after which she carried her heart for service into her professional life as a special education teacher for fourteen years and a counselor for eight. Now retired, she has been guiding the social ministry at Grace Lutheran, inspiring a core of members to invest themselves in action ministry.

The Grace Lutheran team came with the loving support and backing of the rest of their church. Members sent them off with baked goodies and prayers. One woman had presented each "missionary" with two handmade beaded crosses—one for them to wear, and the other to give to someone they met during their trip. My treasured cross hangs on a peg near my bed.

Like Nancy at the Easter build, mission team members Marjorie, Bob and Helen set a beautiful example of how any task, no matter how mundane, can be transformed into a loving gift. Taking the same randomly mixed boxes of food we had had to work with the week before, they conjured up marvelous culinary surprises for each family-style meal. When we arrived at the church hot and tired after work, cold juices, fruit and snacks were set out and waiting for us. At the end of the week, the trio received a well-deserved standing ovation.

Larry and I, now "experts" in stringing barbed wire, were assigned to lead a team composed of two high school girls, Hilary and Veronica, and Linwood, a high school English teacher. Our mission was to repair and/or replace a length of sheep and barbed wire fencing for Dorothy, a 71-year-old widow. Much of her fencing still lay under water, but the section we were to repair separated two grazing ranges for her cattle and her son's horses.

Dorothy worked part-time at a nearby cafe so she was gone much of the time, and since she had no tractor, we had to do everything by hand—all the while keeping an eye out for the herd. Dorothy had warned us to "Watch out for the Red Angus bull. He's very protective of his females!" And sure enough, on our third day of work, we all had to spend a half hour in our truck as the herd passed through the gate. The wild-eyed bull was something we definitely didn't want to tangle with.

Our little group worked extremely hard in the sometimes-scorching heat, but there was something exhilarating and freeing about being out in that vastness, attending only to the task at hand as the sun beat down on us and the breeze cooled our perspiration. The girls were "plucky," a term my mother was fond of using, weathering insect bites, heat, rain and sore fingers. Lunches around Dorothy's kitchen table were a welcome respite and a chance to get to know each other.

Little by little, Dorothy, the colorful and "feisty Scotswoman," as she referred to herself, opened and warmed to us. As she sat up on her kitchen counter talking with us on Thursday after we had completed our work, her voice became noticeably emotional. "I didn't need any of the food they offered me after the storms, but I sure do appreciate a hand with this," she said gratefully.

We All Need To Help Each Other

During the evening before the Grace Lutheran team was to head home, I sat down to talk with Charlie—in everyone's eyes the most inspiring member of the mission team. Charlie had been a mechanical engineer for Baltimore Gas and Electric, when at age 35 he had a life-changing accident while tobogganing down a hill on a refrigerator door with his eight-year-old son. His son escaped injury, however Charlie became a hemiplegic, the left side of his body paralyzed. He suffered a broken neck, a blood clot on his brain, double vision and loss of hearing in his right ear. It took him a year to recuperate to the point where he could walk again with a cane.

Charlie returned to work, but over the course of the next ten years it became increasingly noticeable that the brain damage had affected his organizing and prioritizing skills, and he eventually retired on long-term disability. He tried to write his autobiography, but only succeeded in becoming severely depressed when he realized he would never again do many of the things he enjoyed—building, skiing, mountain climbing, etc. Finally, Charlie's wife, who was a schoolteacher, convinced him to consider substitute teaching. Reluctantly, he tried it one day and loved it. Charlie had been subbing for the past two years, and especially enjoyed teaching in the special education department where he could "role model" a disabled adult for students with disabilities. When he heard about the mission trip, he was determined to go.

Charlie's contribution was considerable—he helped clean a shelterbelt, took down two chicken coops, and painted the children's playhouse. But it was by no means easy. The long drive was wearying, and the work required all of Charlie's stamina. However, his deep satisfaction overshadowed the physical challenges. Charlie's reason for pushing himself to the limit was simple and straightforward: "A lot of people gave to me after my accident. This is my opportunity to give back. We all need to help each other!"

III-17. THE HEART OF THE MATTER

It is these undeniable qualities of human love
and compassion and self-sacrifice that give me hope. . .

Jane Goodall, ***Reason for Hope***

The Worst That Can Happen

The pivotal moment in Larry's and my decision-making process, as we contemplated embarking on this new lifestyle, was when we asked ourselves, "What is the worst that can happen to us?" Facing the worst that can happen, either in our imaginations or in reality, is often an epiphany. For the first time perhaps, we see more clearly than ever that life is so much more than security, possessions, getting ahead or any of the other things we have spent it striving for. This is often the case with people who have had near-death experiences and "come back" with clarity of purpose and an altered perspective and vision of life that is drastically different from before.

As a result of such an experience, Dale and Jeannie Peercy are full-time missionaries for Lutheran Disaster Response. We met the Peercys when they joined forces with us in Timber Lake, South Dakota, to lend their experience and skills to help manage the projects of the large mission group from Ohio. The couple had been in the mission field for almost two years and had spent the last 7 1/2 months coordinating the repair of 123 homes damaged by the winter storms in the area of Opal, about 100 miles west of Selby. Like Ramona, they helped to mend broken hearts and spirits, as well.

Dale, who had his own successful construction business for 20 years, was stricken with pancreatitis (inflammation of the pancreas) in 1995 and was so near death that his family and friends were called to his bedside to say their good-byes. Dale survived, however, and during his recovery he learned hard, humbling lessons about being in need and accepting help. They changed the direction of his life. In January 1996, Dale sold his business, Jeannie closed her house painting and drywall enterprise, and they

149

signed on with LDR. "I really think it [missionary work] was our purpose, our calling," Dale proclaimed in an interview in the February 23, 1998 *Rapid City Journal*.

I believe that, in one way or another, people who have encountered and survived a major catastrophe have a similar revelation—some stronger and more lasting than others. If only for a brief time, they see clearly that, stripped of all its outer trappings, life is sweet and precious, and that love is its true essence. As much as anything, I believe it is this realization, augmented by its visible manifestation through the outpouring of caring, generosity and support from others, that sustains disaster survivors along the lengthy and arduous road to recovery.

The Primacy Of Relationships

To be sure, not all people remain open to that understanding and, in some measure, their ability to maintain it may depend on their faith and outlook on life prior to the event. However, many whose lives are most changed are those who had little faith before, yet report that the "hand of God" touched them and "saved them for a purpose." Though they still must deal with all the stages of the healing process—frustration, anger, periods of depression—overarching all, they have caught a glimpse that the good in life is far greater than the bad, and that our lives are not separate entities but, rather, are intricately connected and interwoven. What we observed in almost all the survivors of the three disasters we were involved with is that the one awareness, above all others, that was gained from their personal tragedy was the *primacy of relationships*.

One young woman in Oak Grove definitely understood. Standing in front of her leveled high school as her class prepared for their graduation ceremony in a cleared field in back, she shared that she "was not going to have my senior year remembered for *one mean wind*. I realize family and friends are what you have. Personal possessions don't matter." While finishing high school in a makeshift classroom, she made a decision to become a nurse.

Feeling connected is one of the most critical factors in the healing process. Because ordinary life (in our country, at least) has become much more complex, mobile, and detached, there has been a growing body of research aimed at determining what factors contribute to a person's resilience in the face of uncontrollable stresses and upheavals. Sociologists and psychologists have begun moving away from an emphasis on victimization toward a focus on survival and resilience. (Thus, it is preferable to refer to people as *storm survivors* rather than storm *victims*.) Companies and organizations are even training people in *resilience skills*.

Although the potential to be resilient seems to be more innately present in some people than in others, researchers now believe resilience can be learned. Factors contributing to resilience, such as strong problem-solving ability and a questioning mind, have been identified. But, interestingly, according to Monika Guttman in her article "Resilience" (*USA Weekend*, March 5-7, 1999), almost all of the landmark studies have concluded that, contrary to our cultural belief that rugged individualism prepares us to face adversity, "*one of the most important skills is the ability to be and feel connected to others*" (italics mine).

Recognizing Our Connectedness

For most of us, however, the awareness of our connectedness does not come all at once. I liken the gradual realization to one of my favorite childhood pastimes—completing connect-the-dot drawings. I was intrigued by looking at a page full of seemingly disconnected dots and knowing that they formed a picture I could not yet see. My anticipation would mount as I moved my pencil from dot to dot and tried to guess what the hidden picture was. Sometimes it was easy to discern; other times it wasn't clear until the end.

I have begun to see life itself like those dot drawings. It is often difficult to comprehend the big picture, to recognize the connection between individual people and events in our lives, but most of us have a deep knowing that there is a picture out there bigger than our own individual dots. And until we can see it, we live with the feeling that something is missing.

I have come to my awareness of our spiritual connectedness through a growing understanding and incorporation of the meaning of the life and teachings of Jesus and my own personal communion with God. As Kathleen Brehony asserts in her book *Ordinary Grace*:

"The belief that all beings are part of a connected cosmic web . . . is informed not only by modern research in physics, bioecology, chemistry, and chaos theory, but by every great religion and tradition of wisdom known to the world.

"But many of us have forgotten our own true natures and the exquisite unity that binds all things together. Our modern world, with its emphasis on materialism, rationalism, and separatism, has lost sight of the cosmos as a coherent whole in which every aspect of creation is vitally related to everything else, and in which each of us is an indispensable part of all that is."

Spiritual Kin

The chief problem is that the picture we are trying to see cannot be perceived through our senses, which are interpreted by our minds. Our minds perceive others as separate entities, disconnected from us—strangers, competitors, threats. In order to see the picture I am talking about, we need to view people through the window of our hearts. Only then will we comprehend that, spiritually, we are all kin to one another.

In more primal cultures such as the one Larry and I encountered in Nigeria, connectedness is fostered by broadening family delineations. Thus, all members of one's tribe or village are referred to as *brothers* and *sisters*. This minimizes individualism and fosters greater concern for the wider circle.

I am reminded of an illustrative incident that took place one day in our home in Nigeria when a painter came to redecorate our kitchen after several patches had been made on the concrete walls. As I cleared away the dishes and remains from our lunch, I offered him a leftover sandwich. Gratefully accepting it, he took a bite and disappeared into the kitchen. A few moments later, he reappeared in the doorway, standing there with the sandwich in his hand, still with only one bite eaten. When I asked if he didn't like it, he answered that it was very good.

Obviously, something was definitely bothering him, but he seemed hesitant to say what. Then, all of a sudden, he blurted out, "Please excuse me. I must go out and share this with my brother." Stepping outside, he called another worker over, broke the sandwich in two, and handed his *brother* half. Only then did he relax and enjoy his share. Such is the profound difference in our relationships when, with our hearts, we recognize our brothers and sisters as extensions of ourselves.

As You Give, So Shall You Receive

However much we may see serving others as an optional, selfless act, I believe that in truth it is fulfilling an inborn "selfish" need to feel connected to the whole body, to the *all* of life. It teaches us that our fulfillment is intrinsically linked with our relationship to others.

As we discussed this very issue, Phyllis, the woman from Rapid City who worked with us at the armory, shared with me a story she had recently heard about a person who was given a glimpse of Heaven and Hell. As the door to the room marked *Hell* was opened, the person saw thin, gaunt bodies sitting along both sides of a long banquet table laden with appetizing food. Their bodies were twisted and contorted as they made vain attempts to negotiate the food to their mouths with three-foot-long spoons, cursing and crying out in frustration, anger and hunger.

In the next room marked *Heaven*, the setting was the same: a long table laden with food and people seated on either side with three-foot-long spoons in their hands. But these people were plump, smiling and content. For instead of vainly attempting to feed themselves, they were lovingly feeding each other!

So many volunteers, whether they helped for a day, a week, or a month, indicated they were responding to "a need to be here." In acknowledging that need, they were feeding and nurturing themselves as surely as the survivors. Dale Peercy discussed this truth in the April 1998 LDR newsletter *Recovery.* "We get a whole lot of praise from people who tell us that we're special, and it's hard for us to accept. Whenever someone thanks us, we want to turn around and thank them. We're getting the blessing. We're getting the joy out of it."

Another aspect of the giving/receiving equation that I observed is that those who had been most generous and giving before disaster struck were the ones most often showered with unsolicited help in their own time of need. We often refer to this truism with phrases such as, "What goes around, comes around" or "What you sow, you reap." I think this principle is also expressed (and not just in the monetary sense) when we say the "rich get richer and the poor get poorer." For in order to "get rich" in any aspect of one's life, one needs to give out—even, sometimes, everything one has. Something there is in the universe that does not like a void, and it rushes in to fill it. Conversely, those who hoard and cling to what they have, generally are stuck with just that!

Ken Moses, a high school principal, who is a member of the Rock Creek Church of God, demonstrates this principle in his daily life. According to Mrs. Staggs (the pastor's wife), Ken was always the first to respond when there was any need in the church or community. Her eyes watered as she elaborated.

At the foot-washing service the night of the storm, Pastor Staggs had just finished washing Ken's feet when the 30 members present were alerted that the tornado was approaching. As most of them headed for the ladies restroom, Ken hopped into his car and drove the short distance to his rental home. He could see the tornado coming and got inside a closet, fell to his knees and prayed. The tornado picked up the house and hurtled it across the road. It exploded on impact, leaving Ken beneath the wreckage.

Everyone in the church searched for him immediately after they emerged from their demolished Family Life Center. He was found disoriented, suffering internal injuries and broken ribs.

Two weeks later, when Ken was released from the hospital, he came to church, barely able to walk with the aid of a cane. The tornado had taken everything he owned, yet Ken was observed putting a large-denomination bill in the offering for tornado victims, and later refused to accept money from the church to pay his renter's insurance deductible. "I don't want it," he said, "but call if you need me for anything."

Though 80% of the congregation had suffered major losses, they were all in agreement about wanting to do something for this man who always set such a high standard of magnanimity for them. Under the coordination of the State Minister, the congregation purchased a lot for Ken, furnished the materials and built him a home of his own.

To Ken, Dorothy, Mariesha, George and Josephine, and others who throughout the course of their lives had given generously of their time, talent and money, in their own hour of need it was returned in "good measure, pressed down, shaken together and running over. . ." (Luke 6:38, NIV).

An Attitude Of Gratitude

It was a constant amazement to us that people who had been so battered and traumatized could respond with such compassion, find so much to be thankful for, and trust that somehow there was goodness beneath the veneer of destruction and despair.

In his book *Spiritual Economics*, Eric Butterworth maintains that "thanksgiving is not just a reactionary emotion; it is a causative energy. It is an effective key by which anyone may 'meet life as a powerful conqueror'" (the words of Walt Whitman).

Seeing all circumstances through the lens of a grateful heart is to view events from a "high level perspective." Butterworth asserts that from that elevated viewpoint we will "see things creatively, leading to an attitude that is constructive and optimistic." Perhaps his assertion explains what we observed in many of the storm survivors: those who were able to see reasons to be thankful were able to endure enormous loss with a remarkable degree of peace and resolve.

I'm reminded of the last afternoon we cleaned up in McDonald Chapel. We were about ready to leave for home after clearing the lot on which Mariesha's neighbors had lived (the couple had died when they were swept under Mariesha's garage). A car pulled up, and a petite lady and a gentleman stepped out. Neighbors from across the road met and accompanied them slowly up the driveway. They stood in front of the barren foundation for a long while just looking, the woman occasionally shaking her head in acknowledgment as her neighbor spoke. Progressing to the back of the yard, the neighbors pointed behind Mariesha's house where the bodies had been found. Then they turned and walked toward us.

"Thank you for being here," the lady said to us. "My parents lived here." We extended our sympathy. After again earnestly expressing her appreciation for what we were doing, she told us that she lived out of town and had called every relief agency trying to get word of her "mama and step-daddy" when she heard about the storm. She knew instinctively that something was terribly wrong. "But I know they're in Heaven," she said confidently. "I want to believe God took them in an eye-blink. I need to hold onto that image, even though perhaps it isn't true," she confided.

"They found only three of my parents personal items," she added. "Mama's charm bracelet, their study Bible, and a tape of them singing together. Each one represents something special about their lives. I believe they are *little gifts from God*."

Larry and I were deeply touched not only by this woman's heartfelt expressions of gratitude toward us, but also by her ability to be thankful for what appeared to be so little.

Great Is Thy Faithfulness

Of course, the role of faith in a God of love, and belief in the continuity of life beyond our present existence, cannot be overlooked as a powerful factor in how people responded to the aftermath of the disasters.

Those, whose faith ran deep, saw the disaster as a happenstance of life to be accepted and overcome. They assigned no blame, and they believed and expected something good to emerge from apparent tragedy. They experienced pain and sorrow, but their inner core remained unshaken. Their faith gave them strength to carry on because they trusted that God's loving arms were around them right there in the midst of the rubble. Such was the steadfast faith we saw exhibited by Dorothy.

I also think of the Seale family in Rock Creek, Alabama, whose home was picked up by the tornado and blown apart, flinging the family into the woods 250 feet away. A week after the tragedy, paralyzed from the waist down, the father lay on a gurney at Children's Hospital next to his eight-year-old son, Nathan, who was losing his hold on life. From those watching on TV, he solicited prayers and shared his desire to one day hold his son again. Then, tearfully, he affirmed, "Even in this darkest time, I know that God will find a way to bring good from this."

Days later, Nathan died with his mother at his side praying and comforting him as he was taken off life support. "We know God is in control of everything, and despite the pain, that makes it bearable and acceptable," she was quoted as saying in the August/September 1998 *Good News* free newspaper formerly published by Shades Mountain Independent Church in Hoover, Alabama. What more powerful testimony could there be to the peace such faithfulness brings.

Accentuating The Positive

Some of the great unsung heroes in my eyes are the spouses and children of the countless volunteers who put their lives on hold for weeks and months to devote their full-time energies to relief and recovery efforts. I'm sure there were numerous children's functions missed and many Hamburger Helper and fast food meals eaten while moms were busy cooking for storm survivors.

I'm inclined to believe, however, that a little old-fashioned sacrifice isn't a bad thing. Children learn compassion and caring by seeing it exhibited in the adults around them, even though they might not fully understand it at the time. Many children who were old enough to help were given the opportunity to feel useful and a part of the effort, also something good for character building. In fact, some of the most touching gestures were from children.

Taped on the kitchen bulletin board in the armory in Salem, South Dakota, were numerous letters and expressions of sympathy sent along with donations, many of them from children. One was a picture with a simple hand-printed message—"I'm sorry." Another child drew a house, tree and animal with a rainbow over the top of them. On a big piece of poster board was a letter from a nine-year-old in Yankton, South Dakota:

Dear Spencer South Dakota,

I'm very sorry about the tornado on Sat. I want you to be safe for a long time. Last night I said a prayer for you to not die and that you would earn enough money. I guess it came true! . . . I donated $2.50 and soap, shampoo, toilet paper, Avon samples, socks, and underwear. I want you to all be safe.

Without a doubt, not everyone responded charitably. There were instances of looting, thievery, greed, and just plain taking advantage in all the situations we encountered—even on the part of some of the survivors. However, in comparison to the overwhelming support and generosity of thousands of decent, ordinary citizens, and the compassion and gratefulness of the majority of survivors, those instances are barely worth mentioning.

Furthermore, I contend that more regular attention sorely needs to be given to goodness. Too often we give recognition to that which we should minimize, and convey the message that goodness is not fashionable or worthy of our attention. If the evening news showed half as many instances of good news as it does bad, perhaps we wouldn't be so amazed by the altruism that is exhibited during an emergency. And, perhaps, more people would be inspired and encouraged to express their benevolent inclinations without needing the impetus of a disaster.

Standing The Test

"Blessed is the man who perseveres under trial, because when he has stood the test, he will receive the crown of life that God has promised to those who love him," reads James 1:12 (NIV). There were, indeed, so many people we observed who stood the test and not only brought blessing and honor to themselves, but were an inspiration to those of us who were there to help them.

My friend Margaret commented after reading this manuscript: "All these people seem larger than life, but taken in context, I somehow feel they are just as ordinary as me. We *all* have that potential for grace and service. We just need to allow it to flow as the occasion arises."

And therein lies the heart of the matter—the strength and nobility of the human spirit, waiting beneath the surface to be called forth and to shine. I have no doubt, after what we've seen, that we human beings can be so much more than we often are.

IV. REFRESH AND REFLECT

*. . . seek ye first the kingdom of God, and his righteousness,
and all these things shall be added unto you.*

Matthew 6:33 (KJV)

IV-18. PRAIRIE PORTRAITS

Blessed are the flexible,
for they shall not get bent out of shape.

Shared by Al Everett
at Habitat RV Care-A-Vanners Conference
March 30, 2000

Restorative Beauty

The plains and prairies have a beauty all their own. As we followed the Missouri River north from Mobridge, South Dakota, there were no imposing forests or majestic mountain backdrops. Just the quiet beauty of the gently-rounded nubs of hills covered with velvet green, variegated by the casting of the clouds' shadows and dotted with cattle grazing or gathered round a water hole. My chest felt like it would burst as I attempted to drink in the expansiveness of the scene. Being on the road has always been restorative for Larry and me, and it was definitely good for our psyches and souls to be enveloped by these tranquil pastoral panoramas after the intensity of the previous months.

Here, also, was confirmation of a realization that we had come to early in our travels—every region of our country boasts its own grandeur—unique and incomparable. We are often asked which part of the country we like best, and invariably our answer becomes an exposition of the special features of each area. There is no way to compare or choose. One thing did amuse us, however, as we drove along miles of fenced-in ranges. We found ourselves noticing fence posts, counting strands of barbed wire, and commenting on the size of shelterbelts. It's amazing what an education one receives by living something for a couple weeks, and how it opens our eyes to things heretofore never even noticed.

Kudos To The Park Service

Our aim was to follow as much of the Lewis and Clark Trail as was possible with a 30-foot trailer behind us. After spending an hour in the Lewis and Clark Interpretive Center north of Bismarck, North Dakota, we stopped at the nearby replica of Fort Mandan (situated 20 miles from the original site, which is now under water), and marveled how 40 people could winter in those tight quarters. After enjoying the evening at Cross Ranch State Park, named after Teddy Roosevelt's "cross" cattle brand, we headed northwest along the Missouri River the next day to Knife River National Historical Site and toured the inside of an exact replica of a Hidatsa earth mound dwelling. This area, which features one of the most complete records of a horse-buffalo culture, was the site of five Mandan and Hidatsa villages for 500 years. Five thousand people lived in the villages at their peak, a number that far overshadows today's population in the area.

Here, I must commend our federal government for their preservation and interpretation of national historic and natural sites, though we are concerned that funding to keep them up has not kept pace with the greatly increased usage. Civil War battlefields, national parks, wildlife refuges—at each site we have taken in, the Park Service has done an excellent job of capturing not only the facts, but conveying the flavor and aura of the setting or event through introductory slide shows or movies, interpretive trails, live presentations, and concise, extremely informative brochures and maps. Believing it is important to give credit when it's due, we always make sure to express our appreciation at the end of each visit.

Our day ended gloriously at the northern unit of Theodore Roosevelt National Park near Grassy Butte, the prairie counterpart of the Grand Canyon. Carved by the winding Missouri, glaciers and wind, the formations of muted earth tones accentuated by the deep green of pine trees were both awesome and quieting. After dinner we drove the 14 miles to the end of the park road and watched the sun slip away.

Getting Settled In Regina

Heading to Regina, Saskatchewan, for the Ed Schreyer Build, we moved west across North Dakota and into northeastern Montana. The ranges became noticeably sparse with vegetation. Much of the landscape was exceedingly desolate. Nothing changed about the terrain as we crossed into the Canadian province of Saskatchewan two days later except that the drab, flat land seemed to stretch even further—clear to the end of the earth. And then, as we drew closer to Regina we began to encounter fields of sunflowers (Canadians eat sunflower seeds like Americans eat popcorn) and expanses of dazzling yellow canola and delicate purple flax—such a sharp contrast to the barrenness that it almost hurt our eyes to look at them.

When we at last arrived at the campground that would be our home during the Ed Schreyer Build, we discovered that Regina does not adhere to Daylight Saving Time, so we changed our watches—again.

Saturday morning we enjoyed a leisurely tour of the Royal Canadian Mounted Police (RCMP) Museum on the grounds of the training academy. Growing up listening to Sergeant Preston on the radio, the RCMP had a romantic appeal to us both. We were surprised to learn, however, that the Mounties are no longer mounted, except for an elite unit that performs the "Musical Dance" on very special occasions throughout Canada.

Already in the "Habitat section" of the campground a large fifth-wheel trailer was parked which belonged to Elmer Shantz, a full-time volunteer for Habitat Canada and coordinator of the yearly Ed Schreyer builds. Later in the day, some of our other camp mates began to arrive, and that evening we all sat around a campfire until midnight getting acquainted, swapping Habitat stories, and enjoying the magnificent stars. Everyone was eagerly anticipating the beginning of the build.

Facilitating Is Rewarding, Too

Every blitz build has a unique tone and flavor, so it is important to be prepared to be flexible. The Regina build began with a crush of people turning out Monday morning to frame five houses; the sixth was constructed with interlocking vinyl tubes into which concrete would later be poured. (This form of construction is almost 100% maintenance-free and provides outstanding insulation.) Regina citizens are known for not signing up, but simply showing up in unanticipated numbers. There were enough people to frame ten houses.

Larry and I made a quick assessment of the situation and agreed that we'd had our opportunities to enjoy the thrill of hammering and raising walls. We decided we would make it our priority to see that first-timers felt useful and had a rewarding experience. With a large number of professional tradesmen there also, we urged the more timid to find a spot and to let it be known that they wanted to do their part.

One of the quiet people standing back observing was Karmel Schreyer, the 34-year-old daughter of Ed and Lily. She had come all the way from her home in Hong Kong to join her parents and participate in her first build. Lily came over from the house next door and stood nearby looking distressed. Noticing, I approached and asked if she needed anything. "No," she replied, "but I'm concerned that my daughter is just standing there. This is her first build and I want her to have a good time."

"Don't give it another thought," I assured her. "My husband and I will get her involved." Lily slipped away, and I immediately went over to Karmel, introduced myself, and said, "You look like you need something to do. Sometimes you have to assert yourself. Just say, 'I can hammer that' and step in and do it." I located an unoccupied spot where studs were being laid out for a wall and told her to claim it. When it was time to join them together, Karmel hammered in her first nails. Her face beamed with satisfaction. For the rest of the morning, I made sure she was by my side as we hammered, stuffed insulation into walls and caulked around windows. It was obvious that Karmel was a quick study and that she was enjoying herself.

The next morning, as we arrived at our house to begin work, Karmel walked up behind me, put her hand on my shoulder and asked, "So, where are we going to assert ourselves today?" From then on, there was little she didn't try or become proficient at. Larry taught her how to use the skill saw while they worked together measuring and cutting siding.

Thank You, Oprah

Our homeowner was Desiree Bank, a baker by trade and a single mother with seven-year-old twin boys and a two-year-old girl. At her mother's house one afternoon, Desiree happened to catch an Oprah Winfrey show about Habitat. She had never heard of Habitat for Humanity, and wondered if they operated in Regina. After a few calls, she reached the director of the local affiliate who mailed her information and an application. Several weeks later, Desiree saw news about the planned blitz build and applied. In just three and a half months, she was informed that she would soon become a homeowner. "The time must have been right," she conjectured. "If I hadn't seen Oprah's show, I never would have even known about it."

Desiree's house was sponsored by Home Depot, a business that supports Habitat everywhere it has stores. Home Depot employees worked hard and enthusiastically alongside us throughout the week, and our house was finished well before the start of the closing festivities. As the house took final shape during the last two days, Desiree wandered from volunteer to volunteer, looked appreciatively into their eyes as her own filled with tears, and hugged them tightly. She was too overwhelmed to express her feelings in words.

After the closing ceremonies, meal and entertainment, Larry and I walked along the alley behind the houses to our van. Our hearts were warmed when we saw Desiree and her children eating their first meal on their deck.

Catching Up

We left Regina with full hearts. Once again we had experienced the satisfaction of knowing that we had contributed to improving a family's life. And, we had been reminded of something very important—building people up is just as important as building a house. In the process, we also acquired two new friends.

On our way to Minnesota, we spent an evening at a wayside rest area with a field of golden ripe wheat growing next to the parking lot. I picked a few stalks. I had never tasted kernels of raw wheat and discovered that they are sweet and delicious. Across the road, farmers had just finished baling wheat stalks after harvesting the grain. Huge round bales of gold glistened in the afternoon sun while hawks circled overhead. Against the deep blue sky and cotton clouds, it was a magical sight.

When we pulled into the campground in Minnesota the next afternoon, there were two things on our minds—rest and cleaning the truck and trailer. Every nook and cranny harbored powdery dirt and sand, remnants of our treks across the plains states and the prairie winds that had disseminated them. For several weeks, we caught up on household chores, relaxation and sleep. Clean at last, we headed for Michigan.

IV-19. WHERE DREAMS MAY LEAD

Rather than get life together,
we might allow life to have its way with us
and get us together in a form that is a surprise.

Thomas Moore, Finding Your Original Self
"Unity Magazine," August 2000

Turning Over The Wheel

One night we lay in bed reflecting on all that had happened in our lives since becoming full-timers. We began to giggle as we enumerated some of the unexpected occurrences and the wild ride we'd been taken on.

When we began our journey with a rather bold disregard for security issues, we had scant appreciation for what we were committing ourselves to or how much we would be stretched and pushed to grow and change. As we attempted to maintain our focus on the road in front of us, we were continually amazed at what unfolded in our lives in both the inner and outer realms—things that would likely never have occurred had we continued making physical and financial security our primary priorities.

When we put ourselves into the flow of life, rather than trying to control it, the right circumstances or resources always seem to present themselves at the opportune time. As the reader may have noted, we were not "one-trial learners" when it came to "turning over the wheel"—and we're still learning. At the very least, we are beginning to recognize more readily, and pay closer attention to, the inner voices and urges beckoning us in a particular direction. We may not always trust them completely—sometimes "hedging our bets" just in case—but at least we are willing to defer when the signs become clear.

This new-found sensitivity or intuition has guided us not only to where we need to be, but also lets us know when it is time to move on. It has helped us to be open to alternate possibilities within situations, such as being facilitators at the Regina build. It has allowed us to recognize our limitations as well, teaching us that we are only responsible for *doing our part*, and enabling us to pace ourselves and give ourselves permission to take a day off when we need rest—either physical or emotional. And, it has guided us in making decisions such as going to the more intimate build in Regina instead of the big Jimmy Carter one in Houston. These are all positive changes from how we tended to approach life when *we attempted to be in control*, and they have been invaluable aids in developing us to become better servants.

Had We Only Known

We have often said, as we've looked back at all the agonizing we did about whether we could afford to follow our dream—"if we'd only known." There were infinite opportunities already out there awaiting us, but with our limited vision we couldn't foresee them. In order for them to come into focus, we first had to make the commitment to trust life, which also meant trusting in the Creator's provision.

Despite our increasing faith, however, we were not immune to moments of panic when we saw our money dwindling faster than we had anticipated. But those instances never held their grip on us for long. When we experienced them, we immediately tried to refocus on our true source of all things. This has allowed us to meet with equanimity circumstances that heretofore would have induced many sleepless nights.

We had spent so much time worrying about money, but when we finally went for it, we found that a door opened and a means was provided for every need that surfaced. We have become more and more convinced that there is, indeed, a divine order to life, and although we may not always be able to see it at the moment, we *can* depend on it.

We were surprised to find how many options there are to support ourselves in campgrounds—some for money, others for a free site over an extended period, or a combination of both. However, it goes way beyond that. It is the timeliness with which opportunities have presented themselves in relation to an unexpected need, and the fulfillment of needs in unanticipated ways, that have instructed and guided us into a more carefree way of living.

I have already spoken of the financial support we received from friends and churches that enabled us to participate in Habitat for Humanity blitz builds. But sometimes money or resources have come in other ways. Learning about less expensive vehicle and medical insurances came at a time when we needed to trim our expenses. Having meals provided by churches and relief agencies when we were working at disaster sites saved us not only time and energy but also money. At the Spencer Relief Fund rummage sale, we were able to acquire needed clothing inexpensively.

Fortunately, Larry's mechanical skills have saved us expensive truck and trailer maintenance bills, but even those we've had to pay for have often ended up costing much less than anticipated. His maintenance background has also made it easy for him to secure part-time work when we are parked at a campground for any length of time. And, as I began processing our experiences and what we were learning from them, I felt compelled to express my thoughts in writing. A number of my articles were published in *Unity Magazine*. In addition to the personal satisfaction derived, I received compensation.

Smooth Transition

At the end of our first year of traveling in our 24-foot Jayco, we both knew we would need to upgrade to something a little bigger for the long haul. We gave ourselves a maximum budget of $6000 for that purpose, and made a list of improvements we were looking for—a living room, bigger refrigerator and freezer, walk-around bed, and higher underbody clearance. It made the best sense to try to make the move while we were up at our camp, so we began visiting trailer lots and eventually set our hearts on a 1991 30-foot Jayco. We were disappointed when the dealer would not give us a fair trade-in price for ours.

The next day we shook it off, remembering that we had been perfectly happy in our little trailer up to that point and affirming that a suitable replacement would come along at the appropriate time. The following Sunday, Larry spotted an ad in the paper for a 1992 30-foot Dutchmen being sold by a couple who lived two hours south of camp. We drove down on Monday and were ecstatic to find the trailer was in mint condition. In addition, it had every one of our essential requirements, plus a 20-foot-long screen room. The colors were pleasing, and most of our accessories would match nicely. It only had 300 miles on the tires.

We did something we almost never do—we decided on the spot to buy it at their asking price, and sealed the agreement with a handshake. Before we left, the couple also offered to include the 20-foot sectional platform they had constructed, along with an Astroturf covering, and even a large gas grill. (I was beginning to feel like we were in one of those ginsu knife commercials!) And as if that wasn't enough, when we came to pick up the trailer, they loaded the platform and grill into their pick-up and followed us to camp.

We immediately felt at home in the new trailer, and set to spit-polishing the Jayco to ready it for sale. Interestingly, although the two trailers sat almost side by side on our property, after we spent the first night in the Dutchmen, our cat Ross never attempted to go back into the Jayco. He seemed to know instinctively that he had a new home. For him, home was wherever we were.

The happy ending is that we parked the Jayco by the side of the road with a "For Sale" sign, and the very next day a family returning from vacation with their two junior-high-age girls stopped to look at it. Three hours later they returned with a check from the bank, and the next day we watched our baby trailer disappear down the road on its way to a new life. There was no sadness—it was time for it and us to move on. In all, the upgrade cost $3000, half of what we had anticipated.

The Express Business

In *Spiritual Economics*, Eric Butterworth describes some of the very transformations that we had been undergoing. I found myself often saying "Yes!" out loud. One of the profound points the author makes is that we inhibit our creative expression and growth when we aim only to "do a job" or "earn money." Instead, he says, everything we do should be for the purpose of expressing and unfolding who we are and are becoming—"You are in the express business, and growth is what it is all about."

As we have sought to listen for our own drumbeat and to march to it, we have found ourselves giving expression to desires and talents which had been suppressed by our former preoccupation with *doing* rather than *being*. We have taken Thoreau's oft-quoted injunction—to keep moving in the direction of your dreams—seriously.

Larry and I have been married since 1978, and although I learned early on that he had regrets about not pursuing two callings—to be a professional baseball player and to teach history—I never knew he harbored a desire to write a novel, just for his own satisfaction. A detail-oriented person who always notices inconsistencies and errors in books and movies, he wanted to write a novel free of such discrepancies. Like many of his other desires, it became buried as he funneled his energies into "earning a living."

Although Larry has read widely, English grammar was his Achilles' heel in school. He often joked about the fact that he married an English teacher. But one day, he pulled out a pad of paper and began writing. The spelling and grammar weren't always pretty, but the characters and story began developing as, hour by hour, he sat in the armchair in our little living room filling page after page. I have never seen him so focused. Although I helped with the mechanics, Larry was determined to do and learn as much as he could himself through the process.

Veil of Vengeance was thus born, a foreign intrigue adventure that takes place in Iran and features a beautiful but lethal heroine. Though it is extremely difficult to break into the publishing world with a first novel, Larry's sense of accomplishment isn't dependent on that outcome. "I've already gone further with this book than I ever envisioned," he muses. His primary reward came from pursuing the dream and seeing it to conclusion. With the new print-on-demand options for publishing, we will likely have it in print in the near future. If the book sells, the money and recognition will be a bonus.

My story is a little different. Expressing myself through writing has been a life-long process. Following my experience in Brethren Volunteer Service, I wrote several articles for the *Gospel Messenger* (the magazine of the Church of the Brethren). However, for the most part, since then, my writing had been confined to long epistles to friends and family, letters to the editor, a little poetry in college, and a political newsletter while I was on the board of United We Stand America in Connecticut. As a young person, like many, I dreamed about penning "the great American novel," but fiction didn't seem to be my natural bent. I didn't think seriously again about writing until we began traveling.

First, I began by sending detailed letters describing our experiences and my thoughts about them to family and friends. The exercise was as much to force me to commit them to paper while they were still fresh as it was to inform others. Then, in the summer of 1997, when we were at our camp in New Hampshire and I was indulging my passion for picking wild blueberries, the inspiration came for a little book that I titled *The Blueberry Connection*. In it, I shared 16 insights on living that God had revealed to me through the process of picking blueberries. Three years later, Peter Pauper

Press published it under the title *Blueberries From Heaven: A Basketful of Wisdom.*

The exercise of writing the blueberry book revved up my creative juices, and I began thinking of a context in which to share the experiences we were having as we traveled. I didn't want it to be just another recitation of travel adventures. One evening in the summer of 1999, while I was washing dishes, Larry was showing our photo album to our friend Lee and elaborating on our Habitat and disaster relief work. As I listened to their conversation, I was struck by Lee's questions and responses to what Larry was describing. They were very similar to others' reactions to our stories. In a flash of inspiration, I had both the title and format for this book. As my daughter had suggested to me earlier, I just needed to "tell our story."

Even in this endeavor, it has been fascinating to observe how often I "happen onto" a pertinent book, am introduced to a person whose story illustrates what I am trying to convey, or catch "by chance" a TV program on the very subject I am working on. I truly believe I have been guided in writing this book.

Planting Seeds In Thoughts

Midway through our travels, there were two other needs we began articulating. By 1998, after two years of travel, our truck was eight years old and approaching 100,000 miles. Though it was in excellent physical and running condition, we were becoming concerned about the number of miles we were accumulating on it—most of them while sightseeing and running around when we were parked at a campground. A new truck definitely had not been figured into our budget.

We began talking about the idea of picking up a used economy car to save mileage and wear and tear on the truck. One day in passing, I mentioned our concern to my daughter, and she surprised me by saying they were planning to buy a new vehicle in the near future and had discussed giving us their Honda Civic, which we had helped her buy when she was in college. She had maintained it in good condition, and it had only 40,000 miles on it.

Also, we did not have a computer. Larry and I were both writing our books on a portable word processor. I was well aware of the limitations of the word processor, but felt sure we could get by just fine with it. After all, people used to write books on typewriters (and in "ancient" times with a pen). As we approached the stage of serious editing, however, I found myself occasionally commenting that it would certainly be helpful to have a computer. By then, I was also beginning to comprehend that if I was expressing a legitimate need, the fulfillment would come in its own time and manner. We relaxed and let the thoughts drift "out there."

Built On Faith

We connected with Larry's brother and sister-in-law at the Wisconsin border and began our trek across the Upper Peninsula of Michigan. As we had promised, we drove to Watersmeet to visit the headquarters and training center of the ALERT team, the young rescue workers we had met in Alabama.

The main building on the campus was a huge, wooden lodge, which had previously served as the conference center for the highly successful Institute in Basic Life Principles, initiated by Bill Gothard who conducts seminars for professional groups on Christian principles for living and working. The ALERT Program was begun in 1994 as an offshoot, and the home education program, Advanced Training Institute of America (ATIA), was established, in which many of the young men who eventually trained with ALERT were schooled.

One of the most impressive facts we learned about the ALERT program was that it was literally "built on faith" every step of the way. From the time of its inception, and at each juncture in its growth and expansion, the staff prayed for God to provide the needed resources as confirmation that they were "in God's will" and heading in the right direction. And, as we were observing in our own lives on a much less ambitious scale, the resources always appeared effortlessly and on time.

As described in their information brochure, "The goal of the ALERT Program is to build young men who possess not only excellent skills but also Godly character and servants' hearts with which those skills are executed . . ." The young men from Unit 14 whom we had encountered in Birmingham certainly exemplified all the qualities that the program aimed for, and it was fun to reunite with them. They gathered around as we shared pictures, updated them on what had happened since they left, and reminisced about working together on Dorothy and Brenda's property.

Thereafter, we spent three glorious fall weeks camping across the UP, which should be on every traveler's itinerary. It reminded us very much of Newfoundland—sparsely populated and relatively unspoiled by commercialism. Bounded by Lakes Superior and Michigan and generously dotted with inland lakes, there is water everywhere. There is also a rich history to explore—mining, fishing, and the Great Lakes commerce made possible by the Sault Ste. Marie (Soo) Locks.

Twists And Turns

Our intentions were to slowly drift south from Michigan, spend some time at our Tennessee campground, then make our way to Texas to try out the winter scene there. However, shortly before we left, we received a call from my daughter saying she and her husband were ready to give us the Honda, and that they had also decided to upgrade their computers and would be passing one of their older ones on to us. They wanted us to come out to Connecticut to pick up both in a few weeks. She also mentioned that they would be moving to a new apartment and could use our help.

By the time we left Connecticut, it was late October, so we decided to forego Texas and winter again at Carolina Landing, our home park, to concentrate on completing Larry's book and to work on mine.

We now had another consideration—where would we put the computer and printer in the trailer? The kitchen dinette was out of the question if we planned to use it for eating. I spent several nights lying awake trying to figure out where to situate them. There just wasn't a spot. I finally gave up the struggle. The computer had come to me without effort, I reasoned; therefore, I would need to trust that a place to use it would also be provided.

The answer to all our needs came together beautifully when we pulled into the campground. After registering, I asked the manager if there was a secure place where I could set up my computer for the winter. After a few minutes of thought, he offered me use of the sales office, which is closed during the off-season. It was perfect. It had a long banquet table on which to spread my work, a window to look out at the woods, and even a private telephone line that we could use—a luxury for us. In addition, he offered Larry the opportunity to work 10 hours a week for pay and to be on call three nights in exchange for our extended stay. And, as if that wasn't enough good news, the campsite I had been envisioning parking on had been vacated just a couple hours before our arrival!

Living Magnets

When such things happen, I am no longer surprised, but I am still definitely in awe. It really doesn't have so much to do with the fact that we have received things we've needed or wanted, but rather that we are beginning to see and understand the supportive flow of substance that is available to all of us. We just need to learn how to open ourselves to it.

Eric Butterworth proclaims often in his writings, ". . . things may happen around you, and things may happen to you, but the only things which really count are the things that happen in you." The importance of this understanding, he says, is that "you are a living magnet, constantly drawing to you the things, the people, and the circumstances which are in accord with your thoughts."

As I said before, I believe the key lies in a grateful heart. When our hearts are overflowing with gratitude—and not a day has gone by that we have not acknowledged our thankfulness for being able to live the life that we are—they are open and receptive to all the good that life is waiting to pour forth. Our needs are then met as naturally as those of "the lilies of the field" and "the birds of the air," resulting in our feeling blessed and abundantly rich. Indeed, we are!

Having An Attitude

One of the greatest challenges to our peace of mind regarding financial matters was the failure of the buyers of our house to make regular payments on the second mortgage, for which we had floated the loan. At the end of a year of frustrating and fruitless efforts to obtain payments, we had to face the possibility that we might never get repaid.

At that point, we realized we were at a defining juncture in our journey: Were we going to let the financial machinations disturb our peace of mind and diminish our enjoyment of our freedom? If we were, then we weren't really free at all. As we saw it, we had two choices: either come to terms with the situation internally or let the outer circumstances "ruin the day." If we chose the latter, we might as well settle down somewhere and work until the concern was alleviated.

Believing that our needs would always be taken care of (as long as we remained focused on being what we were called to be), we made a conscious decision to trust that if the money due us was not collected, another avenue to replace it (if and when it was needed) would open up. We absolutely stopped worrying about it, or even talking about it.

Trust me when I say that I would never have imagined us dealing with such a challenge in the way we did. There was a time when we would have exhausted ourselves trying to figure out what to do. We would have lost sleep; we would have been angry and bitter; we would have felt unjustly taken advantage of by people we had tried to help. Of course, none of those reactions would have accomplished anything except to inhibit our enjoyment of the present. Instead, we simply decided we were no longer willing to sacrifice our dream and our continuing happiness for the fleeting satisfaction of angry and spiteful feelings. The lessons we learned were of far greater value than the money.

Follow Your Dream

One of the reasons I felt compelled to share our story is to show that ordinary people can make their dreams come true. To be sure, it takes courage (some may even say a little recklessness) and a stepping out on faith. Nevertheless, we can heartily attest that the rewards are a peace and contentment well worth the effort it takes to overcome fear of the unknown. Like others, it took us a long time to understand that truth.

Nowadays, there is little time for people to dream. We are so caught up in the externals and noise of life, that we seldom are still long enough to listen for our inner voice, which holds the key to our real happiness and contentment. Even our children are too programmed and distracted to spend time just laying on their backs watching the clouds drift by, as Larry and I did when we were young.

I am convinced, however, that it is our dreams that are the vehicle to our growth. In them lies the call to risk—the known for the unknown; running in place for moving forward; wondering for discovering; having for finding; security for adventure; and comfort for ecstasy. Our dreams come from the deepest recesses of our being, from our core. They call us to be what we were created to be. That so few people dream, and even fewer actually pursue their dreams, is doubtless why many are so dissatisfied with life.

At the time of our first wedding anniversary, I was assembling a collage of pictures of our courtship, marriage, and first year together. In the center of the arrangement, on a piece of 5x7 rainbow stationery (rainbows were "in" then) my daughter wrote in her beautiful calligraphy:

FOLLOW YOUR DREAM—
LARRY AND CAROL
JUNE 30, 1978

Though the pictures in the collage have been updated several times, the rainbow has remained at its center, leading us, at last, to truly follow our dream.

V. RAINBOW'S END

The legacy of this disaster is not the destruction
but the manner in which people like you
joined together in unity
to help rebuild hope and rebuild lives.

From invitation letter by the
Unmet Needs Committee for Disaster Recovery
Birmingham, Alabama

178

V-20. BIRMINGHAM REVISITED

*The power of love is stronger
than the power of the tornado.*

From Unmet Needs Committee invitation letter

Back To Birmingham

As winter at Carolina Landing drew to a close and buds began to appear on the dogwood trees, we were faced with a difficult decision. We had wanted to attend the second Holy Week Build in Americus, Georgia, that spring of 1999 but, unfortunately, Easter fell on April 4, just four days before the one-year anniversary of the Birmingham tornado. Since we hadn't made it to Birmingham during Thanksgiving to help build Habitat homes as we had promised Jan Bell, and also because we wanted to participate in the recovery celebrations, we opted to go there. We called Jan in mid-March to let her know we were heading her way.

I reached her on the cell phone in her car as she was dashing from one building site to another. In her usual effervescent manner, she exclaimed, "Oh, my gosh, Carol, this is a God Moment! I was just this minute feeling overwhelmed and needing help, wondering how I was going to accomplish everything to get ready for the anniversary day—and here you call and say you're coming! Praise Jesus!" If we'd still had any question about where we were supposed to be, we'd just received our answer.

We were met by Brother Steve shortly after pulling into the parking lot at Faith Baptist Church the next day. After chatting a few minutes, setting up the trailer and relaxing awhile, we enjoyed pizza and volleyball with a number of the church families. It felt natural to be back, and we were warmly welcomed during worship the next morning.

Sunday afternoon, we drove over to surprise Dorothy and Brenda. The first thing we noticed as we turned onto Mitchell Drive was that the house to the left of the road, which had been severely damaged, was now rebuilt. Also, there were big new houses on the two lots to the west of that one, where previously there had been only driveways leading to nothing.

Up on the hill we were excited to see Brenda and Lonnie's new house, situated to the left of its original site. Not thinking they would have the finances to build a "real home," they had at first constructed a cement block building where their former house had stood and had been using it both for their plumbing business and living quarters. However, the Unmet Needs Committee (which I will discuss in the next chapter) eventually put together the resources to build them a home. We knocked on Brenda and Lonnie's door, but no one answered.

Eagerly walking across the road to Dorothy's, we immediately noted how different her house looked—the new siding was on and a large covered deck had been built off the kitchen. Dorothy was indeed surprised when she opened the door. She quickly put on a pot of coffee, and as we caught up on each other's news the air was charged with the excitement of reuniting with someone with whom a deep and intense bond had been forged.

Much had been finished inside Dorothy's house as well—the ceiling had been sprayed, flooring laid, walls painted, the bathroom finished—and she had power! But as we looked around, we became aware that there were many little things still undone.

Dorothy had spent the winter with a relative and had just recently moved back into her house. Her clothes were piled in bags on the bedroom floor because she had no closet pole, and she needed help moving furniture and appliances so she could get organized and feel like she was really settled. Her air conditioner had been incorrectly wired, and the company wanted $700 to fix it. Dorothy looked tired and lacked her normal spark. We promised that as soon as the celebration was past, we would get everything in shape for her.

Getting Out Of The Way

Arriving at the Greater Birmingham Habitat office in Fairfield on Monday morning, we talked with Jan Bell for a few moments, and met some of the staff. Jan has an irresistible magnetism. Her upbeat, positive, and exuberant personality draws people to her and makes them want to do their best. In her forties, Jan is a mother of five whose boundless energy and enthusiasm are by no means all she has going for her. Years of working with her husband to create and run their highly successful Confrontation Point

Ministries in Tennessee, and her positions as Administrative Services Manager for a large HMO and Executive Director of the Alabama Kidney Foundation, all contributed to gaining essential skills and savvy for "working *with* the system" to accomplish a goal.

After her stints in the corporate world and with maintaining an already established charity, Jan felt drawn back to a position of ministry. When their family had lived in Tennessee, she had enjoyed working with her local Habitat affiliate. Just as she was beginning to feel restless for a new challenge, Jan saw an ad for Director of the Greater Birmingham Habitat affiliate. The affiliate had been struggling, and the morale of the staff was low. The affiliate was building just one house at a time, averaging four homes a year. The job offered an opportunity for Jan to do what she loved most—"to build up and turn things around." And so, in May of 1997, she took a large cut in salary, moved into a hole-in-the wall office and began working her magic.

Jan's desire is to serve "by emptying myself, and letting God be God." Framed and sitting on her bookcase is a personal reminder which says, *"Do not feel totally, personally, irrevocably responsible for everything. That's my job. Love, God."*

After taking the leadership position at Greater Birmingham HFH, Jan attracted a diverse and equally positive and skilled staff, whose talents were pushed to the maximum during the year after the tornado. "It is amazing the power of God when it is unleashed, when we get out of the way," she proclaims. The Greater Birmingham Habitat affiliate had since moved into a large church that was donated rent-free, including utilities, for two years, and had increased the number of houses built by 50% each year. Their goal was to complete100 homes by the end of 2000.

The Overview

Demian, a construction supervisor who in his earlier days had participated in the Civil Rights marches and voter registration drives in Birmingham, was asked to show us around the area and fill us in on what Habitat had accomplished since the tornado. It was definitely impressive. By the one-year anniversary, six homes had been completed for tornado victims. The first was built in a one-week blitz just two months after the tornado struck, and the other five were finished within the first six months. The affiliate also built fourteen additional homes.

Not too far from the office in Fairfield, we stopped to see the house we would be working on for the next week. Fairfield is a predominantly black community that had deteriorated and become riddled with drugs and crime. In 1988, the citizens elected Larry P. Langford as mayor, a black man who made it clear that drugs and crime would no longer be tolerated, and that the laws would be equally applied to all offenders. In fact, the signs as one enters the city read: *Fairfield—An older city moving in a new direction.*

By standing behind his commitment to firmness and fairness in cleaning up the city, Mayor Langford quickly gained the respect of the entire community and dramatic changes took place. One of the mayor's bold actions was to condemn rundown houses and ones used for dealing drugs and donate the properties to Habitat.

The house we were going to help finish was being financed by two Methodist churches whose members were also providing the labor. The on-site coordinator was Paulette West. We were introduced to her and discovered an amazing coincidence that immediately connected us. After five minutes of the usual introductory chitchat, we realized we had worked together that first day we had been sent up to Brenda's. Paulette was among the Methodists who had come in the van to help and had later left, leaving Larry and me gazing down into the ravine feeling so utterly alone. Paulette was happy to hear that Brenda's situation was looking much brighter than when she had left that day.

We visited the site on Grassilli Avenue where a 20-lot subdivision had been developed by Habitat through a grant from Jefferson County. Four homes were already completed and the families moved in. The foundations for three more had been poured, and we would later help put on the decking.

Finally, we headed to McDonald Chapel. We had anticipated that moment ever since we arrived. It was hard to imagine what it would look like, because our last memory was of curbsides piled high with debris. Many of the properties had not yet been cleared when we left the year before.

Our First Look

We came in the back road, which is elevated above the old mining camp and parked across from the first Habitat home built in Mac's Chapel. Exiting our vehicles, we stood with Demian looking out over the bowl-shaped community. We were bombarded with intense emotions and memories. Demian directed our gaze to two more Habitat homes before leaving us.

We climbed back into our car and started down the hill to get a closer look at the changes, stopping first by the "twin houses." Since the elderly sisters had stated adamantly in a newspaper interview that they would rebuild (at the very least, one home for the two of them), we were surprised to see that both of their lots remained vacant. Earnest Chapel, the marquee of which had read "Spring is a time for rebirth," had not yet been reborn, but we later learned that the Open Door Church near the highway deeded them a parcel of land which would enable their lot size to conform to new planning codes.

However, Mr. Johnson's house across the street, the one that was being rebuilt while we were working there, now looked as though it had never been disturbed. And in between the sisters' lots and the little chapel there was a beautiful new brick house replacing the one that we remembered peeking into and shaking our heads in disbelief. On the front porch an elderly lady was sitting in a chair, and a woman in her late sixties was standing near her. They watched us as we pointed and looked around. We thought we better introduce ourselves and tell them why we were there. We asked about the elderly sisters and learned that one had moved out of the area and the other was living with her daughter.

The 91-year-old lady told us how she had survived the storm sitting in her rocking chair in the little back bedroom that we had looked into. "Something just kept holding me down in that chair," she said, "even though I kept thinking I should get out of there. It felt like a strong hand on my shoulder making me stay put. Everything in the house was swirling around. When the tornado passed, the neighbor boys came looking for me and wanted to carry me out through the broken window, but I told them I wanted to walk out by myself if I could. They helped me over the jagged window ledge and shined a flashlight ahead of me so I wouldn't step on any of the downed wires."

This was the first instance, though there would be many more, of survivors recounting their frightful experience as though it had happened the night before.

Continuing down the street, we debated about what had been where. It all looked so different now, with a few big houses situated here and there in between barren stretches of land. Only a few tall, scraggly trees dotted the landscape. The corner lot we first cleared was still empty, as was the entire block. Many of the old lots were too small to satisfy present-day building requirements. Consequently, they had been consolidated or left vacant.

There was no continuity to the style of the houses, either. The whole area looked sad and disjointed. It didn't look anything like a community. I felt myself being overcome by depression.

I perked up a bit when I spotted Mariesha's house in the distance. We never learned whether it had been declared salvageable or not. The Chapel Hill Baptist Church on the corner of Xavier, the street Mariesha lived on, had been taken down to its foundation by the tornado. It was now rebuilt and the finishing touches were being added to the interior. We walked inside and looked around. It made us feel a little better to see a church coming back to life. The man across the road whose modular home had blown to the next lot had a new one set up on his site.

Turning left, we proceeded toward Mariesha's. Her block was the only section in Mac's Chapel that appeared to have reclaimed any semblance of a neighborhood. There were several modest, new homes across the street from her house, most of which had been constructed by the Mennonites. A couple of the neighbors had received enough insurance to have their homes rebuilt—and Mariesha's house now had a roof and new windows.

I knocked on the door and waited expectantly, wondering if she would remember me. But when it opened, it was her husband standing in the doorway. I'd forgotten that Mariesha worked. I explained who I was and told him I was hoping to talk with his wife. Without hesitation he gave me their phone number. As we walked back to the car I found myself feeling relieved that Mariesha hadn't been home. I suddenly felt very tired. We drove back to the trailer in silence.

Called To Build

By 8:30 a.m. Tuesday morning, we were painting—Larry doing his magic with the roller, and I with my trim brush. The home we were working on was for Faye Williams, a tornado survivor who, along with her children and grandchild, had been living in Oak Ridge (across from McDonald Chapel) in a home owned by her brother. Though they had all survived by gathering in the hallway, the house had been lifted off its foundation and twisted. The final blow was delivered by four pecan trees crashing down on it. The entire family was displaced.

Though Faye had heard about Habitat some years before and immediately after the tornado, she was not motivated to apply until her six months of temporary housing expired and she discovered she was ineligible for an extension of subsidized housing because she would not be moving back into her brother's home. If she wanted to stay in the shelter house, she would have to pay $600 a month—extremely difficult on what she earned from her job at the Jefferson County Tax Assessor's office. Faye was greatly relieved when she was selected for a Habitat home.

It was a genuine pleasure working with Paulette, a wife and mother in her early forties who was born and raised in Cullman, Alabama, a town where not a single black person lived. Fifty miles south in Birmingham, it had been much different. Paulette remembers watching on TV the ugly rioting and hosing of freedom marchers when she was six years old. She had been perplexed by what she saw, which was so contrary to the examples of love and caring for all people, without regard to race, exhibited by her parents.

Growing up with a love for people and a heart for service, Paulette was always involved in volunteer projects at her church and her children's school. However, for 20 years she had been praying for a distinct call to a specific service and, at last, believed she had received it. As Chairperson of the Outreach Committee at Trinity Methodist, she was asked to help lead a mission trip to Panama to address both medical and construction needs in the summer of 1997.

Her positive experience building in Panama (which she has done every year since) encouraged Paulette to become involved in her Methodist district's endeavor to build one Habitat home a year. She was asked to be chairperson of the steering committee to build the district's second home, and agreed on one condition: she wanted to learn how to build a house from the ground up.

For that, she turned to Rick Connelly, overseer of the district projects and an ordained minister and master builder who works full-time with the United Methodist outreach program called Kingdom Builders. The ministry provides construction resources for small-membership churches and addresses low income housing needs. Most of their work is done in conjunction with Habitat.

Rick was a patient instructor, and Paulette a quick learner. When we first worked with her on Faye's house, we assumed she had been in construction for many years. It was obvious she had found her niche.

Today, Paulette continues to build with Rick, though in a different capacity. Beginning in 2000, the two Methodist districts in Birmingham, consisting of 90 churches, committed to an ongoing program of sponsoring and building clusters of homes with the Greater Birmingham Habitat affiliate. This is an excellent example of how the work of Habitat is expedited through cooperative partnerships. Rick is the overall building coordinator, and Paulette guides the work of the steering committee.

Holy Week

During Holy Week we helped tie up loose ends at Faye's. On Good Friday, after several days of rain, a cement truck backed into the alley behind the house to pour the sidewalks and driveway. As it pulled forward to unload more cement, it became hopelessly entrenched in the infamous Southern red muck. A huge winch truck came to its rescue, and we all carried our lunches outside to watch as numerous attempts were made to extricate the tilted giant. Finally, it was coaxed out of its hapless predicament, and we all resumed work.

In the meantime, the crew had been filling wheelbarrows and buckets with cement and carrying them around front to pour the sidewalks. I told the foreman how impressed I was by his calm demeanor in such a frustrating and embarrassing situation. He shrugged it off. "When you've done this as long as I have," he said, "you learn that things don't always go right. It makes it a lot easier if you just accept it."

Easter Sunday we sang with the Faith Baptist choir. After enjoying a delicious meal and warm fellowship with one of the church families, we stopped by to see Dorothy and Brenda and drop off some cookies. Brenda was sick, but handed us a box in return. When we arrived at the trailer and opened it, we found a number of little gifts she'd been saving for us over the year and a collection of cards and letters she had begun writing but had never mailed. In them, she had poured out her feelings about how much the time we had spent with them meant to her and had affected her life. It was a poignant ending to a day that commemorates resurrection and new life.

Countdown

The excitement began to mount as everyone geared up for the anniversary celebration on Thursday. On Monday and Tuesday, Larry and I helped put decking on one of the foundations at Grassilli Avenue. At 6 a.m. on Wednesday, the first eight-hour shift of Alabama Power Service Organization workers began building "The 24-Hour House," which would be completed by 6 a.m. the following morning, April 8—the one-year anniversary of the tornado. Months of careful planning and preparation preceded the ambitious undertaking.

We spent Wednesday doing touch-up work on another Methodist-built house for a tornado survivor, up the street from Faye's. On our way home, we stopped to see the progress of the Alabama Power workers. The building site resembled a country fair.

A big tent was set up behind the home, providing continuous food, drinks and snacks for the hard-working volunteers. Radio broadcasts were taking place from a bus, and TV camera crews were everywhere conducting interviews. Habitat's construction manager Reg Olson, a man who had built major multi-million-dollar projects worldwide, aptly described the atmosphere, as well as his own feelings: "The organization and spirit here are like a revival! I can't think of one day more thrilling in my lifetime."

It was six p.m. when we arrived—just 12 hours after the first shift had begun. All the landscaping was in and the garden shed finished and painted. The last bits of siding on the front porch were being tacked in place and, inside, the sheetrock crew was at work. Using quick-drying spray-on mud, the interior would be ready to paint in about an hour. The Alabama Power workers seemed oblivious of all the commotion as they focused intently on carrying out their assignments. It was a truly magnificent feat. The house was finished by 5:30 a.m.—a half-hour ahead of schedule!

Celebration Time

The anniversary day was kicked off with a 7:30 a.m. prayer breakfast at the Fairfield Civic Center. We were welcomed by Mayor Langford, who chose the occasion to announce that his city was accepting Habitat's 21st Century Challenge to set a specific date by which to eliminate all substandard housing. After breakfast, a video prepared by Alabama ABC 33/40 TV was shown, followed by special recognition of the key people and organizations involved in the recovery. Millard Fuller gave the keynote address.

The closing challenge by the Bishop of the Episcopal Diocese of Alabama was delivered through a story. A small boy had become lost in a large cornfield. Many individuals searched diligently, but were unsuccessful in locating him. Finally, in order to systematize their efforts, someone suggested that all the volunteers join hands as they walked through the field. In a short while, they found the little boy's body, but their discovery was too late. One of the rescuers lamented, "Why didn't we join hands sooner?"

"We look back at how the tornado has united the church community and have to ask ourselves the same question," the Bishop remarked. "Why didn't we do it sooner?"

In step behind a bagpiper, Jan Bell led the crowd in a jubilant parade from the dining room out to the parking lot. Following a commissioning prayer, we gave a rousing cheer of "Oyee" before climbing into our cars and caravanning to the Grassilli site.

The families who would occupy the new homes on Grassilli stood beside Millard Fuller on a makeshift platform as he spoke with his usual passion to them and the volunteers and onlookers. He explained some of the reasons why Habitat continues to grow and spread. "One reason," he said, "is because it is God's idea. The plan is plagiarized from the Bible: it is based on interest-free loans and the precept that it is more blessed to give than to receive.

"Another reason is that Habitat does not look at homeowners as customers or clients; it does not operate like a lottery, bestowing houses on lucky winners or a special few." Habitat, he maintained, is a true *partnership* that makes it possible for the recipients to give also, through their faithful payments that help buy homes for others.

The new homeowners had lived in Pratt City (the last to be hit by the tornado), and one lady standing next to me said proudly, "These were my neighbors. God took a terrible thing and made a blessing for them. Before the tornado they had no hope of realizing their dream to own a decent home, but now they are! I am so happy for them."

Faye's house dedication was scheduled next. After Jan welcomed everyone and spoke about the incredible year that was culminating on that day, we joined in the litany of celebration as Millard dedicated the house.

Paulette expressed her appreciation to all the volunteers who worked on the house and to the members of both Methodist churches for their support, and shared about the special relationship she had developed with Faye. Then, she began to talk about angels, declaring that two very special ones had been sent to lift her up and keep her going at the very moment she had needed them. She asked Larry and me to come up onto the porch and presented us with a personal gift—a mosaic serving bowl she had purchased during her trip to the Holy Lands.

We were overwhelmed by Paulette's gracious gesture, but at the same time felt unworthy of the special attention. I thanked her, adding, as I have on other occasions, that it is our privilege to "drop in" for awhile, but we feel the real credit goes to those who are there for the long haul—day after day, week after week, month after month. Still, it felt good to know that our contribution had been so appreciated.

After the dedication of the other house, we went back to the trailer and rested awhile—before round two.

The Power Of Love

Larry and I decided to split up for the evening. He attended the local Birmingham Barons baseball game at Hoover Metropolitan Stadium, for which passes were mailed to tornado survivors and all who had helped in any way with the recovery. During the pre-game salute, all the survivors and volunteers were asked to come onto the playing field to receive a certificate of appreciation. The commemoration also included a video presentation by NBC 13 recognizing the many agencies and organizations involved in the recovery, and a moment of silence in memory of the losses suffered by so many.

After the Barons presented Millard Fuller with a check for $40,000 to finance a Habitat home, which they themselves would construct, Millard (who had been a pitcher during his college years at Auburn University) threw out the first ball. An ironic bit of information is that the year before, while the tornado was delivering its deadly wallop to the surrounding community, the Barons were playing a game in the Hoover Met. Late at night after the game ended, many returned to their homes unaware of what had taken place around them until the next morning.

Tools Of Redemption And Nurture

While Larry was at the Met, I was at the Rock Creek Church of God with Brenda attending the celebration and dedication of the new Family Life Center. Brenda's husband Lonnie had installed the plumbing. This event, also, was a joyous tribute to love and rebirth. The huge gymnasium was already packed with people, and they continued to file in. A large number stood throughout the program.

Celebratory music from the church's various choirs was the thread which wove together the evening. Four of the many members who were profoundly affected by the storm gave testimonies, including Ken Moses, the principal who had been flung across the road in his rental house. The church members completed his new home in five months, and after a

189

lengthy period of rehabilitation, he is now in good health and serving on the church's Board of Trustees. He travels all over the country with the Red Cross speaking about his experience. "Good things do come out of bad," is his reassuring message. "I'm at peace. I've never been happier in my life or had more."

Pat Williams thanked God for the new Family Life Center and all the ways in which it is used in reaching out to the community. "And last, but not least," he added, "it's an excellent tornado shelter!"—the response to which was hearty laughter.

We were all moved by the haunting song "The Storm," written by former Church of God member Luvenia Roberts, who herself has a harrowing story to tell about her face-to-face encounter with the tornado. Though the tornado spared her home, it altered the course of her husband's and her retirement plans by wiping out their three rental houses on adjoining lots.

After learning that Luvenia was an author and was also writing a book about the storm, I paid her a visit. Her book will concentrate on the effects of the tornado on the people in the Rock Creek area, fifty-five of whom she has interviewed extensively. "I already know the title," she told me. "It is *The Big Black Wall*, because that is the most common description given by people who saw it." The refrain of her song echoes:

> *We have lost some best beloved ones;*
> *We have seen the storm cloud run,*
> *But we've gained life's precious secret;*
> *We're God's children every one.*

In a later letter, Luvenia shared: "Rock Creek is slowly but surely building back, filling in gaps and healing, but it will never be the same Rock Creek of my childhood. We had our sense of safety stripped away, along with the ten members of our community and the hundreds and hundreds of ancient trees which shaded our grandparents and our great-grandparents. That link to our past has been broken, but we have not looked back very much, only forward."

In his dedication remarks, Pastor Staggs declared, "Our blessings are so many, we cannot enumerate them. We have become rich by getting acquainted with so many new friends. Never again will we take things for granted! These new buildings are tools of redemption and nurture."

As his voice choked with emotion, Pastor Staggs gave a moving tribute to Brother Steve, proclaiming that he was indeed his brother's keeper. "He was there for me *daily*," he marveled, "praying with me, encouraging me, funneling money to us, giving us contacts for our building and other needs. I don't know what we would have done without him." Brenda and I were not in the least surprised at his assessment.

After the program, we were invited to enjoy refreshments and tour the new center. Each room was decorated with beautiful murals and delightful wallpaper borders. I was surprised to learn that, with the exception of some extra storage space, the building is an exact reproduction of the previous center, which had been dedicated exactly one year before the storm. I was asking questions of one of the teachers standing proudly in her room when I realized she was the same young woman I had spoken with the year before while she was outside tending children in their temporary quarters. She'd had the same serene smile on her face even then.

The Theology Of The Hammer

We counted ourselves honored to be invited to join the Habitat staff for their own celebration dinner the following Thursday. After thanking her outstanding colleagues, Jan presented Larry and me with official Habitat hammers inscribed with our names. They are among our most prized possessions, for they symbolize what had been so profoundly demonstrated in Birmingham and the message of a humble carpenter many years ago: *love is not real unless it is translated into action.*

V-21. ANATOMY OF A RECOVERY

The race has won—the human race.

Dr. Mike Harper, UMCOR, at Volunteer Appreciation Dinner

OVERVIEW

God's Spring Cleaning

Everyone I spoke with about the recovery in Birmingham echoed the observations and sentiments expressed at the Volunteer Appreciation Dinner hosted by the Birmingham Interfaith Tornado Recovery Group two weeks following the anniversary celebrations. Not only was the recovery remarkable for its swift success in addressing the physical and emotional needs of the storm survivors, but it was agreed by the key players and many others that that success was due in great measure to the efforts of the community-at-large to confront, redress, and heal old injustices and wounds.

Birmingham's accomplishment can be attributed to its willingness to clean out the corners instead of simply attempting a surface makeover. I was startled at first when Jan Bell referred to the tornado as "God's urban renewal plan" and, likewise, when Mariesha called it "God's spring cleaning." Later, I realized how insightful those statements were. The tornado had blown away the old status quo and cleared a path for both physical *and* spiritual renewal to take place. Failure to address the spiritual needs of a community is sometimes one of the reasons that other cities recovering from a disaster cannot boast the same positive results as Birmingham.

Following is an overview of the many elements that must be present in order to render a recovery successful. A great deal of soul-searching and a monumental amount of time and hard work preceded the happy ending we were all praising and commemorating in Birmingham.

Official Statistics

The statistics provided by The Unmet Needs Committee For Disaster Recovery and The Birmingham Interfaith Tornado Recovery Group are, in themselves, impressive. Fifty-four agencies and organizations comprised the two groups. The former included the city's trusted Community Foundation of Greater Birmingham, Habitat for Humanity, the Children's Aid Society, American Red Cross, Salvation Army, United Way, both the Alabama Power Foundation and Alabama Power Service Organization, NAACP (National Association for the Advancement of Colored People), the JCCEO (Jefferson County Commission on Economic Opportunity), and numerous other civic and religious organizations.

The Interfaith Group included all the churches, church associations and outreach ministries. A number of church organizations were also represented on the Unmet Needs Committee. The two committees met separately and jointly each week.

Of the 2200 families affected by the storm, 2180 were located and contacted by the Disaster Recovery Team, and 1538 were provided with information and services. Property damage was sustained by 1140 residents, 820 incurred major damage to their homes, and 432 homes were totally destroyed. Assistance with demolition and debris removal was provided at 900 sites, 208 sites received repair and rebuilding support, 144 homes were repaired, and 64 homes were rebuilt.

Over 6,000 volunteers assisted with disaster emergency and relief services during the first six weeks after the tornado, and another 6,000 helped with disaster recovery, including rebuilding and repairing homes, case management, counseling services and community support groups. It is estimated that 96,000 volunteer hours were contributed in the first twelve months following the April 8 tornado!

The amount of money pumped into the effort was also exceptional. Excluding private insurance and private funds, $12 million was provided by nonprofit organizations, $6 million by the federal government, and $30 million by Jefferson County, the City of Birmingham, and utility companies. This large infusion of money was one of the critical factors in the success of the recovery.

Response, Relief, And Recovery

When a disaster strikes, *emergency response* groups are the first to arrive. In most instances, the local Emergency Management Teams, relief agencies, churches and volunteers are on their own to handle the first 24 to 48 hours. This includes search and rescue, medical treatment, emergency food and shelter, fire suppression, disconnecting dangerous utilities and securing the area. The National Guard will most likely be called upon to aid in the emergency phase, including protecting the disaster area against looters. The emergency phase in Birmingham lasted five days.

In both Birmingham and Spencer (Salem), we were involved primarily in what is known as the *relief phase* of a disaster. That phase usually begins as soon as all victims are accounted for and the area is safe to enter. It includes clean-up, getting people into temporary housing and providing food, water, clothing, medications and other household necessities of daily living. The greater the magnitude of the disaster, the longer the relief phase will last. In Birmingham the relief phase stretched to seven weeks. In Spencer, the major relief work was accomplished in less than two weeks.

Temporary housing is the greatest relief need. It is important to the emotional well being of disaster survivors for them to be situated in private living quarters quickly. Prepared meals, groceries and household supplies are plentiful and easy to come by, as I have earlier described. The Red Cross may provide housing assistance for up to a month for those who have no other recourse. In addition, they give each person a standard sum of money to replace clothing, personal effects, lost medications and eyeglasses. They also give vouchers for medical-related accessories and services and deliver meals during the active relief phase. In most cases, however, these direct services are only available for a few weeks, although the Red Cross later sits as a member of the long-term recovery team.

The *initial recovery phase* begins even as the relief phase is still in progress. FEMA's initial role is to get people into apartments or houses for at least two months (with the possibility of extending to 18 months) until an assessment can be made of the status of their homes and the length of time required to repair or rebuild. They also provide grants of $100 to $5000 for uninsured victims to make their homes safe, secure and sanitary.

Usually, during the process of evaluating the extent of damage, determining which properties are salvageable, and getting people connected to insurance companies and government and other agencies to apply for the financial assistance they will need to proceed with rebuilding, many of the faith groups are already at work repairing homes. Our work in Birmingham for Dorothy and her family was part of this phase.

Often in the initial recovery phase, people are still numb or in a state of denial as to the full impact of what has happened to them. They may tend to be unrealistic about what it will take to put their lives back together. As in other situations, people vary in their response to major catastrophes. Some react like Dorothy and Brenda by getting right to business. Others are immobilized and refuse help or fail to apply for the services they are eligible for. It is essential for relief workers to be aware of these variances and to make sure such people do not "fall through the cracks."

Business, Business, Business

The amount of business that needs to be taken care of is mind-boggling. Anyone who has ever lost their wallet can attest that losing the money was the least of their aggravation. Duplicating driver's licenses and canceling checks and credit cards are tedious and time-consuming. Imagine adding to the loss of your driver's license the disappearance of your birth certificates, medical records, Medicare or Medicaid cards, insurance policies, vehicle registrations, bank statements, income tax records, etc.

During those first few weeks, the major relief agencies and FEMA make themselves as accessible as possible, setting up in central locations in the communities and doing their best to inform people through TV, flyers and newsletters about what is available. But even for those who are not in crisis, much of this information is complicated and difficult to understand.

Many people do not realize that FEMA is primarily a loan broker. When they hear it announced on TV that FEMA is on the way to help, there is a tendency to picture the "men in blue" arriving with shovels, rakes and hammers. Instead, they come with brochures, telephone numbers and forms to fill out. "For one thing," explained Faye Williams, "you are so dazed, you are unable to answer questions such as 'What items did you have in your house and what did they cost?' One time I couldn't remember my age when asked. In some places before they will help you, they want to see your ID— but it was blown away!"

Wanda Long, former family coordinator for the Greater Birmingham Habitat affiliate, described in Habitat's 1st Quarter 2000 *Affiliate Update* how some of the storm-related variables frustrated the application process for tornado survivors. "The Application Review Committee had difficulty gathering the necessary documentation because the applicants' documents had blown away. The credit counseling team had difficulty for the same reason, but also because the applicants were still in shock. The home visit team had difficulty because many families didn't have a stable place to stay—some were moving from relative to relative every few days. Site visitation was difficult because there was not a house standing for blocks. There were no house numbers to refer to, and much of the land had been declared environmentally unsafe."

Under normal circumstances, it is tedious and often frustrating to come up with all the required payment records, loan numbers, financial assets, copies of income tax forms, etc., when applying for a bank loan. For the person who has just lost not only all their records, but their home, furnishings and family mementos, their vehicles, their eyeglasses, perhaps a family pet, or even worse, a family member, neighbor or friend—being required within a week or two to contact all the myriad agencies that are offering assistance, make major decisions about rebuilding, and fill out loan applications greatly magnifies the stress they are already under.

Another one of our concerns about the role of the agencies is that they are often gone before some people are even out of the hospital or many others are finally able to begin recognizing and coping with their needs. Wanda stated in her Habitat assessment, "Nearly two years later we still are learning about the needs of the survivors with whom we are building. Many feel that . . . the service agencies withdrew too soon and that they should have stayed for at least 18 months, or until families got on their feet again."

Should It Happen To You

The following list of steps a disaster survivor must take in order to stabilize their situation and procure the services and help they need to recover may be of benefit in bringing home the enormity of the task and the implications for long-term recuperation:

1) Get help with immediate survival needs, contact family members who may be concerned.
2) Cover or secure any furniture or valuables which were not lost.
3) Get situated in suitable living quarters, procure necessities such as food and clothing, try to salvage any household remains.
4) Find out what services and help are available, contact insurance companies (if insured), bank, places which may have copies of needed records.

5) If insured, wait for the adjuster to arrive and determine whether the home can be salvaged or if it is a complete loss, and get an estimate of what will be paid. (This is when one finds out if they have a good company and/or whether they had adequate coverage.)

6) If uninsured, determine if there are enough personal resources to rebuild or whether one qualifies for any kind of conventional loan. (Depending on the income level of the affected area, oftentimes a large percentage of the people will not qualify. In addition to losing their homes, their jobs or businesses also may have been lost or severely affected. Many survivors are often elderly, dependent on social security or small pensions.)

7) If unqualified for a regular loan and not independently wealthy, apply to FEMA for a low-interest loan through the Small Business Administration (SBA). (Even if they qualify, they may or may not receive the full amount needed to rebuild.)

8) If unqualified for an SBA loan (and many won't qualify), apply to FEMA for a grant to help rebuild the home. (In Birmingham, the maximum grant was $12,500!) At this point, since obviously they cannot build a house for $13,000, *they are now dependent on the generosity of their community for their future housing needs.*

9) If insured, but coverage is inadequate to rebuild (For most, what they receive will not come close to replacing their house. Most people, particularly those in older houses, are grossly underinsured.), follow the same steps as the uninsured to secure the balance of the financing to rebuild (with the likely outcome that they, too, will end up dependent on the mercy of their community).

After all that, even if financing is secured, they still may not be able to proceed because they may find that their lot no longer meets building and zoning requirements, or their property does not pass the perk test for a septic system. They may, therefore, discover that in addition to having to build a new house, they also need to purchase a new piece of property.

It is at this juncture that a well conceived, efficiently administered *long term recovery plan* is vital if there is to be any hope for the majority of the people affected by the disaster.

As one can see, the agencies we most associate with disasters, the ones which are so visible on television in the early days after a tragedy strikes, do play a significant role in the initial phases of meeting survivors' needs.

However, when it comes to the long-term, nitty-gritty work, it is our local governments, businesses and agencies, our churches and ordinary citizens like you and me who will determine whether our neighbors remain simply survivors or are able to put the pieces of their lives back together and resume normal living. That is the part of the story we never see on television—except, perhaps, in the immediate broadcast area of the disaster.

The Necessity Of Money

All the conscientious efforts in the world are impotent without money to back them up. When people hear about a disaster, they respond generously, sending millions of dollars to relief agencies. Therefore, it is essential that they understand the process so they can make informed decisions about where and when they contribute their money.

As just outlined, the large relief agencies play a significant role in the emergency and relief phases and, for that reason, it is important that they be supported as a part of one's regular charitable giving. However, when it comes to getting money quickly, directly, and with the least expense and red tape to the people and places where it is needed most, their flexibility is often thwarted by the guidelines they must adhere to.

In the case of the Red Cross, for instance, their response is directed strictly to *emergency needs* on a case-by-case basis. Once other options are available, usually within a few weeks, requests for help will often be denied.

In addition, it is important to know that unless one's donation is designated for a specific disaster, it may be used for other purposes of an organization. There are a number of options if one wants their donation to have a direct impact in a community. For immediate needs, it may be sent to a church of preference in the affected area. If the desire is for it to be used in rebuilding and recovery work, money may be sent to a local relief fund such as the governor's fund for Spencer, to the interfaith or unmet needs committees, or to one of the churches or agencies that comprise them. It is always important to designate the gift to be used only for the disaster.

If a more personal connection is desired, one can call a church or agency and ask about the needs of a particular family. Money can be sent directly to them, or an account set up in their name at a builders' supply store for purchasing materials. Some communities even establish an adopt-a-family program. It may take a few phone calls and a little more effort, but there is satisfaction in knowing one's money has truly made a difference in someone's life.

CRITICAL SUCCESS FACTORS

Money

The *first critical success factor* for Birmingham was that very quickly nearly $1.5 million in donations from private citizens was received and directed to trusted local agencies and churches.

FEMA also came through in a timely manner (which is not always the case) with $4 million in loans through the SBA, $1 million in individual family grants, and another $3 million in other monies and services, including a $300,000 grant to provide crisis counseling and support groups—all critical to the long-term recovery.

Once the money was in hand, however, there had to be agreement as to how it would be disbursed. This is often where communities become bogged down in power struggles, thereby delaying or diluting the effectiveness of their efforts.

Trust

Trust between the groups and agencies working together for the recovery is the *second critical success factor*. Doris Harris, Case Manager Coordinator for the recovery, states in her final report, "Divisive issues have a way of surfacing during crisis. This crisis was no different. The question before us in April was 'how do we take what we know of each other and create something new for the good of all?' That is not an easy question to answer in good times. It becomes even more difficult during hard times. This disaster qualified as a genuinely hard time for the City of Birmingham."

On April 22, the President of United Way of Central Alabama called the first meeting of what would become the Unmet Needs Committee. The committee reached a consensus to recommend that three of the community's most highly respected leaders serve as co-chairs. In Doris' words, "Their presence raised the trust factor 150%." One of the first things that was agreed upon was a covenant stipulating how members would work together and respect each other.

Two days later, the first discussions about an Interfaith Recovery Group were held. That group chose two co-facilitators to guide its meetings, and agreed to recommend the appointment of one person to oversee the rebuilding process and one to guide the case management work. They confronted the issue of personal agendas head on, agreeing that whenever they met, personal agendas would be left outside the room. The only agenda on the table was to be the *tornado agenda.*

Although there were a great many dynamics to work through in both groups, agreement on the spirit in which they would operate helped to expedite the process. Gradually, the role of each group was defined, a communication link established, and an orderly process to meet the needs of the tornado survivors carved out. The Unmet Needs Committee would focus on determining the amount of funds necessary to satisfy needs on a case-by-case basis. When an amount was established, the agencies would in a sense "bid" on who would contribute what to whom, in addition to providing whatever other services were their fortes.

The Interfaith Group's focus would be on providing leadership, coordination and labor for the rebuilding. Habitat for Humanity had a presence on both committees, as did some other faith groups because, as well as providing labor, they brought the $1 million dollars (contingent on matching funds) pledged by Habitat International to add to the mix. Of course, any tornado victim who rebuilt through Habitat needed to meet Habitat's financial and credit requirements, adjusted in minor ways to take into account the special circumstances created by the disaster.

Thus, an organizational plan and a plan for disbursement of funds were formulated which gave the agencies control over how their money was to be spent, and at the same time provided crucial flexibility. The early infusion of the large sums of money and the unusually quick resolution of the process of disbursement enabled the recovery effort to get a jump-start and to leverage additional dollars received from government sources.

Case Management

Developing an orderly, integrated system for managing cases was another critical factor. Many agencies—both government and private—had procedural policies that needed to be adhered to. FEMA normally turns over to the Red Cross the cases of families who have received maximum grants. In order to access those cases, a release procedure had to be devised. It was also critical to define and coordinate the whole process from beginning to end in order to uniformly gather and report the necessary information, prevent duplication of services, insure that survivors were all receiving the same information, safeguard confidentiality, assure donors that their money was being spent responsibly, and to thwart those few who would seek to take advantage of the system. After countless hours of hammering out the details, a system was set in motion that proved to be highly efficient.

The Interfaith Group asked Doris Harris, who had been a staff member of the Birmingham Baptist Association and involved in the disaster response from day one, to be the Case Management Coordinator. Ricky Thacker, the pastor who had coordinated the clean-up efforts in Mac's Chapel and had in his background hands-on maintenance and building experiences, became the Construction Coordinator. An Area Coordinator was assigned to each of the eight communities affected.

The Unmet Needs Committee enlisted eight Case Managers, all persons on loan from cooperating social agencies in Birmingham, and developed a working file for their use. An additional 25 social workers were also involved. The mental health grant, which was administered by the Jefferson/Blount/Shelby Mental Health Authority (JBS) profoundly impacted the effectiveness of the effort by providing for ten mental health workers who set about the task of contacting every affected family.

Ricky Thacker, and the leadership team of the Interfaith Group, paved the way for a smooth, efficient and orderly process for the rebuilding by first meeting with the City of Birmingham to discuss the procedures and permits for rebuilds and repairs. They were given the necessary forms, codes, contact persons, and fee structures. Likewise, they met with both the Jefferson County Commission and the Jefferson County Board of Health to iron out issues with them, particularly with regard to sewer and septic systems.

Ricky developed a file to be used for each rebuild, which proved to be an invaluable, timesaving tool. It included a procedural checklist with instructions for 53 steps leading to completion, a map, copy of the intake form and release forms, procedures for obtaining building permits and inspections and the necessary applications, and a worksheet for figuring materials needs and costs.

Seven areas were delineated for rebuilding, and a church denomination providing rebuilding service was assigned to each. Money from insurance, loans, and government and private sources could be leveraged to finance the building of houses by using the volunteer labor. At the end of the year, when volunteer labor became more scarce, Outreach International, a nonprofit agency that builds government subsidized housing, was contracted to finish up the last of the work.

What I have described is only a partial picture of all that has to take place in order to achieve a smooth and satisfactory recovery. In addition, an Internet database program was developed to help prevent duplication and to share information, a procedure for bringing the recovery to a proper conclusion was devised and, last but not least, plans were made for the community to celebrate its accomplishments and have a sense of closure.

At the end of her culminating report, Doris emphasized the need to remain organized and prepared in the event of a future emergency—good advice for any community to consider. The official report on the Birmingham Recovery is available to any community desirous of being ready to work as a cohesive unit in the event of a disaster or interested in benefiting from what was learned in Birmingham.

SEEDS OF CHANGE

Human Relations and Race Relations

Doris Harris describes in her report the daunting task of uniting all the diverse agencies, groups, individuals, and communities to work toward the single goal of recovery. "One day we all woke up and there were over 50 agencies and faith groups sitting in the same room wanting to help the same 2200 families. Everyone was moved to action by their compassion, and at the same time overwhelmed by the enormity of the task at hand. Add to that the need to arrive at a single agenda and a direction in which everyone could work. Then throw in a sense of urgency to help families begin to rebuild and recover, a state of shock throughout the community, and the fatigue that existed due to involvement in the emergency and clean-up phases, and you have one anxious situation." Now factor in an undercurrent of racial tensions, and you can begin to see the enormity of what Birmingham faced.

Doris schooled me on the role of "stake holders" or "pillars" of a community. What they say and how they react has far-reaching influence in setting the mood and tone of a community. It has been discovered that communities also have negative stakeholders who use a crisis to vent their personal anger and discontent publicly, feeding and fueling gossip and misperceptions. Unfortunately, the media is often quick to give these negative voices a platform.

In one case, the cry of the negative stakeholder was that their community was not receiving the same resources and aid as others. In another, the stakeholder instigated the pitting of neighbor against neighbor—"he or she got more than I did." Identifying these negative stakeholders and defusing them was handled very effectively by the Disaster Response Crisis Team, the mental health workers funded by FEMA.

It is only natural that the thorny issue of race would surface during a disaster. Both the black and white communities in Birmingham had a long history of being guarded, at best, and openly distrustful and suspicious of each other at worst. If contingents from both groups were going to work closely together to maximize the recovery endeavors, efforts needed to be made to break down those barriers of mistrust. Countless behind-the-scene hours were spent by mediators with that aim and, to their credit, there gradually emerged a feeling that the "system" could work for the benefit of everyone. "You have to trust the system," Doris would often say to some who had long felt outside or victimized by it. Overcoming distrust was a gigantic step and another critical factor in Birmingham's successful recovery.

Communities, like people, have distinct personalities and reflect a representative consciousness of their members. Some are more healthy and able to cope with stresses than others. It is also my observation that the collective faith of a community is a key factor in how it will react when under pressure. Some communities are resilient, used to being cooperative and self-reliant. Others feel powerless and dependent, unable to help themselves. And though the members of some communities live in close proximity, they are disconnected and distrustful of each other.

The tornado shook every community to its very foundation. It left people with no recourse but to rely on each other, to help each other, to trust each other. By so doing, a transformation, a shift in consciousness, took place that, hopefully, will not easily be reversed. One of the most common statements people made to me was that they now knew their neighbors and were more mindful of the needs of those around them. The storm brought with it not only winds of destruction, but also the seeds of change and an atmosphere of good will. Its legacy is renewal and hope for a better tomorrow.

Sixteenth Street and Sixth Avenue North

I was in my late teens and early twenties during the Civil Rights Movement, living at the time in California, far from much of the action. Nevertheless, my heart was with those who were trying to effect the changes that would free our black brothers and sisters to take their rightful place as equals in our society. I remember the tumultuous scenes on TV—the police dogs straining at their leashes, the policemen's sticks clubbing freedom marchers, the jets of water from fire hoses knocking people off their feet, and Governor George Wallace standing defiantly in front of the University entrance. My heart was heavy with sadness over the bombing of the 16th Street Baptist Church and the four precious, innocent lives that were snuffed out. Those incidents etched so vividly in my mind all took place in Birmingham, Alabama.

Paulette and I spent an afternoon in the Birmingham Civil Rights Institute, which portrays the Civil Rights struggle through multi-media displays. It brought to life the sounds, images and urgency of those days, and caused all the old feelings to wash over me. I had been so engrossed in our work in Birmingham, I had never taken time to make the connection with what had happened there 35 years before. But as we started across the street to enter the 16th Street Baptist Church, the fact that I was standing in the very intersection where so many of the "images" were created jolted me as though I'd been hit with a stream of water from one those hoses years ago. How fitting that the Institute was erected at that very spot, so that one could not only relive those events pictorially, but also stand on the very ground where they had occurred and absorb the vibrations of the past. It was a moment I find impossible to adequately describe.

It had slipped my mind that there once were "separate" baseball leagues. In the days of segregation, Birmingham fielded two Barons teams—one black and one white. I saw Willie Mays pictured in one of the team photos, and thought about how far Birmingham has come since then. Perhaps not far enough and fast enough for some, but far, nevertheless. Several nights before, an integrated Birmingham Barons team had joined their community in celebrating a healing—not just from the physical wounds of a tornado, but more importantly a healing of the spirit. Yes, I thought, Birmingham has come a long way. I'm glad we were here for this pivotal moment. We can now replace the old memories of Birmingham with kinder, gentler ones.

The Courageous Survivors

The process of healing takes time and cannot be minimized or rushed. There are many wounds and scars and haunting memories that will take many years to heal and fade. Many have needed help in coping with their emotions and the formidable obstacles they face. Weathering a storm is a recurring challenge for most.

As with any human crisis, there are distinct stages everyone goes through to a lesser or greater degree until they arrive at acceptance and can move forward with their lives. But most ministers and counselors I spoke with were heartened by the dignity and grace with which the survivors were working their way back to wholeness. It goes without saying that there are probably some who will never fully recover, but the majority seem to be taking one day at a time, thankful that they are alive and mindful of what a precious gift life is.

That's What It's All About

Dr. Mike Harper of UMCOR, and Moderator of the Interfaith Group, was the host of the aforementioned Volunteers Building Together appreciation dinner. In his opening remarks he stated, "We have crossed all kinds of lines to deal with a situation bigger than race, creed, religion, gender, politics. . . Not since the days of Civil Rights have so many people crossed so many lines for something bigger than themselves. God's work," he continued, "is to bring order out of chaos, and we are all called to be co-creators in that task."

Every speaker echoed those sentiments in one way or another that evening. Dr. Harry Brown, Moderator of the Unmet Needs Committee, called the April 8 tornado "a defining moment for the Birmingham community." Appreciation from the victims was expressed by Rev. Staggs of the Church of God, who confessed that they had always been a fairly independent group. "After the tornado," he said, "we only knew need. We were broken, in need of repair. After 51 years in ministry, my life has been forever changed because of all of you who loved and gave so much."

Wendy Garner of News 13, before the viewing of that station's video tribute to the volunteers, read from the Gospel of Mark: ". . . whoever wants to become great among you must be your servant." (Mark 10:43 NIV) "That is what has happened here," she proclaimed. Someone that night quoted Martin Luther King, Jr.'s hopeful statement that "the moral arc of the universe bends toward love." I believe those words capture the promise of what took place in Birmingham.

All of the leaders who had devoted their entire lives to the recovery during that year reiterated that every single person was essential to its success. The ongoing presence of fresh volunteers from out of town not only lent physical support, but also moral strength, reminding community leaders and survivors who were mired in the everyday nitty gritty that they were not alone, and rejuvenating them when they were weary.

No one person or group was more or less necessary than another. Leaders, organizers, financial supporters, businesses, long-term committed volunteers, short-term volunteers, emergency service organizations, the religious community, mental health workers, media, all levels of government, agencies, the churches and businesses which loaned key workers, and the survivors themselves—all were vital links in the chain of recovery.

There were few dry eyes when Claire Gross, grandmother of Austin Lowery, a six-year-old boy who had survived the tornado in McDonald Chapel huddled and praying in a closet with his mother, finished reading Austin's Story. She had composed it from Austin's account of his ordeal. When the worst was over, Austin "had been real worried about my dog Bear and my friends. Well, I found out Old Bear was in the basement with the Methodist folks, and they didn't even care that he was a Baptist chow. Mama said it was the same with people. She said it didn't matter what church you went to or what color you were. She said we were here to help each other—even an old smelly dog like Bear."

V-22. SAVING GRACE

To me, faith is not just a noun but also a verb.

Jimmy Carter, *Living Faith*

Beacons Of Hope

No discussion of the recovery process could be complete without looking at the role the churches played. In my opinion, there aren't enough superlative words to describe the work of the faith community in the response and recovery. Their responses were exemplary in all phases— emergency, relief, and recovery. I completely agree with the assessment of Wilbur Litwiller, a regional director for Mennonite Disaster Service: "If the faith community doesn't work, many victims of disasters are lost." It would be almost impossible to raise enough money to pay for the labor and other services they provide.

Almost every church left standing in the areas hit by the storm, as well as dozens on the outskirts of the communities, was a beacon of hope. They instantly sprang into action, becoming stores and restaurants, as well as places where one's needs could be made known and addressed. Not a single church that was damaged made any move toward repairing its buildings until the relief phase had ended and they had done everything possible to meet the immediate needs of the survivors. All their normal activities were deferred until the crisis was past. Let me recount the efforts of a few of the congregations in the Rock Creek area.

On The Spot

Union Hill Baptist sustained $80,000 worth of damage and 37 of its families' homes were either lost or heavily damaged. Rev. Howard Thompson, his wife, and nearby members were out with flashlights in the dark immediately after the storm passed over. Unable to clear the road in

207

front of the church where the fallen tree lay and the deputy sheriff was trapped, they set about checking on neighbors and parishioners. As soon as the lights came on 30 minutes later, they brought food from their homes and began preparing meals for the workers and victims.

I will digress a moment here to assuage any lingering curiosity about the fate of the deputy sheriff. It took several hours for people to cut away the tree in which he and his car were entangled. Able to move his hands, he kept in radio contact with his dispatcher, who warned him that a second tornado was headed their way. Turning on his loudspeaker, the officer told the people to leave and take cover—but everyone kept working to free him. The tornado passed over without touching down, and the deputy sheriff was at last extricated and taken to the hospital. He was dismissed later that night.

The intense relief effort at Union Hill Baptist Church continued for six weeks, during which three home-cooked meals a day were served in their fellowship hall and delivered to many families at their temporary sites. A well-organized "grocery store" was set up, and clothing filled offices and classrooms. Money funneled in from all over and was dispersed according to need, to anyone in need, and without respect to their church affiliation or whether they even lived in Rock Creek.

Bethel Baptist in Pleasant Grove, about ten miles away, spearheaded the collection of supplies and channeled them to Union Hill. Two refrigerated trucks were parked outside for perishable food. Countless hours were spent cooking, cleaning up, and stocking shelves and organizing donations. One couple from Florida, who had previously owned a thrift store, came in their RV and spent a week lending their professional touch to the operation. Toward the end of the critical period, meals were tapered to two, then one a day, and finally discontinued when it was apparent that most people were able to provide for themselves. However, a storehouse of goods was maintained for anyone who needed them for a full year afterward.

Concord Baptist, about a mile from the storm zone, also mobilized immediately. Though they soon stopped serving meals because of duplication of effort, they continued to dispense goods, and their building became the center for numerous storm-related services and meetings.

Every Little Bit Helps

Though the amount of donated items is sometimes overwhelming, particularly in respect to clothing, they are vital to the survivors—if they can be convinced to take them. From a monetary standpoint, they are invaluable.

Remember that these people have lost everything—right down to their underwear. The money they would otherwise spend to replace their clothing and household furnishings and restock their pantries, as well as ongoing purchases of food, toiletries, laundry detergent, light bulbs, etc., can be directed instead toward the task of rebuilding. Even those who had insurance quickly found that it did not begin to cover all their expenses.

Almost as important is the energy that is conserved by not having to run to stores and battle crowds. Survivors need every ounce of available energy to cope with the myriad facets of recovery and rebuilding. In the initial weeks, people could eat their meal and pick up what they needed in one stop, grabbing some moral support, as well.

The Little Church With The Big Heart

On the outskirts of Rock Creek sits the West Concord Church of Christ (50 members), whose building sustained $90,000 damage. Though none of their own parishioners were affected, they held services in the church basement and concentrated on dispensing help in any form they could.

A year later, Rev. and Mrs. Pilgrim's eyes still teared as they spoke about that terrible night, exacerbated for them by Rev. Pilgrim being in Georgia in a revival while Mrs. Pilgrim anxiously awaited the arrival of their daughter-in-law and two young grandsons who were en route from Tennessee. The Pilgrims pulled out a map of the storm path and showed me where their daughter had missed intersecting the eye of the storm by no more than 10 minutes.

Armed with maps and accompanied by volunteers from other churches, members began canvassing the Rock Creek area to find out who needed help and to spread the word that they were available for assistance. As their efforts became known, they learned of situations by word of mouth and other churches and agencies referred people to them.

In addition to donated food and clothing, the church was the repository and distributor of a tractor-trailer load of blankets and Family Food Boxes (packed with staples to feed a family of four for a week) delivered by the Churches of Christ Disaster Relief Effort headquartered in Nashville, Tennessee.

Besides supplies, monetary donations were also pouring into the West Concord Church. A former member who lived in St. Louis called and said her congregation would send $10,000, but when the check arrived it was for $25,000! The Pilgrims' daughter, who lived in Mississippi, spread the word over the Internet and donations began arriving from all over the country. Mrs. Pilgrim literally worked herself to exhaustion coordinating their church's relief efforts.

Little known before the storm, the Church of Christ's exceptional response has drawn it into the community, and its members will be forever remembered not just for the money sent by Church of Christ members nationwide, but for the loving way in which it was dispensed—not only to provide appliances and furniture (such as Dorothy received) to as many people as they could reach, but also to help people with rent, motels, car rentals, clean-up, roof repairs, and even something as small as a new pair of shoes for little Scott to attend church, personally delivered by Jan Smith, their "delivery angel." The nearby May town Church of Christ (90 members) mirrored West Concord's efforts. Between both churches, close to a half million dollars in goods and services was dispersed!

Coping With Faith

One morning I visited with Mrs. Carolyn Staggs, wife of the pastor of the Church of God, which had been so profoundly affected by the storm. We met in their rented fifth wheel trailer situated next to the damaged parsonage. She and her husband were doing their best to cope with the loss of six of their members as well as the overwhelming needs of their parishioners. Pastor Staggs spent literally hundreds of hours in those initial weeks counseling and supporting members, as well as trying to meet their needs in concrete ways such as paying their insurance deductibles. The need was staggering, and that didn't take into account the complete rebuilding of the Family Life Center and the major repairs to the church and parsonage. Their faith and having the entire community behind them sustained them through their long ordeal.

The Gentle Giant

Three miles down the road from Rock Creek is Faith Baptist Church, shepherded by the "gentle giant" Brother Steve, who was extremely frustrated the morning after the tornado struck because he and members of his congregation were not allowed into the storm site to help. The next day Ed Cruce, Director of Missions for the Bessemer Baptist Association, called and requested that Faith Baptist serve as the volunteer headquarters for the Rock Creek and Oak Grove areas. Brother Steve was more than willing, but having never done anything like that before, he asked: "Lord, how are we going to handle this?" The answer appeared to be: follow your intuition, shoot from the hip, fly by the seat of your pants. If your heart is in the right place, the right answers and moves will come naturally.

As Brother Steve described, much of what he remembered of those next few weeks was a continuous blur of answering phones, gathering information and assessing needs, assigning people to jobs and shuttling them back and forth. The appropriate people or supplies always appeared when they were needed. In addition to organizational and assessment help from Association pastors and volunteers, three groups of Baptists came from South Carolina because "you were here for us when Hugo hit," and people from Florida and California showed up to lend a hand.

A man from South Carolina who was in Birmingham on business drove over to the church in his business suit because "he was led to come help." He stayed for three days, combining his knowledge about equipment and his organizational skills to guide the early coordination efforts. One man arrived with a wrecker and donated his services for two days, during which time he extracted Brenda and Lonnie's vans from the trees and ravine. Another provided walkie-talkies when the cell phones were overloaded, so those who were in the field determining needs could radio the information back to the church. Wanda Barnhill from the Pleasant Ridge Baptist Church organized the telephone crew of 12-14 women and oversaw all the paperwork.

The toughest thing for Brother Steve to cope with was the bureaucracy and red tape of the governmental and relief agencies; he often viewed their guidelines as exclusive, overly rigid, and inequitable. Wherever possible, he circumvented those entities by garnering resources through church and private avenues and channeling them directly to where they were needed. As I have previously indicated, Brother Steve was an omnipresent dispenser of comfort and hope and a dispatcher of swift relief. Without him, many people surely would have languished. There is almost no one in the Rock Creek and Oak Grove areas who was not touched in some way by Brother Steve's compassionate heart and pragmatic action.

Brother Steve is quick to defer the praise to others. He gives credit to all the Baptist churches in the Bessemer Association who were invaluable help, and special kudos to Ed Cruce, not only for his leadership, but also for his role as "the money line," and to Johnny Fox, State Director for Baptist Disaster Relief, "who was our supply line for everything under the sun— from portable bathrooms to chain saw oil" and the liaison to the federal and state agencies. He also acknowledges all the other denominations whose pastors and members helped. "Without all of the loving people, I could not have done anything. Love made the difference!"

In fact, every minister I spoke with agreed that the byproduct of the churches working together to respond to the great human need created by the tornado was that the barriers between them melted away, giving rise to a fresh understanding and appreciation of each other's unique role and of their common mission.

Prepared For Disaster

In addition to the response and relief efforts, people from the faith community representing almost all denominations were often the key leaders and mediators of the various committees and groups, as well as the work force that wielded hammers and offered on-site counsel and comfort. In Birmingham, and at all the other disasters we worked at, we were continually amazed at the extent of the role played by the churches. Most denominations or faith groups have some form of outreach ministry for emergencies, and many have highly delineated national disaster response and recovery networks.

Spearheaded and directed by Elder Joe Dudley, the relatively new Churches of Christ Disaster Relief Effort has made a substantial contribution to disaster response in the United States with its highly organized distribution of emergency food and supplies, beds, furniture and appliances since its official organization in the spring of 1991. Supported by donations from individuals, churches, corporations and other non-profit agencies nationwide, Churches of Christ Disaster Relief has disseminated $35 million in aid to disaster victims in the eleven years since its inception.

In the summer of 2000, we visited their 48,500-square-foot center in Nashville, touring the well-stocked facility and worked alongside some of the regular volunteers (several in their seventies) readying supplies to be included in the Family Food Packs, Personal Care, Infant Care, and Cleaning Kits. Such love and thought go into this ministry that food boxes are packed to appeal to different regional tastes, and a personal letter of encouragement and a Bible are included in each. Because of their efficient operation, a truck can be loaded in two hours and on its way for distribution by a local Church of Christ in an affected area. In addition to material aid, follow-up ministry and support are provided.

Mennonite Disaster Service (MDS) is usually one of the first to begin repair and rebuilding efforts, and the last to leave. Local Mennonite groups will be active in the response and relief phases, and move swiftly into repair and rebuilding work before that phase has officially begun. Once an unmet needs process is in place, they work in coordination with it. They also work in conjunction with the Red Cross, providing the labor to rebuild homes for the recipients of FEMA maximum grants.

MDS, organized 50 years ago, is divided into four regions in the United States and one in Canada. Each state has a unit and a state coordinator, and each church has a unit and a contact person.

MDS, which worked primarily in the Oak Ridge community across from McDonald Chapel, made a two-year commitment to work in the Birmingham area, continually rotating in volunteers and completing 136 jobs—from rebuilding roofs and decks to constructing new homes. As they do during any sustained effort, a housing facility was obtained for their volunteers and an on-site project director provided for coordination. MDS' special emphasis is on "helping those least able to help themselves."

Another Mennonite group known as Christian Aid Ministries were the rebuilders in McDonald Chapel. Even after the anniversary celebration, it was the Mennonites who put together a team to build Becky and Greg (Dorothy's grandchildren) a home. Without their support, it may have been a year or two more before little Scott and Jonathan had a place in which to feel settled and secure. All of the Birmingham community was deeply touched and challenged by the steadfast example of faith in action set by the Mennonites.

The Methodists, likewise, are active in all phases of disaster response, and are especially strong in building skills. Supported by UMCOR (United Methodist Committee on Relief), which is funded by churchwide special offerings, the Methodists will send a person to be at the disaster site full-time to maintain a stable presence in the community and assure continuity in their efforts.

The Methodists were assigned to Edgewater, a relatively poor mining community that did not function cohesively before the tornado and was struggling greatly afterward. In all, approximately 1000 United Methodists worked anywhere from a day to several weeks at rebuilding. A contingent of Methodist NOMADS, the equivalent of Habitat Care-A-Vanners, also pitched in for several weeks.

After the anniversary celebrations, I visited Rick Connelly (who had supervised the construction of the Habitat houses built by the Methodists) while he was working at one of the last homes being built in Edgewater, and got a feel for the positive influence of the Methodists' presence in the community. People were constantly waving or stopping by to talk. It was clear that the Methodists were not merely building homes, but building up people and modeling what good, supportive relationships are all about.

The Church of the Brethren, though a very small denomination, also makes a large contribution to relief efforts around the world. Every Brethren district has a disaster response team, with overall coordination taking place from their headquarters at Church World Service in New Windsor, Maryland. Each district is responsible for raising its own funds which, in addition to paying the costs of their team's transportation and lodging (usually donated), contributes to the church-wide Emergency Disaster Fund.

In Birmingham, nearly 100 Brethren volunteers served at least one week, some returning for a second tour of duty. Their efforts were concentrated on rebuilding Pratt City. At the volunteer appreciation dinner we sat with four members of the Shenandoah District from the area of Harrisonburg, Virginia, who when they returned would plunge into the final work for their seventh annual Disaster Relief Auction. When I received a copy of the auction catalog, I realized it was no small undertaking. Held at the county fairgrounds, in previous years they had raised anywhere from $111,000 to $151,000 auctioning everything from livestock to quilts to handmade furniture and much more. Their 1999 effort netted over $140,000.

Eldon Zimmerman, the LDR Coordinator for the Lutheran Ministries of Alabama, had already had a busy spring making weekly trips to southern Alabama as a member of the Interfaith Committee responding to severe flooding there, when he was asked to coordinate the Lutheran response in Birmingham. The decision was made to join forces with the Episcopal Church, creating Lutheran/Episcopal Disaster Response. The Episcopal Church provided administrative support and the office out of which was coordinated the work of 400 Lutheran volunteers who contributed approximately 4000 hours to the recovery. They shared oversight responsibilities in McDonald Chapel with the Mennonites, took down one house, financed the building of a second, and built a home in Edgewater for one of the maximum grant families.

Countless hours were also spent counseling survivors and their families, a specialty of Lutheran Ministries. The Episcopal Church helped provide training for counselors. With money provided by the Lutheran Aid Association and the Episcopalians, a tool trailer was purchased and furnished with tools and equipment. The two church organizations contributed approximately $100,000 each, and were so pleased with the results of their combined effort that they have decided to continue the partnership to meet future disaster needs.

Other churches played essential roles, as well. The Presbyterians coordinated the housing of out-of-town volunteers—no small task. The Adventists organized and staffed the warehouse at the fairgrounds—first for emergency supplies, then for building materials. The Salvation Army provided money for building materials, canteen service to volunteers in the field, and clothing and furnishings for survivors. Catholic Charities worked on an ongoing, consistent basis with families in need, giving them supportive counsel as well as providing furniture and other assistance. The Jewish community was active in the overall process, serving on committees, providing volunteers, locating resources and supplying outstanding social workers. Church World Service (CWS), with an organizational structure similar to FEMA's, helps with creating and coordinating interfaith efforts, provides seed money for that purpose, and also sends blankets and clean-up kits when needed. CWS contributed $3000 to the Birmingham Interfaith Recovery Group.

The monumental role played by the Baptist church has already been made evident. Although not active in Birmingham because they were engaged elsewhere, the Southern Baptist Convention Disaster Relief volunteer mission program is also highly organized and effective. Disaster volunteers complete a training program, which includes general disaster relief information and hands-on training to operate chain saws and other equipment. Each state has a Disaster Relief unit and director. Nationwide, Disaster Relief has built more than 220 mobile mass feeding, recovery, communications, and child care units, including airlift kitchens.

Our faith communities deserve the highest praise—"Well done, good and faithful servant!" (Matt. 25:21 NIV)

V-23. HOPE FOR A BRIGHTER DAY

Lord, make me an instrument of Thy peace;
where there is hatred, let me sow love;
where there is injury, pardon; where there is doubt, faith;
where there is despair, hope; where there is sadness, joy.

Prayer of St. Francis

The Rest Of The Story

"And now," as Paul Harvey says, "for the rest of the story." When I told our mentor Topsy that I planned to write a chapter following up on the people and situations we'd been involved with, she responded with an enthusiastic "Good! So often we're left wondering." So, this one's for you, Topsy, and for all who may question whether the efforts of so many really give people hope to carry on or produce lasting changes in their lives. Judge for yourself.

The Mitchell Clan

Keeping our promise to Dorothy, we made tying up the little loose ends in her house our immediate priority when the anniversary remembrances concluded. As we spent more time with Dorothy, we could see that she was mildly depressed, having difficulty getting motivated. We knew she needed to be *settled*, not merely *in* her house, so we hung curtains, arranged pictures on the walls, installed a closet pole, made shelves, moved her dryer downstairs and wired it, and fixed the air conditioner. I brought her home-baked goodies, and Larry spent long coffee breaks chatting with her while I was out conducting interviews for this book.

It was amazing to watch Dorothy's transformation and see the sparkle gradually return to her eyes. After the first day or two, each morning when we arrived at her house there was clear evidence of what she had

216

accomplished the night before, and she would proudly open cupboard doors and drawers to show us that they were cleaned and organized. She began greeting us with make-up on, and made an appointment for a long-overdue permanent.

When everything was completed in her house, we took pictures of Dorothy posed on her couch and at her eating bar, as well as several views of the outside. Later that day, we all enjoyed a barbecued steak dinner up at Brenda's. We felt satisfied when we left Birmingham that we had done all we could to assure that Dorothy was finally "at home."

Brenda and Lonnie's situation was more complex and not as easily remedied by us. They still had a temporary power line running to their house that gave them only limited electricity and caused them to have to juggle what they did in the house. They had had no air conditioning during the scorching summer months. Their siding and a few other things remained unfinished until workmen could get back to them. On the positive side, they were in a beautiful new house, and it was obvious that Brenda has a flair for interior decorating. Using donated items, she had created a stunning decor in the living room and master bedroom.

Brenda was in the throes of trying to recreate all their business records, tornado-related losses, and other information before the income tax deadline. We didn't see much of her until after April 15. Lonnie had been working almost seven days a week over the past year. They were both exhausted and often ill. They were also struggling with long-time personal problems.

What we were most able to give to Brenda was moral support and encouragement. We reminisced and shared our pictures with each other and attended the Church of God celebration together. Like before, Brenda stopped by the trailer now and then, "just to get away." It was also a relief for her to see Dorothy settled and back to her old self. It would probably be another four to six months before Brenda and Lonnie's lives would regain a semblance of normalcy, but knowing what I did about Brenda's strength and determination, I felt sure they'd make it.

Greg and Becky and the children were still in FEMA housing, but they were finally getting enough assistance to meet their basic needs. Although Greg's health had stabilized, heart surgery was being considered with the aim of restoring him to a more normal and productive life. The Unmet Needs Committee and the Mennonites had just finalized the package to finance and build a home for Greg and Becky on a parcel of Dorothy's property. The work on it began shortly after we left. Becky and the boys took me to see their lot and showed me how the house would be laid out. Becky was especially excited about all the wildflowers on the property.

Later in the summer, Scott and Jonathan called and excitedly described their new house. Brenda's home was also completed and order gradually returned to their lives. Greg's heart surgery went well, and he has felt better and been able to do more, although he still ends up in the hospital at times.

The Mitchell family has recaptured many of their everyday rhythms and, in some ways, their living circumstances are better than they were before the storm. Scott and Jonathan once again enjoy making the rounds between their home, grandma's and great-grandma's to grab a hug, read a story or share a meal, and both are doing well in school. However, Dorothy has had ongoing health problems, undoubtedly exacerbated by the stress, and Brenda often has severe back pain, the result of too much heavy lifting. The sense of security everyone had up on "their hill" is gone, and the all-too-frequent tornado warnings still strike fear in them—a vivid reminder of the night when everything in their lives was blown apart.

Mariesha

I was tingling with anticipation as I approached Mariesha's house in McDonald Chapel, hoping for the same immediate connection I had felt with her the year prior. I need not have been concerned. Mariesha opened the door with her signature broad grin and warmly greeted me.

As I stepped inside the door, it was almost as shocking as the last time I had been in her house. My mind was struggling to juxtapose what I now saw with the images it still held from the year before. In the middle of the front room was the pool table under which her husband had crouched during the storm. The smell of baking bread—a gift Mariesha was making for me—greeted me as we walked through the TV room into the kitchen, the room where I had tried to find a bare spot amid the broken glass and debris to place the jar of jam. It was now completely restored—bright, inviting and colorfully decorated.

Mariesha showed me around the rest of the house, pointing out the few changes that had been made. For the most part, however, they had been content to rebuild their home pretty much as it had been, and had refused free furniture and household items, feeling other people needed them more than they. "Just before the storm, we had been approved for a loan to remodel," Mariesha explained. "We combined that loan with our insurance money and a generous donation from the employees at my bank and considered it our remodeling—just a little more extensive than we had planned!"

We sat down at the kitchen table to talk, and I quickly remembered why I had been so taken by Mariesha. She knew exactly what her priorities were. She told me what the loss of her home had represented. "When you lose your home, you lose your family base," she explained. "This was the first time I didn't have a home for my son." Mariesha recalled how deeply touched she had been by the intuitive understanding of a friend she had known through the bank. The woman had handed Mariesha money, saying, "I want you to go out and buy David anything he needs."

Though David had done well in school and was anticipating graduation, he had suffered from nightmares and been haunted by the memory of finding his dead neighbors. The week of the anniversary was especially stressful for him. And while Mariesha's attitude was upbeat and positive, I noticed that as we talked she began unconsciously wringing her hands. I wondered how long it would take before mention of the storm would not evoke such visceral responses. Perhaps it always would.

I asked Mariesha how the tornado had changed their lives and the nature of their community. "Our family is a lot closer, now," she confided. "We spend much more time together. We know that if we lose our new stuff, it doesn't matter as long as we have each other. As for our community, we've pulled closer together, too. I know I am much more aware of my neighbors now—where they are and what they need. We all want to be there for each other if there is ever another emergency."

We stepped outside so I could take an "after picture" of her house. I asked about the beautiful wreathe at the bottom of her former neighbors' driveway. "I put it there for the anniversary," Mariesha said quietly. "I had to show I remembered them. My neighbor across the street said she was glad I had. She had been focusing too much on herself, and the wreathe reminded her of what was really important—that their friends were not coming back." As I drove away with the smell of fresh bread flavoring the air in my car, I felt a warm glow of gratitude that Mariesha had allowed me to see the depths of both her pain and joy. It was a rare and special gift.

ALERT Acquisition

If anyone is thinking of visiting the ALERT Headquarters, don't look for it in Watersmeet, Michigan. The International ALERT Academy now

219

operates on the beautiful 2,200-acre campus of the former Ambassador University located in Big Sandy, Texas, approximately 100 miles east of Dallas. The acquisition and move were once again a result of faithful prayer and trust in God's promise to provide.

With ALERT and other programs of the Advanced Training Institute continually expanding, the purchase of the property (which includes two lakes and a mile-long airstrip) was timely. Besides training increasing numbers of young men from around the country for emergency work and volunteer service, young orphan boys from Russia and Romania will be educated and raised family-style on the campus and also participate in the ALERT cadet program until they reach the legal age to return to their countries. In addition, whole churches will gather at the academy for weekend trainings "on how to apply the seven basic factors that made first-century churches and homes so powerful." Since we are curious to see the new facility, we were also happy to learn that there is a 220-acre RV park on the grounds.

Newfie News

All the children on Hillview Drive East in St. John's are happily settled into their new homes, schools and neighborhood. Someone's house is always full of children. In fact, Cindy Walsh says she's learned that "it's more important to have a happy house than a clean one." She believes "that our children will do so much better in life not having to grow up in poverty housing," and echoes all the families when she says, "They are now so proud to invite their friends over to visit and play in a beautiful and loving home in a safe environment." The Walsh family built a recreation room and bathroom downstairs, and planned to add a bedroom for their oldest daughter.

Dramatic changes took place in many of the adults' lives, as well. Shortly after moving into her house, Cathy Carroll was laid off. After her initial panic, she decided to go back to school and complement her physical education degree with one in education. The Cabot Habitat supported her efforts by lengthening the payback period of her mortgage, thereby lowering her monthly payments. For a year and a half, Cathy marshaled all her resources and completed her degree with a minor in English.

Though it usually is not easy to land a permanent job immediately after graduating, she was offered a position at the first independent Catholic school in Newfoundland, where she taught physical education classes and served as Vice Principal. "It seems like God was waiting for me, and the time was ripe for me to be chosen for this profession. We are all so happy with the way life has taken a very positive turn, and Habitat for Humanity was definitely the pivotal point. Habitat has given us a home and dignity and very many wonderful people in our lives, as well." Cathy is now a full-time P.E. teacher for grades K-12, and uses her musical talents to direct the junior and senior high chamber choirs, as well as a parents' choir.

Likewise, Rick Walsh's new lease on life was the impetus for him to venture onto a new career path. "After 20 years in various facets of the automotive business, I decided I needed a new challenge. I put out the word to all my friends and relatives that I was looking for that perfect job. Then one day my father-in-law heard about an international property management company that was looking for an administrative assistant for their contract properties here in St. John's. I have been working for them since August 1998 and love going to work each and every day." Who can doubt that a decent environment has uplifting and far-reaching effects?

Jerome and Elaine Barry, who were featured in a follow-up article by Jill Claflin in *Habitat World*, indicated life is much less stressful now that they have a home of their own. Unlike the Walshes who resorted to staying inside to cope with their former housing environment, the Barrys "used to get out and drive in the evenings, just to get away," according to Elaine. Now they can relax and not worry about keeping Jillian quiet or blocking out the noise of others. The article points out that "perhaps most importantly, however, the spiritual despair that so gripped Jerome . . . has been replaced with belief." Realizing that so many people cared, just as he remembered they had in the small town where he grew up, "has given me back my sense of childhood security," Jerome relates. Jerome was promoted at the Health Sciences Complex where he had worked for many years; and after 15 years as a hairdresser, Elaine "now works as a product technician at a local manufacturing company," and hopes to return to school.

Lois Kaulback recalled that as they opened and walked through the door into their new home after receiving their keys, "we felt like we had opened a new and wonderful door in our lives. My husband and I felt a sense of pride we had not felt before. We no longer felt like failures to our children." Their new home has fostered many positive changes. "We have privacy and security for the first time ever," Lois shared, "and our outlook on life is better because we learned that it pays to never give up on your dreams. We also learned that there are more wonderful people in the world than bad. Our children have adjusted so well, it's as if we lived here forever. For the first time, they have playmates and their own back yard."

Shortly after receiving their Habitat home, Lewis was fortunate to be transferred to a local position and, since their youngest is in school, Lois now has a satisfying job at the same manufacturing company as Elaine. "Habitat for Humanity has changed our lives completely. It has fulfilled our dreams, and we will be forever grateful," Lois concluded.

In a letter to me in 1999, Cathy expressed her appreciation to everyone for the new life she has been given: "Thank you to Millard Fuller for putting his love into action. Thank you to the committee here in Newfoundland. Thank you to all the volunteers who showed me there are Christians who know how to love one another. And a special thanks to you, Carol and Larry, for creating this book and saving all the cherished messages that Habitat for Humanity has to speak."

Let it also be said that Lois Kaulback's "promise to be there" to help future recipients of Habitat homes was not an idle one. All of the homeowners have been active participants in the subsequent builds in the St. John's area, and raised funds for Habitat by building and selling playhouses for Christmas in 1998. It is their way of sharing the love and special feelings that they received, and keeping them spiraling continuously outward.

Easter Blooms

The Easter Morning Community in Americus was completed in the fall of 2000 during the Jimmy Carter Work Project. Margo Mitchell pitched in at the second Holy Week Build in Americus in 1999, and the Taylors sponsored and worked on a home for that build, as well as funding a third house in April 2000.

Jo Taylor says, "Kyle frequently talks about Margo or Alonzo and Lucille (recipients of the second house) and about how he helped to build a house for them. We believe he is beginning to understand what it means to follow Christ's teaching when he says, 'We built a house for a family that did not have one. Now they have a good place to live.'"

It happened that Larry and I and Hank and Sue, who had also helped build Margo's home, were in Americus at the same time in the fall of 1999. Margo invited the four of us over for a traditional Southern dinner. She was excited to show "her parents" the "personalized changes" she has made to her home. And it definitely is Margo. Plants (one of her passions) abound inside and out, as does her favorite color, black. She has painted the outside trim and foundation blocks black and added black shutters, which combine richly with the tan siding. Inside, the bold and striking black and white decor mirror both Margo's audaciousness and her grateful pride. Indeed, Margo says, "I am very thankful for my home. No one will ever have to prompt me to maintain it."

As Margo showed us around the house, we each pointed out things we had worked on and tried to remember how the house had looked when it was empty. Then, it was just a house, but now it was a warm and inviting home. Margo's son Nakia looked comfortable stretched out on his bed sketching. A variety of posters and historical documents were neatly arranged on the walls, and everything had a place in his tidy room. As Nakia quietly helped serve and clean up after supper without instructions from his mother, it was evident that he and Margo are still a supportive team. Following dinner, he and Larry settled on the living room floor to play a game of chess, while the rest of us reminisced about the special week when we worked together on Margo's house.

Margo, who over the last several years has worked for a travel agency and in the produce department at a local grocery store, is hoping to pursue further education and a career in criminal justice in the near future. She is also actively involved in her community "to assure that its great promise is fulfilled." And after 10 years of single parenthood, Margo now has a very special person in her life. Niki is happy about that, also. He has just turned 18 and will soon be enlisting in the U.S. Navy. Our hearts are very full when we think of Margo and the positive results that perseverance has produced in her life.

Sarah, the young construction supervisor who had shocked her parents by choosing volunteering over "gainful employment," worked for Habitat until the fall of 2000. For a year she was the Campus Chapter and Youth Programs Manager for the Midwest Regional Office of Habitat in the Chicago area. Then she came back to headquarters in Americus and coordinated short-term mission trips in the U.S., Canada, and Mexico for the Global Village Department. During her time with Habitat she acquired a broad range of skills, enjoyed enriching travel opportunities and met many inspiring people.

Co-leading a Women's Build in Kentucky, turning on other students to the joy of volunteering with Habitat, and seeing firsthand, as a member of a Global Village team in Guatemala, the life-saving benefits of decent housing for the children of that impoverished country—these highlights of her career with Habitat have given her a deep sense of pride and satisfaction.

Though most of her peers are making much more money in their corporate careers, she says, "I definitely see myself working in the non-profit area all my life. I like the sense of purpose in this sector and will stay with it as long as I continue to be inspired. I feel like I'm making a difference for the better in the world." In her mid-twenties, Sarah says she can always try her hand at corporate America—if she ever feels the need. She is currently enrolled in a social work program at the University of Chicago.

Struggling In Spencer

The little town of Spencer, South Dakota, is still struggling. A combination of factors conspired to prevent it from achieving the level of recovery reached by the Birmingham communities. For one thing, "The whole support system was drained, instead of one part being lost and the rest being able to step up and offer support," Randy Quevillon, a member of a team from the University of South Dakota's Disaster Mental Health Institute, was quoted as saying in the May 23, 1998 *Argus Leader*. According to former Town Board member Donna Ruden, with no previous zoning laws or agreed-upon parameters to bind them together, the various constituencies were often not of one accord to begin with.

The lack of cohesiveness, job base and grocery or medical facilities, as well as the large number of elderly people who saw no benefit to themselves in rebuilding had, by the end of 1999, resulted in only 22 new houses being constructed or moved onto properties. The spunky antique lady was living in a nursing home in Salem. She had not fully regained the use of her legs. Only four elderly former residents were living in the rebuilt apartment building, and only one of the five churches destroyed had been completely resurrected; the Catholic Church has put up only a parish hall.

Donna and newspaper reports indicate there was considerable dissension over the distribution of money and the planning process. The Governor's Tornado Relief Fund and other donations were managed by the Spencer Area Relief Interfaith Network (SARIN), and were used to assist people in a wide variety of ways based on their individual needs, as well as for infrastructure and other community rebuilding needs. However, a few people felt they were "owed" money without having to follow any application process or give evidence of a recovery plan. Some of those people had been delinquent on property taxes and other bills previous to the tornado. There was also frustration that the assistance promised by Vice President Gore was slow in passing through Congress.

The cooperative plan to consolidate the new town into a five-block area (which had been presented by the governor at the meeting I attended), in large part, did not sell either. Some speculate that having lost so much, it was too soon for people to consider trading their property, which in many instances was all they had left. In any case, the new houses are widely scattered. A small, modified version of the proposed centralized community facilities has been erected, which includes a combination fire station and city garage that also houses the bookmobile, and a city building which incorporates the post office, a sitting room and the library. The Security State Bank, which had temporarily operated out of Donna Ruden's home, has been rebuilt, as well as the Spencer Automotive Services, a combined gas station, convenience store and coffee shop. Spencer's rebirth is now guided by a zoning ordinance, and the town has been connected to a rural water system.

At the end of 1999, the town consisted of about 60 homes (130 were destroyed)—the 22 new ones plus the remainder on the northern end of town which were either repairable or left unscathed. The population declined from 320 to around 150. In a follow-up conversation with Donna Ruden, who is now the mayor of Spencer, only 3 additional homes have been built in the last three years. The antique lady died in 2001.

"Although the restructuring eliminated some of the less desirable elements of our community," Donna says, "we would never have wished for it to come about in this way. Those of us who are still here do our best to support each other, but it will never be the same." Having lost so much, those who have remained, and those who may choose to make Spencer their home in the future, will need to work together to forge a new sense of purpose and meaning for their community, a task which will undoubtedly take more time.

The *Argus Leader* reported that on April 30, 1999, 300 trees were planted by volunteers as part of a three-year plan to reforest Spencer with a thousand trees. A large portion of the trees' roots were removed to encourage reestablishing themselves in the new soil. "They will grow slowly until the roots are replaced, then they will take off," wrote staff reporter Peter Harriman. "In this way, the trees are a hopeful metaphor for Spencer itself."

Back At The Ranch

Ramona Yohe reported that the outreach to the embattled South Dakota farmers and ranchers by Lutheran Social Services and Lutheran Disaster Response was "both a financial and physical success." They were not able to completely remedy everyone's situation, but they were able to offer enough assistance to each to give them a jump-start and the moral support of knowing they did not have to do it completely alone. For most, that was all they needed. Many expressed their appreciation on evaluation forms and indicated that their faith had been restored. "It was so nice to know that others care," wrote a dairy farmer. "It was wonderful. You were Christ to us," added a rancher. And a single rancher, referring to the fencing volunteers, said: "I was so impressed by their perseverance in the heat, their ability, and their gracious generosity."

Only a couple ranchers LDS worked with eventually sold out. Ramona was happy to tell me that all the families assisted during the two-week period we were there are still living on their farm or ranch and that the people are healthy. For more than a year after the active aid ceased, LDR/LSS, Orphan Grain Train and the South Dakota Food Pantry distributed groceries once a month to the 200 families they had serviced. Two subsequent mild winters also greatly aided the majority of the people to get back on their feet.

One hundred seventy-three volunteers worked in the Selby area between October 1997 and August 1998. Volunteers worked 4500 hours at the sites and spent a 1000 more commuting. Ramona didn't need to remind us that travel time was one of the biggest challenges in that area—over one-fifth of a volunteer's time was spent getting to and from the work sites. Forty-four different jobs were completed, and 128 farmers and ranchers received fencing or corral materials. Volunteers spent 340 hours helping to distribute them (after they were brought into the area), and 1200 volunteer hours were invested in helping repair the fences and corrals. It was, most definitely, a substantial and effective undertaking.

We hear from George and Josephine once or twice a year. Josephine reported in her January 1999 letter that she and George completed repairing and replacing the remainder of their fences after we all left. It was slow going due to the extreme heat, but it was a heavy load off their minds to have it done. They hear from some of the other volunteers occasionally, as well, and always extend invitations for a return visit. "You won't have to work so hard next time you come," Josephine promises.

In another letter, Josephine wrote that she had put together six more quilts, and she enclosed a newspaper clipping with a picture of George in front of a B24 bomber at the airport in Pierre, South Dakota. After 55 years, he had fulfilled his dream to once again ride in the same type plane in which he was shot down—only this time, he was able to walk away from it. For George and Josephine, the help they received from LSS/LDR made the difference between spending their later years broken and dispirited and being able to enjoy the fruits of their hard work and service to others.

The LDR missionaries Dale and Jeannie Peercy completed their work in northwestern South Dakota and have since served in the community of Webster, South Dakota, and the towns of Cuero and Victoria, Texas, both north of Corpus Christi, where there was severe flooding in October 1998. "We can't seem to get away from floods," Jeannie mused. They manage to sneak off for a week or two now and then, but otherwise continue their relentless pace of working to ease the suffering of others.

Revival In Regina

For Desiree Bank, our homeowner in Regina, Saskatchewan, her Habitat house represents the beginning of a whole new life. From the time she was young, all she remembers doing was working and getting nowhere. She had very little self-confidence, was stuck in a rut, and had lost faith in people. The father of her children, with whom she had lived on and off over many years, had not been ready for the responsibility of a family. At the time of the build they had been separated for a year.

Desiree says the fact that so many people felt she was worth helping made her feel she was a valuable person, and she became motivated to improve her life. After many years of putting it off, she learned to drive. And although she still bakes for people from her home and took over her mother's wedding decorating business on weekends, Desiree became a full-time substitute teacher's assistant in the Catholic school district, working individually with students who need encouragement and support. "This is the most rewarding thing I've ever done," she bubbled. "I never would have attempted anything like this before. I see so many troubled children, and I tell my own how much we have to be thankful for."

For their twin boys, Justin and Jason, the move from their co-op home, which was cold and dank, into their Habitat home meant a dramatic improvement in their health, since both had developed asthmatic reactions to the molds in their previous house. Little Jessica, who so proudly showed me her bedroom when their house was completed, is a bright and happy little girl. Desiree's father is helping the family construct bedrooms downstairs for the boys, as well as a rumpus area and laundry room.

With the aim of continuing to publicize Habitat's presence and mission, Desiree spearheaded the building of a Habitat float by the six homeowners for the popular Regina Buffalo Days parade for three years. She spoke with pride about their accomplishment and was enthusiastic about helping to build the affiliate's next house.

Desiree has now graduated to being the full-time nutrition planner for the Catholic school district. She oversees all the menus for breakfast and lunch, and works with individual children who have special nutrition needs. The twins are now in sixth grade and little Jessica is a first-grader. Desiree credits Habitat for becoming a confident and self-sufficient woman.

Habitat And The 21st Century Challenge

In the year 2000, the number of homes built by Habitat exceeded 100,000 worldwide. The benchmark was reached during Building on Faith week in September 2000, as part of the Jimmy Carter Work Project that took place at three sites. The 100,000th house was completed in New York City (where in 1984 Jimmy Carter first became a Habitat volunteer), and the 100,001st house went up in President Carter's hometown of Plains, Georgia.

As momentous as that is, there is a larger picture to consider. The December 1999/January 2000 edition of *Habitat World* stated that "As the second millennium comes to a close . . . in the United States alone, some 5.3 million families live in substandard shelter; in developing countries, more than 1 billion people lack adequate housing and live on less than $1 a day." In response to those sobering statistics, Millard Fuller wrote in the Founder's Note in that same publication:

"The missing component that allows miserable housing conditions to continue in this world is the will to resolve the problem. The financial and human resources are available in abundant supply. All that is lacking is the determined will to conquer the problem.

"That is what Habitat for Humanity seeks to do: To create the will to move from the darkness of the 20th century's poverty housing into an illuminated 21st century that is filled with adequate housing for all.

"We want to make shelter a matter of conscience. Inadequate housing and homelessness must become politically, socially and religiously unacceptable."

To address the critical need for decent shelter, Habitat for Humanity International has instituted the 21st Century Challenge Program which "challenges communities to set a date no more than 20 years out by which to eliminate substandard housing in their communities."

Although the task may be more daunting in some areas than in others, the most important steps are making a commitment to the initiative in partnership with the local Habitat affiliate, and involving the major constituencies of the community in setting realistic, achievable goals toward that end. Any community certified in the program will receive support and guidance from both Habitat for Humanity International and the local Habitat affiliate to develop the resources to accomplish its goal. Meeting the 21st Century Challenge will require committed, dedicated, collaborative work, but there will surely be both qualitative and quantitative rewards for a community that so cares about *all* of its members.

Sumter County, home of Habitat for Humanity International, has led the way, making its commitment in 1993. It reached its goal during the Jimmy Carter Work Project in 2000. Over 100 other communities have expressed interest in setting a goal, including three in the Birmingham area. Seven communities have been officially certified for the program, and by the end of 2002 another 13 may be ready to proceed. Habitat's aim in their next 25 years is to eliminate substandard housing one community at a time. What a wonderful tribute it would be if hundreds of years from now the 21st Century is remembered as the last in which there were people living anywhere in the world in debilitating housing and environments.

Clive Rainey, Habitat's first volunteer, has been entrusted with the oversight of this ambitious and far-reaching program. His keen insight and comprehension of Habitat's mission serve him well in this important responsibility. Clive sees other challenges, as well, for Habitat in the 21st Century. With the accelerated pace of building homes, he feels care must be taken not to lose the vital supportive connections with the families, and he sees a need to develop a partnership program to address major repair needs that will begin to surface as Habitat homes begin to age. Clive also believes it is critical that Habitat remain committed to Christian precepts. In that regard, it is crucial that "the churches of whatever stripe, denomination, etc., claim Habitat, make it their own and hold us (Habitat) to our principles," he remarked in an in-house news interview.

Habitat is now one of the largest homebuilders in the United States. As Habitat for Humanity grows and spreads, the same temptations will be encountered as when any vision becomes popularly embraced. Care will need to be taken to introduce people not only to the joy of building houses, but also to the vision and mission, which are the foundation of that building.

If Habitat is to remain true to its vision, it will need to be watchful that it does not become just another business building houses. As the drive to construct more and more homes escalates, creating a need to generate more and more money and ally with businesses and government, Habitat will need to remain vigilant that it does not lose its soul in the process. It is vital that the vision of servanthood remains the foundation upon which every house is built—for lives are not changed, nor wounded hearts healed, by houses alone. The transformative power lies, rather, in the individual acts of love that resonate from each swing of the hammer.

A Final Word About Birmingham

On April 27, 2000, a breakfast was held in Fairfield, Alabama, during which that community reiterated its commitment to systematically address the issue of substandard housing. "Any community can do what Fairfield is doing," said Jan Bell, the then-Executive Director of Greater Birmingham Habitat for Humanity. That is exactly what is happening.

Not only did more than 70 organizations join the coalition to confront the need in Jefferson County, but concern for the quality of life for citizens has spread throughout the Central Alabama region where, in a grassroots initiative called Region 2020, over 5000 people participated in a visioning process to define their priorities and what they would like to see happening in their communities by the year 2020. Decent housing for everyone was identified as a primary concern.

Birmingham stands as a beacon to any community that chooses not to tolerate dehumanizing living conditions within its boundaries. Millard Fuller stated in an address to Samford University students that it is easy to love our "generic neighbor" in the abstract. The hard work comes when we get to know our real neighbor by name, learn what his/her needs are, and address them. I might add: We don't need to wait until a tornado or other tragedy strikes. We can begin today.

After almost three years of Herculean efforts on behalf of the Greater Birmingham HFH, Jan Bell stepped down as executive director to restore normalcy to her family life. She presently serves as executive director of the Juvenile Diabetes Research Foundation in Birmingham. Charles Moore now ably guides the Birmingham HFH affiliate. By the end of 2002, the affiliate will have completed 101 houses since 1998. Fifty-one homes have been built in Fairfield, leaving that community with approximately 50 more properties needing attention. In the community of Edgewater, which was severely affected by the tornado, a newly developed subdivision of 81 homes is being erected, with 12 homes already completed. Each house has a "tornado safe-room."

Jan believes the deadly tornado was the catalyst for much of what is transpiring in the Greater Birmingham area. In the affiliate's fourth quarter 1999 newsletter, she wrote:

"Drive through western Jefferson County today and you will see the results of love in action in the rebuilt homes and restored hope made possible by a caring community coming together. . . Our community largely overcame one of the worst natural disasters in our nation's history in less than two years. Guess what: We can overcome the chronic crisis of poverty housing in the 21st century. Let the legacy of the tornado be that it propelled us forward, brought us together, and focused our attention on the needs of our brothers and sisters. . . Folks, we can solve any problem together."

V-24. VEHICLES OF HOPE

From a distance, we are instruments,
Marching in a common band.
Playing songs of hope,
Playing songs of peace,
They're the songs of every man.

Bette Midler, *"From a Distance"*

The Need For Hope

Our story has exhibited conclusively that despite the glut of bad news, there is an abundance of goodness quietly expressing all around us. Most of us need to become more accustomed to looking for it and acknowledging it when we see it. Newspapers and magazines, radio and TV talk shows, and most recently the ubiquitous TV magazines—all highlight what goes wrong in our society and in the world, until many are left to conclude that there is very little going right.

I remember a brief period after our move to New Hampshire during which I was searching for a job. For a two-week period I watched the morning and afternoon talk shows. Day after day, I was bombarded with alarming statistics about sexual abuse, murder, rape, stalkers, infidelity, fraud, etc. I began to feel that I, and the few people I knew, must be the only normal ones in the world. Out in public, I found myself looking around, trying to figure out who was a wife-beater, a child molester, a rapist, or a serial killer. After all, according to the statistics, there had to be a fair number of criminals and perverts right there in the grocery store.

Recognizing that I was on the verge of becoming a misanthrope, I gave up the talk shows cold turkey. However, my reaction did make me wonder how many other people were insidiously becoming convinced that there is little to celebrate in life, and I contemplated the effect it must have on them and on our society. If we are without hope that goodness prevails over evil, it becomes easier "to mind our own business" (i.e., not come to a stranger's aid, not protest injustice), degenerate into hedonism, withdraw into our living rooms with our big-screen TV's and wrap-around sound, and interact with our computers instead of people—all an attempt to make the perceived bad world go away.

Larry and I were teenagers during the Cold War, with the threat of global annihilation just a push-of-the-button away. Many used that as an excuse to drop out, turn on and tune out. They threw away a big chunk of their lives because they had given up hope in a tomorrow. But look what happened—peace between Egypt and Israel was achieved (by three people who were able to see beyond the appearance of irreconcilable differences), the Berlin Wall came down, the Communist Empire dissolved, and the chasm of apartheid was breached—all occurrences we never dreamt we would see in our lifetimes. All proof that *within mankind there is a deep-seated will to make things right.*

In the fall of 1999, PBS aired the documentary *Reason for Hope*, based on Jane Goodall's book by the same title. Jane Goodall has soared to the heights of ecstasy living among the chimpanzees in the forests of Gombe, Tanzania, and dwelt in the pit of personal heartache and anguish. She has observed not only the best and worst in the human species, but has documented the same proclivities in chimpanzees. Though she is convinced that the capacity for great evil is innate in both, she has refused to acquiesce to the notion that it must dominate.

Jane Goodall has committed the later years of her life to traveling around the world promulgating the message that we all have the option to choose our innate goodness over our darker side; that we can create a better world when we understand the connectedness of all life and base our decisions and actions on that awareness. In her suitcase Jane Goodall carries physical symbols of hope, reminders that we have that capability: a leaf from a plant which sprang forth out of the ashes of Nagasaki, a piece of the Berlin Wall, and a stone from Nelson Mandela's prison.

We must be able to believe that within every injustice and tragedy the seeds of reconciliation and new life lie waiting to be nourished so they can blossom into a brighter tomorrow. I was greatly encouraged by the 100-plus college students from across the country, and leaders from three established peace activist groups, who made Koinonia Partners (the birthplace of Habitat for Humanity) their headquarters for several days. They were

233

preparing for the annual demonstration outside Fort Benning, Georgia, to protest continuation of the School of the Americas that trained Central and South American soldiers in techniques of counter-insurgency.

For me, the hope lay not in *what* they were protesting but that they *were* protesting. Many believe that such actions accomplish little and are simply the expression of misguided idealism. But, even if that were true, it does not diminish the importance for me of what they represent. Such action tells me that there are young people (and older ones, too) who still have hope that they can make the world better, who believe they can make a difference; who—in the words of George Bernard Shaw which were so passionately reiterated by Robert F. Kennedy—"instead of seeing things as they are and asking 'Why?', see things as they can be and ask, 'Why not?'"

Hope impels us to light a candle; despair reduces us to cursing the darkness. To see what *can be*, despite the seemingly overwhelming evidence of what is, requires looking at the world through a different set of lenses. It requires looking beyond *appearances* to the realities that can only be observed through our *spiritual eyes*. Larry and I have encountered so many people who, on the face of it, had every reason to curse the dark, to give up hope, to withdraw into self-pity and despair—and yet they didn't. They were ordinary people—like you and me—people who, when put to the test, were able to see hope where there didn't appear to be any and to marshal the strength to build upon it.

Hope that life can be different is what gives us a reason to act—and when we act, we become a vehicle of hope to another, and they to another, and they to yet another—and so it inexorably grows. Ultimately, this is what we have gleaned from our experiences of the past several years. In the movie *Starman*, the "visitor" comments as he prepares to leave our planet, "You (humans) are a strange species—you are at your very best when things are worst." But seeing how we can be when we are at our best gives us a glimpse of what our noblest potential is, as well as hope that *we can some day fully actualize it*.

Jane Goodall arrives at similar conclusions in her spiritual journey. She believes that ordinary people have the capacity to become saints or, at the least, "just a little bit more saint-like. . . A life lived in the service of humanity, a love of and respect for all living things—those attributes are the essence of saintlike behavior," she writes. Such behavior, she maintains, will help us "hasten our moral evolution, (and to) progress a little more quickly

234

toward our human destiny"—to fully comprehend our spiritual kinship with each other and with our Creator.

Adding Our Weight

People are thirsty for hope. They are hungry to touch—heart-to-heart—to know they are not alone. We fulfill these basic needs for each other by giving of ourselves, by being there for one another. Protests of busyness or lack of time are only indications of a lack of understanding of what contributes to our highest good. Serving others enlivens our souls and lifts our spirits as surely as exercise energizes our bodies. It heals many of our modern-day neuroses, frequently brought on by self-absorption, as surely as antidepressants.

Peace Pilgrim, the woman who from 1953 until her death in 1981 walked more than 25,000 miles across our country sharing and teaching her message of peace, always emphasized service as a key element in acquiring inner peace. She asserted that the only way to truly experience harmony in our lives is to have as *our motive in all that we do*, "to be of service to your fellow humans." She further contended that when we do this, we will be "in contact with the source of universal energy and you [we] cannot be tired."

Life is designed to be a shared adventure, one in which we rejoice in each other's triumphs and help lift each other's burdens. In other words, life is about love, and although that word is often used as a noun, it can only be expressed as a verb—through action. We begin with those closest to us, then, hopefully, as we grow and mature and come to understand that our lives are all interwoven, we will reach out in ever-widening circles to eventually embrace the whole world. Though there are many hopeful signs that "the moral arc of the universe bends toward love," it still has a long way to go. Each of us must decide in which direction we will thrust our weight.

Golden Opportunities

Our life stages and life circumstances will more than likely determine the ways and means by which we are able to give and serve, but the possibilities are endless—regardless of age, health or income. The smallest gesture of kindness produces a powerful ripple effect.

However, those of us who are retired have a *special* opportunity to make these years "golden" not just for ourselves, but also for others. No longer saddled by the everyday responsibilities of earning a living and attending to our families, we have a plethora of vital resources at our fingertips begging to be put to good use—time, freedom, wisdom, and a lifetime of accumulated skills and experiences. For many, it may be the first chance they've had to step outside of familial and societal expectations and explore their hearts' longings. "Retirement," according to Jimmy and Rosalynn Carter in their book *Everything to Gain*, "offers the chance to be bolder than ever before and to do worthwhile things that have been avoided or postponed . . ."

RVers' mobility and flexibility, as I stated earlier, further enhance their ability to serve others. Most RVers count campground camaraderie as one of the greatest joys of their lifestyle. However, Larry and I can attest that there is a comradeship even richer than sitting around the campfire drinking coffee and swapping travel adventures and mishaps. There is no more meaningful bonding than when a group of people shares together the experience of raising a roof, picking up the broken pieces of someone's life, or otherwise engaging in helping others.

Provoked Unto Love

I am convinced there is an *extra special blessing* for those, in any stage of life, who extend their service beyond what affects or directly benefits them. The truth, of course, is that such selfless action cannot help but accrue to them the indirect benefit of deep and lasting satisfaction.

Brother Steve spoke to the point one Sunday morning. Reading from the King James Version of the Letter to the Hebrews, verse 4 of chapter 10, an exhortation given for members to be "provoked unto love and good works," he speculated about how we might act if we provoked each other to love; if we were excited and stirred up to help others. Perhaps, he mused, we would find ourselves knocking on doors pleading, "Please, let me help you. They provoked me down at the church!"

The tornado, he asserted, did just that. It provoked individuals, churches, businesses, even government, to set aside their own narrow concerns and to become excited about helping others—not just their relatives, or their neighbors, or their parishioners, or their employees, or even the people in their own city or state, but anyone—simply because they needed it. And, as he pointed out, it felt good.

The Happy Prince

Looking back, I believe my heart was first opened to the abiding joy of service by the childhood tale, *The Happy Prince*, which I often read and which always profoundly moved me. At the time, I didn't understand why the story brought tears welling up from deep within me.

The statue of the handsome Prince stood on a high hill overlooking the European city that he had defended with his life. One day, a small bird migrating south for the winter stopped to rest at the statue's feet. When the bird felt wet drops land on him, he looked up and saw tears falling from the Prince's eyes. The Prince explained that he was sad because as he looked out over the city he loved he saw so much suffering and was helpless to do anything about it.

The Prince then asked the little bird if he would stay an extra day to help him. The next day the bird reluctantly delivered the ruby from the Prince's sword to a little girl who was shivering in the cold, selling firewood for her family. This made the Prince very happy. Day after day the Prince, despite the bird's protestations that he must leave soon, convinced the bird to help him just once more. And so, the little bird continued delivering jewels from the Prince's sword until they were gone and, finally, the emeralds from the Prince's eyes. The Prince then told the bird to be on his way south.

By this time, the bird had become completely bound in love to the Prince and, refusing to leave, remained to be the Prince's eyes, seeking out those in need and delivering the gold leaves that constituted the Prince's clothing. Each evening when he returned, the little bird would bask in the glow of the Prince's happiness. Eventually, everything that the Prince could give was gone, but the bird still refused to leave him and finally froze to death at his Prince's feet.

The following spring the city fathers, appalled at the dilapidated condition of the statue, decided to have it removed. When city workers tossed the dead bird's body aside, they heard a loud cracking sound. Later, when the statue was being melted down, they were dismayed to see that the Prince's heart was broken.

As a child, I didn't understand why this story moved me so. But today I recognize in it the Prince of Peace who asks us to be his loving eyes and feet and hands, and to deliver his gifts of compassion and love to a hurting world. Like the little bird, we too may be reluctant, desiring instead to fulfill our own agendas. But as we submit to the wishes of our Prince, we become bound to him in love. The things of this world no longer matter, for we are fulfilling the purpose for which we were born—to be light and love and hope to our fellow travelers through life.

EPILOGUE: PILGRIMS' PROGRESS

Only the ones who believe
Ever see what they dream,
Ever dream what comes true.

Beth Nielsen Chapman, *"The Color of Roses"*

Another Crossroads

One of the most frequent questions we've been asked since we took to the road is, "Isn't it hard always being on the move?" Our response usually is, "We really aren't continually on the move (as the reader has observed); actually, what will be difficult to come to terms with is when we're feeling called to stay put somewhere for an extended time."

I have known in my heart that sooner or later we would arrive at that crossroads, if for no other reason than we were resistant to the idea. I firmly believe life has a way of placing in our path opportunities to grow and stretch and move beyond patterns of living which have become too comfortable—even RVing. Naturally, it is always up to us whether we respond and move to the next level of challenge or remain entrenched where we are.

Summoned To Koinonia

In the fall of 1999, we were faced with just such a provocation—as always, unplanned and unexpected. We were on our way to the Natchez Trace Wilderness Preserve in Tennessee to spend the winter. Larry was to work as the nighttime caretaker and I would have use of an office in which to finish this book. However, since negotiating the deal, a number of circumstances had changed, and we both had a nagging feeling that something wasn't right about our going. I'm sure the fact that our beloved travel companion, Ross, had died from a deadly tick bite at that campground

238

the previous spring also weighed heavily on our minds. Nevertheless, for lack of an apparent better option, we continued to head toward Tennessee.

En route, we received our mail packet. It included the quarterly Habitat Care-A-Vanner Newsletter bearing an appeal from Millard Fuller for all Care-A-Vanners to carve out some time to help renovate the neglected and deteriorated buildings and guest houses at Koinonia Partners. Koinonia had just recently weathered a serious threat to its survival as a result of several years of mismanagement.

Of course, when Millard Fuller speaks, Habitaters listen! When I read the letter, I immediately understood why we had been experiencing the persistent misgivings about going to Tennessee—I felt sure Koinonia was where we were supposed to be. In any case, I definitely wanted to volunteer there for a week to experience firsthand the roots and birthplace of Habitat for Humanity, if for no other reason than it would deepen my understanding and give me valuable insights for my book. But, in my heart, I believed that once we were there it would somehow work out for us to spend the winter. And that is exactly what happened. By the third day, after learning of Larry's skills, they were extremely desirous of keeping us there.

We worked out an agreement to stay through the following spring. Larry would do maintenance, and I would be able to work on my book in an apartment across from our trailer and volunteer at my discretion. We received further validation of our "call" when the staff at Natchez Trace was warmly supportive and understanding of our decision not to come.

A Quick Indoctrination

We knew a little of the Koinonia story before we came, but almost nothing about founder Clarence Jordan. I had heard about Koinonia's mail order products in the 1960's, and we had read Millard Fuller's books in which he always pays tribute to Clarence Jordan—the man, friend, spiritual leader and mentor.

As providence would have it, we arrived a week before the 30th anniversary of Clarence Jordan's death. Habitat for Humanity would host a grand all-day celebration on October 29, the date Clarence died, and Koinonia was planning its own special observance and dinner for the 30th, the anniversary of his burial on the farm at "Picnic Hill." Koinonia's new Board of Directors was also arriving for the anniversary and meetings.

Following on the heels of the big weekend, twenty members of the First Congregational Church in Old Lyme, Connecticut, were scheduled to come and work. Old Lyme Church had played a pivotal role, through both leadership and financial support, in saving Koinonia from an ignoble demise.

Throughout the week leading up to the commemorative activities, a resident or worker at Koinonia shared after the communal noon meal about their experiences at Koinonia and what the place meant to them. From their accounts and a number of private conversations, we began to catch a glimpse of its rich history and meaning. On Friday and Saturday, we would be exposed to the full emotional impact.

Friday morning a couple hundred people congregated in front of Habitat Headquarters and, with the local high school band in the lead, processed to the conference center and office complex being dedicated as the Clarence Jordan Center. Throughout the day and evening—by means of personal tributes, recollections, and video and theatrical presentations—a picture was painted of an extraordinary man of faith and vision whose legacy we had been asked to help preserve.

Saturday's activities, remembrances and the culminating celebration at Clarence's writing shack, where he died, also moved us deeply. We became aware of unfamiliar stirrings within us and began discussing the idea of making a longer commitment to this special place. But as a result of what we learned over the previous four years, we decided the best course was to simply remain open and attuned to our inner guidance. If this was where we were supposed to stay, we would receive confirmation.

In November and December we were caught up in the rush of "products season"—producing, packaging and mailing out Koinonia's specialty chocolate, pecan and bakery products. During that time, Larry's experience in production and his mechanical ability prompted one of the coordinators to approach him about taking a management position. The question for us was—were we willing to make the commitment to stay somewhere for an extended time? Much to our surprise, we found it relatively easy to answer "yes."

In due time, an acceptable working agreement was forged with the Board of Directors, and we committed to stay for a couple years. We also negotiated some time off in the summers to seek a little respite from the oppressive heat and humidity and the omnipresent gnats.

Divine Order

And so, for the past 3 years, we have been closely associated with Koinonia, and feel blessed to have contributed to its rebirth and revitalization. For me, it has also been a nurturing and enriching setting in which to flesh out our book. Both of us have grown and been stretched by the inevitable lessons that living in close community provides, and we have enjoyed the stimulating exposure to the many diverse and committed people who pass through here.

One special joy has been the opportunity for regular contact and fellowship with Margo and her son Nakia. Another is that we, along with others from Koinonia, had the honor of working on the "Victory House" in the Easter Morning Community during the Jimmy Carter Work Project 2000. It was especially poignant because Sarah (the young woman who had helped supervise Margo's house) worked alongside us before heading up to college. The Victory House represents both the coming full-circle of the dream of partnership housing envisioned by Clarence Jordan and Millard Fuller in 1968 and the elimination of substandard housing in Sumter County (the first county to meet the 21st Century Challenge).

Hundreds of people gathered in the local stadium on the culminating evening of the build to celebrate this first-in-the-world accomplishment through music, video, and acknowledgments. I looked down at the ball field where President and Mrs. Carter were seated alongside other local supporters and marveled at what has taken place in this little corner of Southwest Georgia amidst pecan groves and red clay farmland. What a privilege it has been to play a tiny part in it!

In a way, we, too, have come full-circle. We have bought one of the feral cement domed houses built by Koinonia in 1976—a two-bedroom, 780-square-foot home nestled on three-quarters of an acre of wooded land. We now have a little place to come back to in the winters and when we are no longer able or inclined to travel. There will always be meaningful things to do there, and a supportive community to welcome our return. Now, if that isn't divine order, I don't know what is.

Reflections

It seems only fitting that we are at our camp in New Hampshire while I put the finishing touches on this chronicle of our six-year journey, for this is where the seeds were first planted. It's been 14 years since our first sight of this spot that was so pivotal for us. Much has changed, and much has remained the same.

The bottlebrush pines we transplanted along the road our first year now touch the power lines, and the two blue spruce that were barely nine inches high (an anniversary present to ourselves) are now over eleven feet tall. There's more traffic on our road, and Wal-mart has arrived in the neighboring town.

Many of the "old-timers" have passed on, including our next-door neighbor Eleanor Bell, who was deeply loved by us. But, her home now belongs to Julie and Kurt, who have added their own special touch to the house and gardens, and who carry on Eleanor's custom of hospitality and helpfulness.

And, we have a new cat named Patches, whose purrs and chirping sounds and cocky strut are a joyful reminder that the only way to mend a broken heart is to love again. Like Ross, he is an excellent travel cat, evoking comments and pets from strangers who ask how we trained him to walk on a leash.

But much has stayed the same as when we first arrived. Our neighbor Julie runs across the road to greet us when we return, although her big black lab, Bear, has since died and Hunter, a golden lab, now accompanies her. Her husband Brad, who was raised in their farmhouse, enjoys filling Larry in on the local history. Over the summer, Julie and I again share long heart-to-heart chats, trade favors, and help each other out as it's always been done in the North Country.

Our mentors, Topsy and Alex, remain cozily nestled in their nearby apartment and are still a powerful guiding light to us—accepting change gracefully, living zestfully in their waning years, meeting adversity with faith and courage, and responding to major health challenges with dignity and determination.

Tom Golden, in his 70s, continues to challenge us with his provocative sermons at the little 200-year-old Dalton Congregational Church, where we are the "youngsters" in the congregation.

Larry still enjoys taking the canoe down river in search of fish or, when he's feeling lazy, casting his line out from our bank. The blueberry fields forever beckon me to harvest their fruits and commune with creation, though the crop was very sparse this summer due to a late spring frost.

The plentiful wildlife, as always, delights us. The great blue heron makes a sweep along the river in the early morning, the haunting cries of the loons pierce the quiet, and the gold and purple finches jockey for position on our bird feeder. This year, for the first time, we were thrilled by the sight of a bald eagle, and surprised to discover six orphaned baby skunks nesting under our garage. We fed them until they were old enough to wander off on their own.

The Connecticut River continues to mesmerize us with its dazzling reflections, broken only by a piece of wood drifting quietly by or a kayaker slipping silently past. And each night the bedroom window of our trailer frames a silhouette of the White Mountains as the variegated colors of the setting sun streak the sky until the mountains disappear into the blackness.

Here, as always, we will listen, reflect, regroup, and prepare ourselves for whatever surprises Spirit has waiting for us around the next bend. Our seedling dream has blossomed into fruition, and these six years have instructed and stretched us in so many ways. If it were to end today, there would be nothing to mourn or regret, for one hour, one day, one year fully lived is to know eternity. However, I don't believe God is finished with us yet.

Perhaps that is what our journey has been all about— trusting, letting go of attachments, taking and learning from each encounter; then moving confidently on to the next "appointment."

REFERENCES

SECTION I

Section quote: Millard Fuller, *The Theology of the Hammer* (Macon, Georgia: Smyth & Helwys Publishing, Inc., 1994), p. 39.

Chapter 1

Chapter quote: Clarence Jordan, *The Cotton Patch Version of Hebrews and the General Epistles* (Clinton New Jersey: New Win Publishing, Inc.), p. 35.

Chapter 2

Chapter quote: Eric Butterworth, *Spiritual Economics* (Unity Village, Missouri: Unity Books, 1983), p. 79.

Chapter 3

Thomas Moore in preface to *Voices From The Heart* by Brian O'Connell (San Francisco: Jossey-Bass Publishers, 1999), chapter quote, p. 9. Text quote, p. 8.

SECTION II

Section quote: Jimmy and Rosalyn Carter, *Everything to Gain: Making the Most of the Rest of Your Life* (New York: Random House, 1987), p. 99.

Chapter 4

Chapter quote: Betty Fine Collins, Jefferson County (Alabama) Commissioner, at tornado anniversary Prayer Breakfast, April 8, 1999. Text quote: Hamilton Jordan, *No Such Thing As A Bad Day* (Marietta, GA: Longstreet Press), p. 123.

Chapter 6

Chapter quote: Millard Fuller, Founder, Habitat for Humanity, in address to homeowners at Grassilli site in Birmingham, Alabama, April 8, 1998.

Chapter 7

Chapter quote: Douglas M. Lawson, Ph.D., *Volunteering: 101 Ways You Can Improve the World and Your Life* (San Diego, CA: ALTI Publishing, 1998), p. 50.

Chapter 8

Chapter quote: Millard Fuller, *The Theology of the Hammer* (Macon, Georgia: Smyth & Helwys Publishing, Inc., 1994), p. 29.

Chapter 10

Lucy FitzPatrick McFarlane, "Solid as a Rock," in *Newfoundland LifeStyle Magazine: Commemorative Edition 1497-1997* (St. John's, Newfoundland Canada: Communications Ten Limited, 1997), chapter and text quotes, p. 64.

Chapter 11

Chapter quote: Eric Butterworth, *Spiritual Economics* (Unity Village, Missouri: Unity Books, 1983), p. 108.

SECTION III

Section quote: Brian O'Connell, "The Impact of Volunteering," *Voices From The Heart* (San Francisco: Jossey-Bass Publishers, 1999), p. 50.

Chapter 12

Victor Hugo, *Les Miserables* ("Saint Denis," Book 12, Chapter 4).

Chapter 13

Chapter quote: Thomas Moore in Preface to *Voices From The Heart* by Brian O'Connell (San Francisco: Jossey-Bass Publishers, 1999), p. 9.

Chapter 14

Chapter quote: Kathleen A. Brehony, *Ordinary Grace* (New York: Riverhead Books, 1999), p. 104.

Chapter 15

Chapter quote: Rob Swenson, "Final cleanup makes room for rebirth," *Argus Leader* (Sioux Falls: Sioux Falls Newspapers, Inc., June 5, 1998), p. 4A. Quotations, statistics, and factual information were gathered from the June 1-6, 1998 editions of the *Argus Leader*.

Chapter 17

Chapter quote: Jane Goodall, *Reason for Hope*, (New York: Warner Books, 1999), p. 148. Text quotes: Kathleen A. Brehony, *Ordinary Grace* (New York: Riverhead Books, 1999), p. 63. Acts of kindness listed in the subsections "Reaching Out in Love" and "Accentuating the Positive" were gathered from the June 3-6, 1998 editions of the *Argus Leader* and the June 6, 1998 edition of the *Yankton Daily Press & Dakotan*. Eric Butterworth, *Spiritual Economics* (Unity Village, Missouri: Unity Books, 1983), pp 86-87; 90. Hoyt Harwell, "God's In Control," *Good News*, published by Shades Mountain Independent Church, Hoover, Alabama, August/September 1998, Vol. 2, No.6, pp 1,8.

SECTION IV

Chapter 19

Chapter quote: Thomas Moore, "Finding Your Original Self" in *Unity Magazine*, August 2000 (Unity Village, Missouri). Text quote: Eric Butterworth, *Spiritual Economics* (Unity Village, Missouri: Unity Books, 1983), p. 34.

SECTION V

Section quote: From a letter by the Unmet Needs Committee for Disaster Recovery, inviting tornado survivors and volunteers to the one-year anniversary celebration of the recovery.

Chapter 20

Chapter quote: From a letter by the Unmet Needs Committee for Disaster Recovery, inviting tornado survivors and volunteers to the one-year anniversary celebration of the recovery.

Chapter 21

Chapter quote: From speech by Dr. Mike Harper, United Methodist Committee on Relief, at the Volunteers Building Together Appreciation Dinner. Text quote: Claire Gross, *Austin's Story* (unpublished, permission from the author).

Chapter 22

Jimmy Carter, *Living Faith*, (New York: Times Books, 1996), p. 4.

Chapter 24

Chapter quote: Bette Midler, "From a Distance," co-written by Henley/Slibar. Text quotes: Peace Pilgrim, *Steps Toward Inner Peace*, printed by Friends of Peace Pilgrim, Hemet, California (no copyright), pp 16, 22. Jimmy and Rosalyn Carter, *Everything to Gain: Making the Most of the Rest of Your Live* (New York: Random House, 1987), p. 189.

EPILOGUE

Chapter quote: Beth Nielsen Chapman, "The Color of Roses," co-writer Matt Rollings.

SCRIPTURE QUOTATIONS marked (NIV) are taken from the *Holy Bible, New International Version*(R). *NIV* (R). Copyright (c)1973, 1978, 1984 by International Bible Society. Used by permission of Zondervan. All rights reserved.

About The Authors

Carol and Larry Tebo are not new to adventure. In addition to residing in numerous regions of the U.S., they lived for a year in an undeveloped area of Nigeria with their two teen-age children. Carol is a former junior high English teacher and administrative assistant. Larry served in the U.S. Army for 9 years, after which he worked in industrial operations and maintenance management. Volunteering has been a lifelong priority for both Carol and Larry who, in 1996, sold their home and belongings and became full-time RVers for four years, dividing their time between service work, writing and touring. Their experiences form the basis of *Vehicles of Hope: Serving Others on the Road to Satisfaction.*

Other published works by Carol include the inspirational gift book, *Blueberries From Heaven: A Basketful of Wisdom*, published by Peter Pauper Press, which features 16 insights on living that Carol garnered while picking wild blueberries near their camp in northern New Hampshire; inspirational articles in *Unity Magazine*; a feature in *Rocking Chair Rebels* titled "Your RV: A Vehicle of Hope", published by the Escapees RV organization; and two pieces in *RV Traveling Tales: Women's Journeys on the Open Road*, independently published. Larry has completed a novel titled *Veil of Vengeance*, which will be published in the near future.

The couple now has a winter residence in Americus, Georgia, where they volunteer at Koinonia Partners and Habitat for Humanity.

For more information about Carol and Larry, to read Carol's other writings, or to view the *Vehicles of Hope Photo Album*, please visit their website:

www.tebotales.com